Sandy Schackel

No Step Backward

No Step Backward

Women and Family on the Rocky Mountain Mining Frontier, Helena, Montana, 1865-1900

by Paula Petrik

Montana Historical Society Press, Helena, 1987

Cover design by Steve LaRance, Artmill, Missoula, Montana
Title page illustration by Biff Karlyn, Helena, Montana
All photographs courtesy of MHS Photograph Archives, Helena, Montana
Text set in Palacio by Artcraft Printers, Billings, Montana, and printed in the United States of America by Thompson-Shore, Inc., Dexter, Michigan

Library of Congress Cataloging-in-Publication Data

Petrik, Paula Evans.
No step backward.
Bibliography: p.
Includes index.
1. Women—Montana—Helena—History—19th century.
2. Family—Montana—Helena—History—19th century.
3. Mineral industries—Social aspects—Montana—Helena— History—19th century. I. Title.
HQ1439.H4P48 1987 305.4'09786'615 87-11334
ISBN 0-917298-13-6

The United States: really a quartering of a continent, a drawer in North America. Pull it out and prairie dogs would spill off one side, alligators off the other—a terrain crisscrossed with geological boundaries, mammalian boundaries, amphibian boundaries: the limits of the world of the river frog, the extent of the Nugget Formation, the rage of the mountain cougar.

—John McPhee, *Basin and Range*

there's a woman in every house. i think of that every time i see hills full of houses. there's a woman in every one.

—alta, *Momma*

No step backward.

—Class of 1879, Helena High School
(all of whom were women)

Contents

List of Tables

Acknowledgments

THIS PROJECT BEGAN some years ago when, as an undergraduate, my friend pointed out to me that I had managed to winnow a population of 14,000 to find my friends among the school's small population of westerners. No one does anything alone, and in the intervening years there have been many people and institutions who have helped bring this book to fruition. First, the members of my committee have been extremely helpful and tolerant of my penchant toward academic nonconformity. Mary P. Ryan, University of California at Berkeley; Harold C. Livesay, Virginia Polytechnic Institute; and Bert Hansen, New York University, have continually been a source of intellectual stimulus and moral support. Together, they have provided the motivation, set standards of stylistic elegance and precision, and laid down a challenge. Among others at the State University of New York at Binghamton, Pepi Levine, Chris Africa, Carol Stevenson, Ann Schofield, and Nina Asher proved to be the best of friends and helpers. I would also like to acknowledge a Fulbright-Hays grant to the United Kingdom that allowed me to acquire the techniques of quantitative analysis and to enrich my knowledge of social history. Some of these research tools were adapted to *No Step Backward*. My special thanks to the University of Essex and members of its staff: Philip Holden, Eric Tannenbaum, and Marcia Taylor. Similarly, I acknowledge an American Bar Foundation Grant in Legal History that permitted me to extend and refine research on divorce that is part of this manuscript.

No social historian could piece together a narrative from various local documents without the assistance of those who work with those records on a daily basis. My appreciation and heartfelt thanks to these Lewis and Clark County officers and employees: Clara Gilreath, Judy Harris, Mary Root, Mary Harris, Hilda Funk, Darlene Johnson, Nancy Jones, Wilma Grant, Dorothy McCarter, and last but not least, the Honorable Gordon R. Bennett, who patiently explained the subtleties of Montana criminal and civil law. The staff of the Montana Historical Society have given unstintingly of their time and interest. This had been especially true of Dave Walter who has often taken his own time to burrow into the archives and of William Lang and Marianne Keddington who undertook the arduous task of editing the manuscript.

Along the way there have been friends who have faithfully supported this and other projects. Memorable in this regard are my aunt and late uncle, Gertrude and William Heitmiller; the "dissertation team" of Kim Sell, Maureen Carroll, and Linda Kelly Nolan; and colleagues Kathleen Underwood and Carolyn Stefanco-Schill. Many people in Helena have contributed to the book by sharing their memories of mothers, aunts, grandmothers, and acquaintances. My special thanks to the late Mrs. Margaret Hibbard, Mrs. John Baucus, Miss Jean Rumsey, Claudia Spencer Sadler, Mr. Rex T. Williams, Mrs. Robert Kirkland, Mrs. Hugh Potter, and Mrs. Pauline Shumate, who helped this historian immensely. Bill and Rita Gowan of Helena Abstract and Title Company took time from their busy day to initiate me into the mysteries of property transactions and title trails. And finally, to Montana State University whose staff and administration threw open the doors of their computer center to me. Georgia Ziemba and Professors Richard B. Roeder, Thomas R. Wessel, and Michael P. Malone have been creative and faithful consultants throughout the course of this project. Montana State University also had the incredible foresight and good sense to hire me. I trust that their confidence has not been misplaced.

Social historians make much of the family economy. This book is the modern product of such an economy. My mother and my father, Helen McKinnon Petrik and Paul E. Petrik, Jr., not only gave me moral support but also had faith in this enterprise and maintained their good humor, but they also came through with the bucks when the time came. The Petrik Dissertation Subsidy in American History (to be awarded once only) financed this venture. I will especially remember those years for their constancy and affection. My brother, Philip Owen Petrik, remained quietly behind the scenes during these last years only to appear magically at critical times with encouragement and financial aid. Like our parents, he never asked questions but had a sibling's faith. His generosity will not be forgotten. My husband, Walter N. Sylva, arrived one New Year's Eve and never left. He has been the best of companions, friends, and partners, never letting me forget what was required and why. His ability to appreciate and to take joy in another's work has sustained me from day to day. This book is for them.

Introduction

CENTRAL TO THIS BOOK is the following thesis: The urban mining frontier transformed its inhabitants, particularly its women, and promoted increased economic opportunity and social equality for its oftentimes unwilling changelings.[1] Characterized by a preponderance of single men in the population, the urban mining frontier's demography (unlike the more settled areas of the nation) created a special social and cultural milieu that disrupted women's familiar nineteenth century sources of influence and confidence, confined women more completely to the home and domesticity, and made reform a crucial undertaking for the benefit and safety of their children. The majority of women—the pioneer wives and mothers of the middling or middle-class sort—who confronted this strange and often inimical society, generally responded by adapting to the new circumstances on the frontier. At first, women did not take advantage of the dislocations in their world but resisted until circumstances dictated that they arrive, however reluctantly, at a re-evaluation of their role. The result was a slow, decades-long metamorphosis of women's perceptions of their public and private roles and a new definition of womanhood. Women's private critique of their situation showed itself publicly in divorce case testimonies and in the addition to the legal canon of "mental cruelty" and a husband's "failure to provide." The process of redefining womanhood, illustrated in divorce documents, involved women's reinstating standard nineteenth century prescriptions, refashioning these dicta to suit themselves, and thereby establishing the terms of their commitment to marriage in law. In sum, women increased their independence within and control over their marital relationships.

The completion of this process was most evident in the lives of the daughters of frontier, middling women, those who came of age on the urban mining frontier. Maturing in an emphatically male environment, frontier daughters accommodated themselves, capitalized on the social rearrangements occasioned by the frontier, and assumed its values. They were less likely to suffer an unhappy marriage, more likely to work, more likely to remain single, more likely to assume leadership positions in the community, and more likely to eschew traditional lifestyles. Ideologies that guided and confined their mothers no longer influenced frontier daughters. The urban mining frontier had an effect on the majority of women that can best be understood as a cumulative change over succeeding generations as women responded to new conditions on the frontier and established a place in its society. These generational alterations manifested themselves publicly in a significant political event: the winning of suffrage.

As grandmothers, daughters, and granddaughters realized a similar perception of their situation and discarded traditional roles, the generations converged in their thinking about their responsibilities and goals. This reconsideration included a belief in the efficacy of the electoral franchise. The composition of these generations, their frontier experience, and their numbers explain the chronology of the woman suffrage movement in Montana and account for its history in terms of women's lives.

Despite the middling women's numerical unimportance, a significant number of women found niches in Helena's service economy, by employing their domestic skills in Main Street businesses to meet the needs of the male population. From this beginning, the number of working women increased as women took command of the service sector. For one notorious group among Helena's working women, the prostitutes, thirty years on the frontier ended differently. Their economic and social opportunities diminished as the frontier period ended and families replaced single, young men as the dominant population in Helena. Having prospered well enough to build an enclave within the city and having acquired the financial resources to guarantee a degree of upward and outward mobility, demimonde entrepreneurs suffered financial reverses when the economy declined. As prostitutes' control of the tenderloin decreased, the probability that they would leave the sexual marketplace also decreased. The substance of this argument is not new. Over the years, historians have debated the thesis that attributed the entire course of American history to the settlement of the West. Named for its author, Frederick Jackson Turner, the Turner or Frontier thesis set a formidable standard for twentieth century discussions of western history.

In "The Significance of the Frontier in American History," Turner explained American development by "the existence of an area of free land, its continuous recession, and the advance of American settlement westward. . . . The true point of view in the history of this nation is not the Atlantic coast, it is the Great West." The frontier, Turner claimed, produced the individualism that is the hallmark of American culture; this individualism, in turn, promoted democratic institutions and economic equality. For Turner, the West with its open land acted as a safety valve: ". . . each frontier did indeed furnish a new field of opportunity, a gate of escape from the bondage of the past. . . ." In short, Turner traced the healthy development of liberty and equality to geographical roots.[2]

The history written in Turner's day paid scant attention to women, and the best that might be assumed is that Turner's singular and consistent reference to the male gender was intended to be generic rather than restrictive. Turner's followers, however, also failed to include women in their discussions. During the first half of the twentieth century, Turner's critics gained the upper hand, and the Frontier thesis fell into disfavor. More recently, historians, aided by the "new social history," have augmented the chronicle of the trans-Mississippi West by including the perspective of women's frontier experience. Either implicitly or explicitly, the Turner thesis has been the focal point for discussions of frontier women.

Historian Carolyn Stefanco has formulated a helpful topology, dividing the historiography of women in the West into three schools: the Turnerian, the Reactionist, and, to coin a descriptive term, the Stasist.[3] Most historians and novelists who considered women in the West, especially those writing in the nineteenth and early twentieth centuries, fell under Turner's spell. They tended to glorify women's contributions to frontier life and attributed the higher status of frontier women to their ability to emulate masculine accomplishment and character. Western women, in Turnerian tradition, were a fiercely independent, capable, and durable lot, free from the constraints binding their eastern sisters. This interpretation implied, sometimes tacitly and sometimes not, that the West provided a congenial environment where women aspired to their own goals, free from constrictive stereotypes and sexist attitudes.[4]

In contrast, the Reactionist writers took the opposite view: the frontier was hell on women. Instead of promoting women's ambitions, the frontier crushed women spiritually, drove them insane, and finally killed them. From the Reactionist perspective, pioneer women were lonely, displaced persons, demeaned and worn out by the rigors of the frontier.[5]

The last and most contemporary of these schools, the Stasist school, sidestepped the good/bad dichotomy and argued that the frontier had little effect on women's lives. The Stasists claim that women's roles survived the overland journey fundamentally intact and continued to shape women's lives in the West in much the same manner as they did in the East.[6]

All three interpretations of women's history in the West are inadequate. The Turnerians chiefly use biography to support their claims, and the result is the history of exceptional women or groups of women. Partisans of the Reactionist school fall prey to criticism of a different kind. Their women cease to be historical actors in their own right and become pawns in the service of much grander schemes—proving the savagery of the Indians or aiding the cause of socialism. Both these schools concentrate primarily on rural women, those who homesteaded or ranched. This emphasis excludes town women, even though on the trans-Mississippi frontier and especially the mining frontier women were urbanites.[7] Both the Turnerians and the Reactionists, in a welter of sunbonnets, flapjacks, Indian massacres, and overland journeys, have lost sight of the female city-dwellers. The Stasists, too, devote most of their attention to farm women, although some have begun to consider women in other environments.[8] Nonetheless, they fail to account satisfactorily for the single most obvious political phenomenon of women's history in the West: the passage of woman suffrage.

While some women's historians view the attainment of woman suffrage as a minor episode in the long history of American women and as generally failing to fulfill the expectations of its proponents, the winning of suffrage in the West prior to ratification of the Nineteenth Amendment does call attention to a curious case of regionalism. Women in the western United States were the first to persuade their male electorate that women deserved the vote. The first congresswoman, Jeannette Rankin, won election in Montana in 1916, four years before ratification of the Nineteenth Amendment. Despite the Stasists' claims for the continuity of nineteenth century ideology on the frontier, both the acceptance of suffrage in the West and Rankin's victory suggest that something was at work in the lives of both western men and women that altered their perceptions of gender roles. Suffragists made the same conservative, nativist arguments in other state campaigns with little success. In the West, however, the male electorate accepted women's claims.

The shortcomings of these three interpretations suggest alternative directions for research. Rather than relying solely on the scattered biographies of illustrious women or taking rural women's experience as the totality of frontier women's history, it is more fruitful to investigate the urban frontier and study the interaction of different groups and generations of women in one locality over time. Such an approach immediately suggests a community study. By focusing on a single city, a historian can reconstruct the lives of many women and examine the relationships between different groups of women and their activities against the backdrop of a frontier town's social and demographic structure.

Representative of several cities in the West that share common patterns of economic development and demographic makeup, Helena is ideal for such a community study. Like Denver, San Francisco, Boise, and Virginia City, Helena began as a mining camp, experienced spectacular growth and instant urbanization, and was transformed into a commercial and bureaucratic center. As did Denver and Boise, Helena became a state capital; like San Francisco, it became a transshipment point; and like all, it survived. Although each city has its own personality, historical idiosyncracies, and distinct chronologies, they are all part and product of that portion of westward expansion known as the Rocky Mountain mining frontier. Some cities on the mining frontier were more mining towns than entrepôt communities, and some quickly became metropolitan titans, while others never fulfilled their urban dreams. Helena falls somewhere between the titans and the ghost towns; it never reached the ranks of the metropolitan elite, but it maintained itself and became the focal point of a limited yet sizable geographical area.

This study aims to accomplish more than an account of the particulars of Helena's local history. With other cities and towns in the Rocky Mountain West, Helena shared a common course of urban development and a preponderantly male population during the pioneering years. A community study of Helena, as an example of a larger phenomenon of western history, can act like a prism and refract women's experience into its component parts and clarify the transformations of the women's varied roles, not only for Helena but also for other female populations in Rocky Mountain cities and towns. Similarly, not only should it be clear that women's history is the focus here and is worth attention on its own merit but also as a means of testing some of the generalizations about the historical development of the Rocky Mountain mining frontier.

The examination of this thesis through a community study is organized by both the chronology of Helena's development in its pre- and post-railroad periods and a crude division of the city's female population into women of the married middling sort and the single working women. Based on both quantitative analysis and traditional archival sources, Chapter 1 concentrates on the general development of Helena between 1865 and 1900 by delineating the basic economic framework and demography that defined the community and by describing critical episodes in its history. It provides a summary of Helena's social and cultural life and establishes a context for the story of women's responses to their environment through the study of Helena's working women. Chapter 2 singles out one particular group of working women, Helena's prostitutes, and tests the validity of a popular frontier stereotype. Through local economic and legal records, it is possible to chart the rise and fall of the tenderloin business empire in Helena, which was one aspect of female opportunity and entrepreneurship on the urban frontier. Turning to more legitimate clientele, the first part of Chapter 3 takes for its subject the majority of Helena women, Helena's middle-class married women. The narrative derives from a statistical model and uses composite biography to examine the effect of the frontier on two generations of Helena women. Because Elizabeth Chester Fisk chronicled her frontier experience in hundreds of letters home, her story and that of her daughter comprise the second part of the chapter. The Fisk narrative substantiates arguments made earlier in the chapter, provides additional evidence, and gives voice and detail to the general description of the lives of two generations of women. Chapter 4 uses divorce records to examine the lives of ordinary women caught in crisis. This investigation confirms the transformation of women's perception of their roles, establishes a chronology for their reinstatement of a refurbished "cult of true womanhood," and, in the end, makes a case for women's reformation of state divorce law. Finally, Chapter 5 moves outside the walls of the county courtroom, beyond the boundaries of Lewis and Clark County, and out of Helena's parlors to explore the connections between the urban frontier experience, the generations of women, and the politics of winning suffrage in Montana.

Metaphorically, the organization and methodologies incorporated in this book owe something to photographs of early Helena. Helena photographers invariably chose to take their pictures of the city from a perch on the slope south of town. The prints were masterful panoramas but framed only a part of the city. Because the tenderloin lay almost directly at the foot of the hills, amateur photographers captured detailed pictures of the red-light district and little else. Toward the end of the nineteenth century, F. Jay Haynes, renowned Northern Pacific Railroad photographer, took a series of photographs that depicted Helena more comprehensively. Evidently, Haynes walked around the city, catching the metropolis from different angles and in different lights. The result is a more fully realized, robust picture of the city. Like Haynes, the chapters of this books make a circuit of Helena, freezing for a time the city's women in their quotidian activity. From different angles and with a variety of methodologies, these historical interpretations overlap and corroborate each other, lending definition and depth to women's experience in nineteenth century Helena.

Like photographers, historians have adopted a special terminology that serves as a shorthand for their craft. In the past decade, women's historians have developed several phrases to summarize complex nineteenth century ideologies regarding women's roles. The "cult of true womanhood" and the "cult of domesticity" appointed women the mistresses of the home and assigned to them the characteristics of submissiveness, self-sacrifice, passivity, maternity, moral purity, and domesticity. The "doctrine of separate spheres" divided social activities into public and private areas. This arrangement alloted to men command of the marketplace, politics, and other recognizable public endeavors; to women, the doctrine meted out the home, its environs, and other private places. Women's isolation in the home was mitigated by "informal female networks," which had both psychological and practical functions. Instrumental in establishing cultural institutions and assisting women in their attempts to regulate society, the networks also bonded women to each other through the consolation they received from each other and the information they shared on topics ranging from health care to fashion. According to some scholars, nineteenth century women derived more of their emotional sustenance from each other than they did from the men in their lives.[9]

Besides terminology pertaining to women, there is "social class," a slippery concept at best on the frontier where an individual could rise swiftly to "capitalist," tumble to laborer, and rise yet again—all in a single year. Despite their chimerical characteristics, there seem to have been several crude class divisions in Helena during the nineteenth century: an elite, a middling or middle-class, an artisans' class, a lower class, and the poor. Except for the middle class, membership in the other classes was self-evident. Most numerous in the community, Helena's middling sort consisted of the petit bourgeoisie or those who, although they had white-collar occupations, did not command the same monetary resources as the "elite" and who perceived themselves one rung lower on the social ladder than their "capitalist" neighbors and one rung higher than their carpenter, butcher, or mason friends. Elizabeth Chester Fisk confessed, in effect, that it took a "long purse" to stay in Helena's social swim and that because of its limited resources the Fisk family could not hope to be numbered with Helena's elite.

Drawing class boundaries in Helena proves as difficult as finding an easy or obvious starting point for the chronicle of Helena's women. No single artifact, document, or event gives any clue to or pinpoints any critical juncture in the history of women and the family on Helena's urban frontier. Instead, the architecture and plan of the city itself provide tantalizing inconsistencies. To look north from the south end of the gulch is to catch a glimpse of one of several pockets of incongruity. Perched on a geological peninsula pushing into the gulch, one structure dominates Helena's skyline: the Bluestone House. Built by architect James Stranahan for his bride in 1890, the Bluestone House is a marvelous piece of Victorian gaucherie topped by a domed cupola. Not as grand as the bastion mansions on the city's west side, the Bluestone House is an apt metaphor for nineteenth century domesticity and suggests the major themes in the lives of Helena's middling women. But the metaphor turns out to be a mixed one. The Bluestone House overlooked Helena's red-light district. To arrive at the front door, guests climbed a steep flight of steps just off the intersection of Joliet and Wood streets, the heart of Helena's tenderloin. This juxtaposition hints at a confluence of two antithetical female lifestyles and invites a variety of questions about the nature of the social relationship between the women who lived in houses like the Bluestone and the fancy ladies who worked the bottom of the steps. These questions naturally lead to others involving less stark comparisons. How, for example, did respectably employed women fit into this scheme? What niche did the Bluestone House's servants occupy in a community that accepted modest homes and *maisons de joies* on the same streets? Stranahan's eccentricity aside, what of the typical middling women who did not share a common property line with the whores?

Yet, one more anomaly shares the Bluestone House's promontory. Almost adjacent to the Bluestone House is another structure. Obscured by contemporary renovation, the architectural design of a nineteenth century public building remains recognizable. It is the last survivor of Helena's Catholic social-service complex, which at one time included an orphanage and two parochial academies. Like the Bluestone House, this collection of buildings had a splendid view of the tenderloin. Father Palladino and his scholars had only to look out the window to be educated about a different sort of life. The school also indicates the presence of children, and this circumstance implies something more than the interaction of adults with the frontier: the education and socialization of generations. Did children, especially girls, mature with an altered view of themselves and their place in society because they lived in neighborhoods like that around the Bluestone House? The Bluestone House neighborhood where roughly the area of one city block included sporting women, middle-class households, school children, and the Catholic priest was bursting with the possibilities for major attitudinal change in its inhabitants.

This chronicle, like an early Helena photograph, begins with a cityscape, a still-life scene of town, men, and women. Unlike a nineteenth century camera, however, it does not preserve a static picture of people frozen in *medias res* but sets out to capture the dynamics of Helena's demography, its shifting economy, and its residents—especially the women.

No Step Backward

CHAPTER ONE

From Urban Village to Metropolitan Town

Helena, Montana, 1865-1900

FIFTY MILLION YEARS AGO near the spine of the continent in what is now southwestern Montana, geologic processes created rich veins of gold and deposited their traces in eastward-flowing streams. In the Prickly Pear Valley, where placer gold glittered for the practiced eye of the prospector, people passed the valley's southern slopes, unmindful of the results of these geologic events, until July 1864 when Reginald Stanley, John Cowan, D. J. Miller, and John Crabb stopped there on their return to Virginia City, Montana Territory.[1]

The gulch looked no more promising than any of the others the four had prospected that summer; but as one of the group later commented, "It was our last chance," and they tested the ground anyway. The four hit pay dirt immediately. As the undisputed claimants, they took their time testing up and down the gulch for the most profitable ground. With their supplies running low, Crabb and Cowan made their way back to Virginia City, where they bought provisions and kept the news of their strike quiet, imparting only the barest facts to a few friends.

The result was not a grand stampede. Small parties of miners left Virginia City to join the original group; others simply blundered into the small-scale placer operation. By the first of October, five cabins dotted the gulch; two weeks later, the camp cast two hundred votes for members of the territorial legislature. By the end of October, the mining camp on Last Chance Gulch, as the discovery party had named it, proved populous enough to be called a town, and its citizens met to choose a name. Among the suggestions were "Helena," "Tomah," "Squash Town," and "Pumpkinville." In a run-off contest between "Helena," the choice of John Somerville who claimed to be a native of a Minnesota town of the same name, and "Tomah," "Helena" won by two votes.[2]

Like other mining camps in cordilleran America, Helena was founded on the principle of impermanence; its inhabitants never intended it to be a permanent settlement. As a result, it bore all the hallmarks of the urban frontier in the Rocky Mountains.[3] First, Helena was instantly urban. The town's residents had barely left their tents for log cabins when the mining camp could boast of its own theater, library, school, newspaper, churches, and social and benevolent societies. Second, Helena was isolated from other metropolitan centers and separated from productive agricultural areas. Most towns on the American frontier had evolved after the surrounding agricultural land had been settled and developed, but the process was reversed on the mining frontier. Third, the community was unplanned and set in a poor location. The bulk of Helena's early population never intended to stay, so street planning, platting, and constructing were abandoned to whim, the dictates of geography, and the pre-eminence of the miners' discovery claims. Situated in the bottom of a steep ravine, Helena's streets paralleled the meandering course of the stream that flowed through the gulch. Buildings, which were constructed on the hillsides, occupied the southeast end of the gulch with no discernible plan of organization. When Captain John Wood had surveyed the town in 1865, he had bowed to the higher claims of the miners; the result was an odd townsite plan with city blocks taking every conceivable shape. Even though each city lot was intended to measure 30 by 60 feet, the lots became odd-shaped plots—some 8 by 42 feet, others 42 by 49 feet, and still others in wedges and polygons. Some streets ran for several blocks only to dead-end or leap to one side. Without grading, some thoroughfares were little more than paths.[4] In later years, when the city council attempted to regularize Helena's chaotic streets, city workers pared portions of blocks or cut through city lots and residences. Fourth, Helena's population was characterized by several outstanding demographic features: the racial, ethnic, and regional mix of its residents; a skewed sex ratio; an unbalanced age structure; and a high rate of transiency.

When the census taker made his rounds in 1870, Helena's boom period had ended, as had the prosperous days of other mining camps in the territory. Gold production in Montana had reached its peak in 1866 and had decreased each succeeding year. At the same time, the territory's population had diminished. Federal census figures and local county estimates put the territory's population at 28,000 in 1866, at between 21,000 and 24,000 over the next few years, and finally at 20,595 in 1870. During its bonanza days, Helena's population probably numbered 4,100 residents; by 1870, its population had declined to 3,108.[5]

Even in 1870, Helena's populace retained the characteristics of its mining-camp beginnings. Helenans were overwhelmingly young, white, and male. Helena was no place for the very young or the very old. Two-thirds of the population were between twenty-one and forty years old. Men outnumbered women by three to one and in some age groups by as much as five to one. Genteel, single women were at an even greater premium; there were approximately five hundred adult women in

Helena, and these women were not always of the best sort. The man who came west to find his fortune and his bride contemplated dubious prospects. The lopsided sex ratio affected the composition of Helena's households. Over 50 per cent of Helena's males lived in households composed entirely of men. By 1870, however, the nuclear family had more than a toehold in the town, where nearly one-third of the population lived in households composed of parents, children, and a relative or boarder. By and large, Helena's households were small, with an average household consisting of three people. Nearly 20 per cent of Helena's residents lived by themselves.[6]

Among the town's citizens, one group organized their living arrangements differently: Helena's Chinese community. In dwellings clustered at the southern end of the gulch on the outskirts of town, Cantonese immigrants comprised one-fifth of the town's population. Predominantly male and without families, the Chinese lived in cadres of ten or more, headed by a foreman who held what money the group possessed.[7] Those Chinese who were incorporated into these work gangs created their own community, complete with all the services available in its white counterpart. Having temporarily forsaken their families, who had remained behind in Canton, the Chinese population had an even greater paucity of women than the whites did and a complete absence of children.[8] They intended to make their fortune in the "golden land" and applied themselves with an even greater single-mindedness and dedication than did the whites.[9] Chinese entrepreneurs contributed to the larger community. For a time, they dominated the laundry business and provided the town with much of its fresh produce from their gardens in the south end of the gulch.

The promise of the goldfields also lured would-be prospectors, mechanics, and merchants from every European nation; nearly one-fourth of the town's inhabitants were foreign-born. Helena's native-born residents represented every state and territory and, with the exception of the West, almost equally represented the northeastern, midwestern, and southern regions of the country.[10] Common to all residents was their penchant for moving.[11] Helena's foreign-born residents were veterans of a number of migrations. For both groups, Helena was the last in a number of ports of call.[12]

Although Helena's mining boom had ended by 1870, 37 per cent of the population was still engaged in mining. The other three-fifths of the workers provided goods and services for those who neither had the time nor the inclination to secure the necessaries of life for themselves. Miners could not hope to become self-sufficient, nor did they want to be. Time was money, and time could be saved by buying ready-made goods and the domestic services of laundering, mending, and cooking.[13]

Women normally provided these services in the nineteenth century home, but familial households with wives were rare in Helena in 1870;

of necessity, single men looked elsewhere for domestic amenities. In addition, there were too few women engaged in the service trades to satisfy the demand. Consequently, male workers and proprietors on Main Street found a ready market for services normally performed by women in the home. Helena's six restaurants kept the miners fed and watered, seventeen barbers kept the men's beards trimmed and offered facilities for bathing, and fifty-four washermen attended to the miners' clothing. A theater, several billiard parlors, a bowling alley, concert rooms, and sporting houses entertained the miners; numerous clothing merchants, hardware salesmen, and sixty grocers provisioned them.[14] These service-brokers dominated and defined a fragile economy that rested on the vagaries of mining and the itinerant miners.

Elizabeth Chester Fisk, one of Helena's matrons, sensed the town's economic vulnerability. Just returned from Connecticut in 1869, she wrote that she found the town much improved:

> Yet it seems to be all *show*. I have an undefined impression for which I cannot give the slightest reason that all is insecure; that we are resting on the brink of a precipice and the least inadvertence may topple us, over. . . . It seems that some terrific calamity is impending. Will the terrible fire again visit us and complete the ruin caused by a whole season of drought and inactivity in mining operations or will the bubble of outside show and glitter burst and reveal the emptiness and bankruptcy within?[15]

Elizabeth understood that Helena stood at a critical juncture in its development. With the surface gold depleted and the town devastated once by fire, Helena could have gone the way of other mining camps and died. But during the early 1870s, silver mining and nearby reduction works revived the town, this time as an entrepôt community.[16] Elizabeth described Helena's transition in 1870:

> The excitement of the new mines in Missoula is taking away a large part of our surplus population. Helena still continues the base of supplies for all the surrounding country and thus new and rich discoveries with their attendant "*stampedes*" are a benefit rather than an injury.[17]

Fire remained an ever-present danger. On April 28, 1869, just weeks after fire had destroyed part of Helena's commercial district, a major conflagration gutted the gulch. Originating in a Chinese gambling house on Main and Bridge streets, the blaze consumed the downtown and more, devastating more than twenty acres. Rocked by destruction, the town's shopkeepers demonstrated their commitment to Helena; within thirty-six hours, they put local mechanics and laborers to work raising their businesses out the rubble. One-third of the new structures, as the *Helena Daily Herald* reported, would be built of stone.[18]

As if to test the town's mettle, another fire started on November 9, 1869, in the Helena Theatre on Wood Street, consuming the theater and eight or nine neighboring houses. Although most of Helena's merchants escaped this blaze, fire once again tried the phoenixes of Main Street on October 1, 1871, when flames flared in the Chinese section of town. This time, the conflagration exacted its toll. Ten days later, the Great Chicago Fire bankrupted dozens of insurance companies, leaving some Helena merchants with no means to recover their losses. Fire again razed Main Street on August 23, 1872, and again on January 9, 1874, in a fire comparable to the ruinous 1871 blaze. The 1874 fire at last prompted the merchants to take action; they revamped the town's fire-fighting equipment and built a watchtower on the hill overlooking the town.[19]

Reassured by its entrepreneurs' confidence, Helena was assisted in another way in late 1874. In February, the territorial legislature had passed a bill giving the electorate the choice of moving the capital to Helena or of retaining it in Virginia City. Unofficial plebiscite returns in August awarded the victory to Helena; but by the time the returns reached Virginia City, the figures from Meagher County had been "mysteriously" transposed, giving Virginia City the majority and the capital. Helena's entrepreneurs immediately petitioned for a recount in Meagher County; and after considerable journalistic squabbling and legal maneuvering, the case arrived in the Montana Territory Supreme Court. The court ordered a recanvass of the vote and ruled that Meagher County's return had been in error.

On January 2, 1875, Helena officially became the new territorial capital.[20] Although the territory's records and furnishings were easily packed in several wagons for the move to Helena and the territory had few officials to relocate, the town gained an extra measure of permanence with the machinery of territorial bureaucracy. The acquisition of territorial offices also made Helena the natural location for federal offices. Acquiring the capital boosted the entire community's morale. Moving the capital to Helena, Elizabeth Fisk wrote, "encourages the people to go forward making improvements in their property, and in every possible way adding to the appearance of the town."[21]

Helena was the seat of territorial government, but it had yet to become an incorporated city. As early as January 9, 1868, the citizens had voted on incorporation, but the measure failed by a vote of 910 to 105. The Republican *Helena Weekly Herald,* which had opposed the measure, called incorporation a scheme concocted by prospective officeholders to line their pockets at the citizens' expense. "They can," wrote the editor, "by their simple fiat, confer an office upon each one of their political partisans, and even upon themselves, and assign to all, from City Marshall on down to Hog Driver an elegant salary."[22] By 1874, the newspaper had reversed its position, but Helena voters again defeated incorporation. While the *Herald* attributed the defeat to a light voter turnout, the editor's wife hinted at the presence of roughs and rowdies as instrumental in the charter's defeat. Between 1868 and 1881, the city charter went down to defeat five times.[23]

Helena lacked more than a city charter in 1880; it still did not possess a rail link with the rest of the nation. It had become clear how critical the railroad's presence would be to the town's stability and growth. Helena suffered from its isolation. Carried up the Missouri to Fort Benton and then over a wagon road the final 150 miles to Helena or overland on the arduous Corinne and Mullan roads that connected the territory with Utah and the Pacific coast, goods came to Montana over slow, expensive, and seasonal routes. Although the territorial legislature had passed three rail subsidy measures in 1876, no eastern entrepreneur was willing to venture the bulk of the capital. On March 27, 1877, Helena's hope for connections with the transcontinental railroad ended with the collapse of Jay Gould's plan to build a northern spur from the Union Pacific at Corinne, Utah, to Helena. "Helena's last and best hope," commented the *Herald* in a headline was a railroad north to Fort Benton and the Missouri River, and then southwest to Clancy, Jefferson City, and Butte.[24] Without this vital link, Helena's prospects were dim. Elizabeth Fisk probably echoed the feelings of many Helena residents when she wrote, "I do not feel as if we would remain here a great while longer without rail communications with the outer world, though we would perhaps sacrifice something in leaving."[25]

A rail line between Helena and Butte could not attract investment from outside the area; it depended on initiative from both cities' entrepreneurs. The *Herald* began mobilizing the community's merchants to that end, and on November 17, 1877, a select group of them met to organize a board of trade, a commercial club and vehicle for "boosterism" that was common across the country during the nineteenth century.[26] A week later, sixty-three merchants, capitalists, and professionals answered the call and organized the Helena Board of Trade in the parlors of the International Hotel. Besides making its voice heard outside Montana and collecting information from similar organizations, the Board worked quickly toward establishing a connection with Butte. If the Board could not build its own railroad, it determined to build the next best thing—an improved wagon road. But such a road, no matter how well-constructed, could not solve Helena's transportation problems. The Board continued to importune rail magnates and to send resolutions to Washington, D.C.[27]

The railroad and incorporation issues revealed the attitudes that Helena's merchants, especially the influential Board of Trade members, held toward their community. On the one hand, their self-interest prompted them to devise railroad schemes, because any improvement in transportation would increase their worth and expand their investment opportunities. On the other hand, the merchants saw municipal incorporation as a hindrance, burdening them with taxes that might go for naught if the town incorporation failed.

Aside from their obvious economic reasons, the members of the Board of Trade had additional motives behind their enthusiastic support of the Board's program. The average age of Board members was forty years, and the majority of them were married and had families. Nearly 60 per cent of them had resided in Helena for over ten years. For them, Helena was the last stop in an itinerant young adulthood.[28]

The rolls of the Board of Trade also show another facet of the business community: 20 per cent of the membership was Jewish.[29] Unlike their Gentile counterparts, Jewish merchants were not dependent on their own capital; they operated as part of a network based in St. Louis, San Francisco, and New York City. Faced with financial disaster—a common occurrence in the world of nineteenth century commerce—Helena Jews could command resources in other cities to rebuild their businesses.[30] To reduce freighting costs and to secure the best prices, Jewish merchants joined forces, bought in bulk, and sometimes absorbed losses together.[31] Locally, Jewish shopkeepers assisted each other in several ways. The agent for R. G. Dun & Company, the arbiters of financial reputation, reported on the house of Poznansky and Bohm: "P is 'an old hand' at the fraudulent assignment business. . . . [They] act as fraudulent assignees for their brethren in difficulties. . . ."[32]

The R. G. Dun agent generally applauded Helena's Jewish merchants, but beneath the surface of his approval ran an undercurrent of suspicion and prejudice. The Auerbachs may have been Jews of the best sort, but "they are real genuine Israelites and hard to understand and merchants here deal with them accordingly."[33] G. Goldberg, a recent Jewish arrival, was ". . . inclined to be oversharp and like most of his tribe will need watching."[34] While the Dun man in Helena may have recommended vigilance where credit and Jewish businessmen were concerned, he understood that the Hebrew merchants had access to cash and credit beyond Helena's entrepreneurial community; as such, they acted as a stabilizing element in a vulnerable marketplace. Merchants on Main Street, although they may have privately harbored anti-Semitic attitudes, never allowed their prejudice to interfere with business or fellowship.

The precarious nature of nineteenth century business, exacerbated by frontier conditions, encouraged some businessmen to maintain themselves by using unusual methods. The Fisk Brothers, owners of the *Herald*, avoided litigation and possible bankruptcy by transferring the newspaper among the five brothers whenever court action threatened the journal. It was impossible, according to the Dun agent, to know which brother owned the business at any time. Wary of this entrepreneurial flimflam, the R. G. Dun man recommended caution in dealing with the Fisk clan.[35] The Kleinschmidts, who were general merchants, operated their business early on under the name of a figurehead, Charles Mayne. As Dun's man reported, "they know they are unpopular . . . K. Bros. are no doubt well-off and sharp businessmen but are entirely too tricky disputing weight and quality of goods and frequently change style of firm. They are generally regarded with distrust."[36]

Some merchants were bolder in their extra-legal business behavior. Of A. J. Davis, a noted capitalist, Dun's man wrote, "He sells extensively to miners, takes mortgages on the pay of his customers, gets exorbitant rates of interest. 'He's a shark.' He litigates considerably and it is difficult to get his means. . . ."[37] All in all, the business community's slipperiness was overlooked by the town's citizens and by the Dun agent. In one passage, the Dun agent reported that W. G. Pruett was not "considered strictly first class" and that he was a county commissioner.[38]

In addition to the vexations of inadequate transportation facilities and dubious associates and practices, Helena merchants relied on eastern credit. Helena was fortunate that it had been chosen as a town worthy of eastern confidence; merchants from smaller communities in Montana were denied eastern investors' confidence. During the 1870s, however, Helena became independent of eastern financiers, adding banking to its services and progressing toward being a financial center.

In November 1878, when the Board of Trade managed to finish the new road between Helena and Butte, only forty-eight hours separated Helena merchants from markets in the territory's second largest city. The merchants also had consolidated their hold on the town by governing the city and passing the major county offices among themselves.[39] But their failure to secure rail transportation had affected the town's growth. In ten years, Helena's population had increased by 17 per cent, from 3,108 in 1870 to 3,637 in 1880.

The Helena of 1880 resembled the Helena of ten years before, but several internal transformations had overtaken the urban village. Despite an increase in women in the community during the decade, Helena remained a man's world. Men outnumbered women by two to one and by as much as four to one in some age groups. Helena had lost some, but not all, of its youthfulness: nearly 50 per cent of the population was between the ages of twenty-one and forty. One-quarter of the men still took up residence together in exclusively male groups, but households containing parents and children had become the dominant living arrangement, comprising 62 per cent of the total. The number of nuclear, extended, and double families had also increased, and their growth accounted for part of Helena's transformation.[40]

In 1870, the average nuclear family in Helena had four members; in 1880, it accommodated five persons. This increase was largely attributable to the greater number of children and boarders. A decade before, 5 per cent of Helena's population boarded; in 1880, 12 per cent of the town's residents, primarily young, single men or husbands without their wives, took up lodgings with a family.[41] The nuclear family, then, drew the community's single males and, to a lesser extent, single females into its circle. This resulted in fewer and larger households and the heightened influence and scrutiny of the family over unattached men and women in the community. The domination of the nuclear family in Helena also indicated the town's increasing inclination toward permanence and away from the instability of a mining camp.

The occupational structure of the community also reflected the town's transition. Helena was still service-oriented, even though by 1880 miners represented only 15 per cent of the population; the town had begun to serve a wider market than its own population.[42] Helena also attracted skilled artisans and mechanics, especially those employed in the building trades: ninety-five carpenters, fourteen brick masons, twenty-three painters, thirty-one stonemasons, one plumber, and one gas-fitter labored to replace Helena's flimsy wooden buildings with lasting ones of stone and to outfit them with modern conveniences. The departure of the miners had eliminated shopkeepers who had depended on the prospectors' business. The sixty grocers of 1870 numbered fifteen in 1880, and the number of laundry workers had decreased by half.[43]

For Helena's workers, the community's continued orientation toward providing services and its reliance on semi-skilled and service workers had far-reaching implications, especially for single, unattached women. From the outset, Helena's single men needed a number of services normally provided by wives or mothers in the home. Because such domestic settings were few on the frontier, initially men provided these services in the business sector. Provision of these services on such a large scale, however, invited women to seek employment as a natural extension of their work in the home. Once the service had become a bona fide Main Street business, women who had performed these services as part of their housekeeping duties seized the opportunity to trade on their skills for cash.[44] The best example of this development was women's competition with Chinese men in the laundry business. Because Chinese laundrymen provided less expensive service, "celestial" washhouses could undercut the prices asked by white women. Helena's laundresses challenged the Chinese on January 27, 1866, when they published a notice in the *Montana Radiator* warning the Chinese washermen to leave town or be visited by a committee of laundresses who would enforce its wishes.[45] The women's militancy indicated the public nature of their work and the women's attitude toward their labor. The laundry women believed their services to be worth the price they asked and that their occupation deserved protection.

By 1880, women also dominated domestic service. In 1870, 46 per cent of the servants in Helena were male; ten years later, women comprised 77 per cent of Helena's domestics.[46] But servants were difficult to obtain and to retain. Although there were opportunities for domestic employment, Helena's women had other alternatives. Business opportunities in the service trades and the blandishments of the town's numerous bachelors lured away many potential female servants.[47] Even children, who were little older than householders' sons and daughters, were pressed into service.[48] In 1870, only 10 per cent of the households could boast a servant of any kind; in 1880, only 11 per cent had servants.[49]

In short supply, Helena's servants could command good wages, dictate the terms of their employment, and force the town's middling women (those in that broad category between the elite and the lower class) to meet their demands. Like the laundresses several years before, a labor conflict in the spring of 1873 demonstrated the servants' bargaining power and solidarity. In May, Elizabeth Fisk's maid, the latest in a long line of household help, made her excuses and left during spring cleaning. "She remarked," Elizabeth wrote to her mother, "to a friend whom she met on the way that she thought she would go away till we were through housecleaning then she guessed I would take her back, and she was going to have fifty dollars a month, too." Earlier in May, Helena's wives had heard that their servants intended to strike for fifty dollars a month. This attitude affronted Elizabeth, and she asked herself, ". . . why may not the mistresses also effect an organization and reduce their servants' wages." Elizabeth gathered the ladies together and, as a group, they decided that not only would they reject the rumored wage demand, but they would also reduce servants' wages from forty to thirty dollars a month.[50]

Elizabeth badly misjudged both the resolution of Helena's domestics and that of her peers. Except for Elizabeth, the town's chatelaines capitulated one by one. Elizabeth ruefully wrote of the whole affair: "The Irish girls are all '*down on me*,' to use a mountain phrase, and I don't suppose I could find one to work for me even for a hundred dollars."[51] Elizabeth was right. She could not engage a new servant until July, and her new servant stayed only a few months before leaving to open a washhouse.[52] Helena's middling women could either pay the market rate or shoulder the work themselves. For female domestics, however, their work was either a lucrative avenue to their own businesses or a means of supporting themselves until marriage. In any case, women both publicly and privately capitalized on their ability to provide household services in the community.

With no industries that traditionally employed women, such as textiles, Helena offered few other opportunities for female employment. In 1870, women comprised 5 per cent of the work force; by 1880, they made up 8 per cent of those who were employed. Not surprisingly, in 1870 and 1880, working women clustered in the semi-skilled and service group; further, they constituted 19 per cent in 1870 and 21 per cent in 1880 of that entire group. Although only a few women had managed to edge their way into white-collar positions by 1870, they moved quickly into the professions during the following decade. In 1870, women had accounted for a meager 4 per cent of professionals; but within ten years, largely as a result of the increase in the number of schoolteachers, their proportion had jumped to 22 per cent.[53]

Despite the tiny percentage of women in the work force, a significant proportion of women worked outside the home. Twenty per cent of Helena's adult women in 1870 listed some form of gainful employment; ten years later, 22 per cent of the women listed an occupation other than "keeping house."[54] The census for Poughkeepsie, New York, a community with several large mills that employed women, tallied 16 per cent of the female population employed in 1870 and 18 per cent in 1880.[55] Even though they did not have the employment possibilities Poughkeepsie's women did, Helena's women entered the labor force in slightly greater numbers. Like Poughkeepsie women, Helena's female workers were young and unmarried.

As Helena entered the 1880s, the most important decade of its existence, one group of women had carved out a place for themselves in the local economy. Because service employment was a mainstay, women gained an entrée into the chinks and crevasses of Helena's occupational structure. Some women made Main Street businesses of their domestic skills; others, most notably the town's domestics, consolidated their position out of the public eye. In a world of few women, Helena's working women were conspicuous, and their visibility underpinned their acceptability in the community.[56] Women's avenues into the work force, however, diverged sharply; they could work in either the professions or the semi-skilled and service occupations. Except for sewing, the skilled trades and large-scale proprietorships remained beyond women's economic reach.

More than anything else, Helena's people were men and women on the move. Even by nineteenth century standards, Helena's population was transient. Of those listed in the 1870 census, only 18 per cent remained to be counted in 1880. In Hamilton, Ontario, a commercial town at mid-century, for example, almost twice the percentage—33 per cent—stayed for a decade.[57] Population growth and stability, however, would come to Helena in the early 1880s when the railroad connected the town with the national market and stimulated a new burst of economic activity.

By 1883, Helena had escaped the grim reaper that haunted the urban mining frontier and turned its towns into ghosts. Additional mineral wealth—the timely development of nearby silver lodes—combined with the persistence and determination of Helena's merchants to bring the town from mining camp to entrepôt community and bureaucratic clearinghouse. Although it remained an urban village in size, in less than twenty years Helena, at least superficially, mimicked the nation's other nineteenth century cities.

The Northern Pacific Railroad's completion of its mainline to Helena in 1883 marked a turning point in the city's history, catapulting Helena from village to metropolis in a few years. The *Herald* followed the progress of the Northern Pacific day by day, jubilantly tallying each mile of track laid. By the beginning of June, train- and track-watching superseded all other social engagements, as city residents jaunted out fourteen miles east of Helena to the end of the track. On June 12, 1883, the construction train and crew arrived in town to be greeted by great fanfare.[58]

Rail connections with eastern commercial centers revitalized business and brought new people to Helena. Silver-mine owners, for example, could now inexpensively ship the ore they did not refine locally to distant reduction centers. As the financial clearinghouse for nearby mining and smelter operations, Helena looked forward to a period of increasing prosperity; those outside the territory and in the territory's moribund towns sensed new opportunities. Between 1880 and 1887, Helena's population nearly tripled.[59] The city directory for 1886 reflected a heady optimism and exuberance bred of easy money and the city's spectacular growth. The directory's compilator counted everyone, even the prostitutes. He honored some citizens with imaginative occupations and addresses. John X. Beidler, former vigilante and U.S. marshal, for example, appeared as "a terror to bad men"; F. Pauntier's residence was reported as "where the woodbine twineth"; and H. A. Smith boarded "all around where the hash [was] good."[60]

The arrival of the Northern Pacific generated more civic improvement in Helena, which had finally incorporated two years earlier. The city council allocated funds to pave Main Street, and in 1885 electric lights illuminated the town's streets.[61] In 1886, a group of venturesome local capitalists established the city's first public transportation, the Helena Street Railway. Drawn at first by horses, the cars were soon converted to steam power and finally to electricity.[62] The city's residents and businesses soon had telephones, and the city also contracted for water and for sewage disposal facilities. The city council handed down countless regulations to improve Helena's sanitation and safety: no longer could draymen leave large rocks on the public thoroughfare; householders were constrained to keep their livestock properly penned and their privies and ditches covered. The council also took steps to elevate citizens' behavior, passing ordinances to curb minor and major vices.[63]

Helenans underscored their financial institutions' belief in Helena's permanence by generating a housing boom, which was aided by the new Home Building and Loan Association and other Helena lending institutions.[64] For most residents, house-building was a modest affair, but for Helena's successful capitalists it became a way to display their wealth and status. Samuel T. Hauser, T. C. Power, Louis Kaufman, and others built enormous residential monuments to their successes on the frontier. Not the typical wooden structure of the period, these Victorian mansions stood solid in stone and brick with architectural filigree, dominating the western side of the gulch.[65] These capitalists also built businesses and civic buildings in the commercial district. In 1888 alone, thirty-one large commercial buildings went up in the gulch; the Gold Block, the Diamond Block, and the Granite Block, named for durable or precious commodities, joined structures called after their successful capitalist owners. The county also participated in this architectural spree in 1885 by building its new courthouse on Broadway.

During this period of expansion, Helena had grown beyond its original boundaries, had platted several new additions, and by the early 1890s had contemplated its first housing developments and suburbs. The Helena and Denver Land Investment Company designed the Lenox Addition, a planned community on the city's east side named for a fashionable New York City neighborhood. Envisioned as an elite residential area connected to the city by its own streetcar service, the Lenox Addition offered Helena's new gentry an imitation of countrified living. By the late 1880s, Helena had become a miniature of older nineteenth century cities, in both its architectural elegance and urban plan.[66]

During the first years of railroad-minded prosperity, Helena merchants had new cause for celebration; in 1887, a second major rail line, the Montana Central Railroad (later incorporated with the Great Northern Railroad), entered the city. Financial pundits promised new rail spurs to connect Helena with nearby mining communities.[67] For Helena merchants and the Helena Board of Trade, the coming of the new railroad was the beginning of their halcyon years. Although Board membership had nearly doubled in ten years, its secretary urged a membership drive to increase the rolls to 200 "wide-awake business men" and formal incorporation to broaden their support of Helena's growing commercial community. In their discussions, Board members entertained suggestions ranging from the installation of salmon ladders to garnering convention business; but the Board's secretary also saw his organization increasingly involved in the city's daily affairs. Despite its city charter, Helena continued to be governed by established merchants. Board of Trade members traded city offices among themselves, and some managed election to territorial offices.[68]

Helena's rapid growth meant money, and chief among the townspeople who joyously displayed their wealth were the wives of the city's elite. Accounts of their expensive entertainments and recreations, lavish weddings, and soirées for their children became commonplace in the city's newspapers. In imitation of their eastern sisters, Helena's wives dressed in the latest fashion, decked themselves with jewelry, and gave costly dinners, dances, and teas. "The ladies of Helena," the *Herald* observed after New Year's 1888, "wore diamonds enough yesterday to pay off the county debt."[69] In their gambling, men matched the women's extravagances. In March 1888, the *Herald* reported a high stakes poker game between "two well known capitalists" and "two of the sporting fraternity." At one point, according to the paper, $40,000 rested on the table and on the draw. The capitalists proved no match for the professionals; the former left the table $16,000 poorer.[70]

Receptions in their westside mansions and the social prominence of their wives publicly confirmed the place of Helena's merchants at the head of the social order. The city's male elite further substantiated its position by creating a private club for themselves—the Montana Club. Initially established in the spirit of public commitment and endeavor, the founders made it clear in the club's constitution, bylaws, and dues that membership was to be exclusive and monied. Not surprisingly, Board of Trade members constituted the club's first board of directors in April 1885.[71]

Mansions and men's clubs heralded another shift in Helena's social structure. During the early years, Helena's heterogeneous population had displayed a relative lack of class consciousness; the town had always had a band of rich residents, a large group of middling folk, a smaller group of skilled artisans, representatives of the unskilled kind, and the poor. Generally, however, the richer and poorer elements had mingled freely, disregarding the boundaries of social class. Capitalists, blacksmiths, bartenders, and shopkeepers lived and worked side by side. At community celebrations, especially the New Year's Day open house, representatives of most stations in life trooped from house to house.[72] Most Helena residents, however, were middle class. They had arrived in the territory with a modicum of wealth, and those who were foreign-born had lost their immigrant status during their successive moves before finally settling in Montana. For the first fifteen years of Helena's existence, no great disparities in wealth divided the city's population of middling merchants into social groups. Far more concerned with other issues, the middling citizens generally ignored ethnic, religious, and class boundaries.

The influx of new arrivals and less acculturated immigrants combined with the infusion of wealth to sharpen social divisions. Although Helena had never been a classless society, the changes and the increase in population made its citizens more aware of class differences, which became an important means of organizing social relationships. The new prosperity had also produced greater economic disparities. For the first time, an identifiable elite influenced social intercourse, and residential patterns in the city changed, reflecting the new class lines. The elite and socially pretentious gathered on the west side of the gulch; the solid middling families remained on the east side. The skilled workers occupied the areas near the railroad depot or lived in or around Main Street near their businesses; the city's lower orders clustered in the south end of the gulch between the Chinese section and the city limits. Beginning in the late 1880s, invitations to New Year's open houses and society weddings were generally reserved for Helena's "best" people.[73]

Ethnic societies and special interest groups further divided the populace. As early as 1883, for example, Helena's Germans published their own German language newspaper and founded a church. Professionals, such as the town's physicians, formed associations, and workers organized unions.[74] The construction of a major smelter five miles east of the city in 1887, which siphoned off a large part of the city's immigrant, industrial working class, further formalized class distinctions in Helena; the working class literally lived at a distance in their own community. Despite the appearance of strengthening class boundaries in its environs, Helena itself remained predominantly white collar and middle class.[75]

Even as the city's mercantile captains congratulated themselves on their successes and looked forward to greater entrepreneurial achievements, some observers looked back and sensed that something had slipped away. In 1887, E. V. Smalley captured the essence of these changes when he wrote:

> The railroad was the great epoch-making factor in the history of Montana. It took much of the romance and adventure from Montana life, it took away the sense of remoteness and daring, made life more commonplace, brought in the Eastern drummer and the Eastern fashions, set people to traveling, made them ambitious for big houses and fine furniture, and introduced a new population which knows not the ways of the "old-timer.". . . It seemed then a wonder of eager, busy, money-getting and money-spending far-Western life, hospitable, buoyant, extravagant, enterprising and courageous. The men seemed of a different stamp from those of the East. . . .[76]

As publicist for the Northern Pacific Railroad, Smalley perceived the railroad's effect in the community. Yet, he was clearly sympathetic to the older community (perhaps touched with a bit of romanticism) and understood that the *arrivistes* (those who arrived after the completion of the railroad) had rearranged the older society and had placed their stamp on the city.

These newcomers had different ideas about respectability and were less tolerant of activities the community had formerly overlooked: gambling, conducting business on Sundays, and prostitution, for example. As they swelled the population, they became numerous enough to win seats on the city council and make their presence and perspective known. Even the renaming of an original street indicated the newcomers' influence. Named for the bridge that once crossed the gulch stream, Bridge Street had been the central thoroughfare in Helena's first commercial area; but by the mid 1880s, it had become synonymous with the city's vice district. Like Smalley, the *Herald*'s journalist paused to reflect, commenting on the significance of the city council's decision to rename the street "State Street":

> As the camp grew, houses and homes were built out on the flats and towards the north, and most of the vice and disreputableness of the wild and bustling mining camp concentrated on Bridge Street. Much of it has stayed there ever since until within the last year when the city council decreed that it should take itself off. Much of it did find other quarters and that is why the remaining residents asked for a change of name. They wanted to blot out the unsavory period of the street's history by letting its very name be forgotten, unmindful of the fact that this would also blot out its still earlier history.[77]

By 1890, Helena's population had nearly quadrupled, numbering 13,854 residents. The city boasted six banks with varying resources and three new business organizations: the Chamber of Commerce, a commercial club, and the Helena Clearing House Exchange. Although the city's newcomers made inroads in local politics, Helena's established entrepreneurs continued their domination of local economic affairs and politics and led state government. E. W. Knight, Henry Klein, Henry Parchen, C. K. Wills, and E. W. Bach were among the Chamber's officers and on the rolls of the Helena Board of Trade; R. C. Walker, secretary of the Board of Trade and of the Chamber of Commerce, won election as mayor in April of 1890; the state legislature chose T. C. Power, one of the original Board members, as U.S. Senator on April 16, 1890; and the legislature met in the Helena Board of Trade rooms in 1891 with Board of Trade members Cornelius Hedges, D. A. Corey, John Horsky, and A. M. Holter, representing Lewis and Clark County.[78]

The new decade, however, brought bad news to burgeoning Helena. Montana's silver boom during the 1880s had coincided with a global increase in silver production and several nations' return to gold as the standard for their currencies. As a result, the bottom fell out of the silver market, and silver-producing states appealed to the federal government for help. Congress responded with the Sherman Silver Purchase Act in 1890, which stipulated that the government would buy all the silver these states could produce and exchange it for U.S. Treasury notes redeemable in gold. While the Sherman Act propped up Montana's and other states' economies for a time, it seriously depleted U.S. Treasury gold reserves and underpinned national financial instability.

The first signs of economic trouble in Helena appeared in 1891. Helena's grand hotels, the symbols of its prosperity and witnesses to its urban sophistication, began to change ownership. The Merchants Hotel closed its doors under assignment in June 1891; the following month, Samuel Schwab and Edward Zimmerman transferred ownership of the Cosmopolitan Hotel to its head clerk and a local caterer. The International Hotel, a Helena landmark for many years, also closed that summer, although the management announced it would re-open as the Mineral

Springs Hotel (which it did under the management of Marcus Lissner). Helena's privately owned utilities and transportation facilities were on shaky ground. The Helena Street Railway went on the block to satisfy a judgment awarded to the Northwest Guaranty Loan Company. Investors, such as Thomas Cruse, who had gone far afield to find profitable places for their money, found themselves pressed. Laborers, too, grew restless. Afro-American workers turned on the Chinese, the former urging employers to dismiss their Asian employees. In East Helena, smeltermen demanded a pay raise from $2.25 to $2.50 per day. Set against these harbingers of economic ill health were two bright portents: a promised U.S. military post and a projected cracker factory.[79]

The promises of the Department of War and the National Biscuit Company were not enough. During June 1893, as banks failed across the nation and began the Panic of 1893, Helena's financial institutions shook, trembled, and fell. At that time, Helena boasted six major banks; no other city, Helena boosters claimed, had a comparable per capita bank capitalization or deposits. During the last two weeks in July, depositors withdrew more than one million dollars; on July 27, 1893, Helena's premier bank, the First National, suspended operations along with the Montana National Bank.

The banks' foreclosures forced many Helena businessmen to make assignment of their property. Commenting on the banks' suspension of business, the *Herald* correctly attributed the failures to the instability of out-of-state investments. "It was not local investments alone," the *Herald* noted, "but the large placing of Helena capital on the outside that created the money stringency." Nevertheless, the paper omitted naming bank officials who had liberally helped themselves to the banks' resources and who had failed to question the houses' lack of cash reserves.[80]

On August 5, 1893, some two hundred businessmen and professionals convened in the Board of Trade's rooms to discuss solutions. After expressions of confidence in the officers of the beleaguered banks and pledges to reduce the number of employees in their businesses, the group called for an immediate curtailment of municipal and school expenditures, including the dismissal of several municipal employees and a reduction in teachers' salaries. Anticipating little opposition from the teachers, who were mostly women, the city council cut teachers' pay and received no complaints. But firing male city workers posed a different problem. Because council members and businessmen feared alienating their constituencies or customers by formally advocating dismissals, the proposal languished and soon died. Conditions improved later that summer when the Second National Bank and the Helena National Bank merged under the latter's name. But for Shirley Ashby, president of the Second National, it was the end; he resigned, assigned his property, and finally filed bankruptcy. Others suffered the same fate.[81]

Events in Washington, D.C., soon exacerbated conditions in Helena. In August 1893, Congress followed President Grover Cleveland's lead by fastening on the nostrum of free silver as chief contributor to the panic, defeating the coinage of silver at any ratio, and passing the Wilson bill that repealed the free coinage of silver. With that, the congressional debate over free coinage effectively ended, as did Helena's salad days.

Badly shaken, Helena weathered the silver coinage repeal and sustained its civic optimism. To all outward appearances, Helena had made a miraculous recovery by the autumn of 1893. Its banks were back in business, and the city had retired over two million dollars worth of debts. But astute financial mandarins would have noted suspicious maneuverings among Helena bankers, indicating their institutions' continued weakness. Helena's banks began a quiet merger program until their number fell to four.[82]

The vulnerability of Helena's financial bulwarks indicated a general worsening of local economic conditions. For marginal citizens and tenderloin capitalists, the situation became desperate. In September of 1893, the *Herald* reported that authorities had arrested Joe Wing, a Chinese, for stealing lunch pails from city street workers.[83] Josephine "Chicago Joe" Hensley, a red-light district entrepreneur, approached the city council for a reduction of the city's "variety theater tax" from seventy-five dollars to forty dollars per month, claiming that the closing of her Coliseum Theatre promised to throw thirty to forty people out of work. Faced with the prospect of greater unemployment, the council majority out-voted its scrupulous members and acquiesced to Hensley's request.[84] What the council bestowed on one element of the vice district, it took away from another. In late August, police officers raided Clore Street, the poorer red-light district, and arrested thirty-nine women and seventeen men on various charges, fining the women ten dollars each and the men twenty-five. In one stroke, the city collected $815.[85] Reduced to shaking down its whores and pimps for revenue, Helena had reached a pretty pass.

The city's economy had ground to a halt by the mid 1890s, but the worst was yet to come. Reorganization could not save the city's financial citadels, and the demise of the First National Bank and the Merchants National Bank in 1896 further undermined depositors' confidence.[86] Both banks went into receivership, and many citizens' savings evaporated.[87] The poor economy meant fewer employment opportunities and a loss of population as workers filed out of the city in search of work. In 1896, Rollin Lynde Hartt, a tedious young Congregational minister, wrote to his mother that he had heard reports that 2,000 people had left the city.[88]

Discovery of gold in the Klondike, the prominence of Butte's copper industry, and the Spanish American War further drained the city's population. Butte's expanding copper production enticed blue-collar laborers who were willing to work in the mines and smelters. In May 1898, the call for volunteers to fight Spain further depleted the city's young male population. When Company L of the First Montana Volunteers returned to Helena in October 1899, only forty-five of the original eighty-one made up the group. Some had re-enlisted in other regiments; others had remained in Manila or stayed on in California looking for white-collar jobs or manual labor someplace other than Helena.[89]

A demographic disaster had overtaken the city between 1890 and 1900; nearly one-quarter of its population had melted away. In 1890, the city had 13,854 inhabitants; ten years later, the number had declined to 10,770. Helena remained a city of families; over 80 per cent of its households were nuclear or one of its variations. Families also continued to supervise the young, unattached residents and, as had been the case twenty years earlier, one-eighth of the city's population boarded.[90]

The most conspicuous absentees in the population at the turn of the century were the Chinese. In 1880, they had made up 8 per cent of the population; in 1900, they constituted 2 per cent. Less obvious was the reduced number of young men. In the twenty-one to thirty-year age group, the sex ratio, so long weighted in favor of men, reversed itself. There were now 123 women for every 100 men in that category, a development that affected women's prospects for marriage. Whereas 29 per cent of the women in that age group were unmarried in 1880, in 1900 46 per cent of them were single.[91]

With the exodus of young men from the city, women entered the work force in greater numbers than ever before. In 1900, women comprised 20 per cent of the city's workers and 27 per cent of Helena's adult women worked outside the home. Women still worked primarily as professionals and semi-skilled and service workers, accounting for 36 per cent of Helena's professionals and an equal percentage of the semi-skilled and service labor; but they also made gains in the semi-professional and clerk classes.[92] In 1889, when the stenographers and "typewriters" had held their annual banquet, their association's membership had been entirely male. Ten years later, only fifteen men called themselves stenographers or typists, compared to forty-three women.[93] As was the case in the rest of the nation, women had taken command of the secretarial field. The two paths into the work force for women in Helena remained sharply divergent: they either entered the world of servitude in one form or another or the elite class of the professionals.

Women made the greatest professional gains in teaching. Not only did women continue to obtain employment as elementary and high school teachers, but they also won positions in Montana's fledgling universities. In 1895, Miss Bertha Reilly and Mrs. William Greenleaf were offered university professorships but declined to accept them because the annual salary of $1,000 was too low. Helena's medical fraternity accepted women as early as 1883. Prominent among its membership was Dr. Maria M. Dean, who practiced medicine in addition to chairing the county Board of Health and sitting on the school board.[94]

The most spectacular advancement among professional women was Ella Knowles's admission to the bar. Disdaining the security of a school principalship in 1888, Knowles returned to a vocation she had begun a few years earlier and commenced reading law with Helena attorney Joseph W. Kinsley. In gaining entry to the legal profession, Knowles faced formidable obstacles, not the least of which was the law itself. The territorial statutes were specific about the gender appropriate to the practice of law, and it was not Ella's. In 1889, with little trouble but serious debate over women's rights, Montana lawmakers amended the statute, making women eligible for the bar. For several years afterward, Knowles engaged in a successful law practice in Helena, successful enough that she caught the attention of the Populist party. In 1892, the Populists nominated her for Attorney General. Knowles campaigned strenuously, and although she ran third behind the winner, Henri Haskell, she made a better showing than her Populist running mates. She also impressed Haskell sufficiently to be appointed Assistant Attorney General following the election.[95]

Two significant additions to Helena's architecture in the early 1890s, C. A. Broadwater's gewgawed and monstrous Victorian natatorium and hotel and U.S. Fort William Henry Harrison, epitomized the new social class divisions that had developed during Helena's post-railroad period. In Broadwater's filigree-adorned spa, Helena's elite had a showplace in imitation of eastern resorts, while the city acquired in Fort Harrison what appeared to its citizenry as a concentrated group of lower-class people. Together, the Broadwater complex and Fort Harrison represented the extreme ends of a new social and economic order demarcated by class distinctions.

Unlike the city's earlier residents who generally ignored social boundaries and tolerated a wide range of behavior, the newcomers of the 1880s introduced more stringent standards of social conduct and imposed new definitions of urban life on the populace. Some of the city's successful entrepreneurs were only too willing to parrot what the new arrivals declared to be the hallmarks of a mature city. And both the newcomers' and elite's inclination in these matters was reinforced by the increase of familial households in the city and the general concern for constructing a beneficial environment for families.

While Helena's history over thirty years exhibited change, it also evinced stasis. Far from ephemeral, demographic characteristics associated with a frontier persisted in one form or another until at least 1885. Helena still had many more men than women, maintained a youthful population, encompassed a various immigrant and regional mix, experienced increases and decreases in population, and remained a service economy, although the nature of the services had altered as Helena had moved from entrepôt to bureaucratic center. Even as the *arrivistes* made inroads into local politics, the commercial ranks kept control of the community's affairs. Although Helena was a village compared to Boston during the same period, the town's occupational structure, except for its larger number of semi-skilled and service workers, replicated that of its giant, eastern counterpart.[96] Despite the similarity of their occupational structures, Helena's demographic makeup and social order were far different. Both visitors and citizens recognized much in Helena as familiar, but they would have marveled at the city's attitude and society. Like Alexis de Toqueville, an early observer of the American scene, they would have been fascinated by Helena's women.

And what of Helena's women? The census and newspapers reveal only the barest outlines of their experience. On the one hand, statistical evidence demonstrates the discontinuity of women's roles; on the other hand, other sources suggest the continuity of women's status. For women, who out of necessity or desire took up employment, Helena's service economy provided opportunity and compensation. This trend, apparent in 1870, did not abate, and the demand for women's skills brought greater public acceptance of working women. Helena's orientation toward a service economy, which remained fundamentally unaltered even during the Panic of 1893, assisted women's employment. By 1900, more Helena women worked than ever before, and a good number of them entered the professions. Work that had been a part of single women's lives as early as 1870 had been confirmed as a stage in women's life cycles by 1900. The departure of young men in the face of Helena's economic decline and the tertiary sector's concomitant growth as Montana's governmental bureaucracy grew created new places for the city's female workers. Opportunity, coupled with social precedent, created a visible group of women workers. At the turn of the century, Helena's women constituted a potent economic force in the community and had the potential to make themselves heard and heeded in the world beyond their workplaces.

Until the post-railroad years, middling women had confronted a society that provided them with few institutional outlets. American society during the last half of the nineteenth century served men's rather than women's interests, but Helena's demographic composition made it even more of a man's city. No matter how concerned they were with the community's survival, the city's men ignored churches, put little effort into schools, and channeled their energy away from family activities and toward financial betterment. Until their numbers increased sufficiently during the post-railroad period, Helena's matrons were strangers in a strange land. When women's activities finally received notice, the journalists in the mid 1880s portrayed them as socialites, as the standard-bearers of the new civic and social morality, and as civilizers of the untamed frontier. Superficially, at least, the city's wives and mothers, pioneer and *arriviste* alike, had assumed the role of "gentle tamer." What described the experience of the majority of women, however, did not encompass the whole.

One group of Helena's working women—the prostitutes—created an economic empire within the city, and the chronicle of the expansion and contraction of their holdings and the transformation of society in the half-world mirrored Helena's own development between 1865 and 1900. A force to be reckoned with, these capitalists with rooms represented the largest class of working women until 1900 and assisted in redefining frontier womanhood both for themselves and for other women.

CHAPTER TWO

Capitalists with Rooms

Prostitution in Helena, 1865-1900

WHEN THE SECRETARY OF THE Helena Board of Trade submitted his first report in 1878, he included mention of wages:

> Laborers wages $2 50 to $4 00 per day; miners, $4 00 to $5 00 per day; mechanics, $5 00 to $7 00 per day; farm labor, $50 00 per month; female labor, cooks and general house work, $30 00 to $40 00 per month.

Propriety forced him to exclude from the list the largest single female employment outside the home until 1900—prostitution.[1]

A miniature of the city's economic world, prostitution experienced the same boom-and-bust cycles as did the city's legitimate economy; like business on Main Street, the demimonde was a dynamic institution, changing its form and organization from the time of the city's founding to the turn of the century. From 1865 to 1880, "proprietor prostitutes," women who worked alone out of small houses that they owned, dominated the red-light district. During the 1880s, several madams consolidated ownership of the demimonde business, established the first bawdy houses, refurbished the red-light district by constructing their own buildings, and rented space to other women who ran a variety of operations. In 1893, however, the "empire" that the fancy ladies had built in the south end of the gulch began to crumble. Pimps appeared and replaced women as prostitution's managers and property owners, turning the sexual marketplace into a dangerous and desperate place. By 1900, women's control of prostitution had ceased.

More than any other female occupation, prostitution depended on the abundance of unattached men in the frontier population and the general populace's tolerant attitude toward male recreations. When the population changed after the coming of the railroad, the fancy ladies found themselves under attack from moral reformers among the parvenus who were concerned about the quality of Helena's urban life. Although the demimonde successfully defended itself, this program of moral reform heralded a reorientation of the city's interests and goals—a direction that did not provide a major role for the skin trade.

Aside from reflecting the economic cycles in the city and attitudinal changes among the populace, prostitution also illustrated the nineteenth century woman's dilemma. Although conditions on the frontier promoted women's participation in service occupations, their opportunities outside marriage, family, and household superintendency were still limited. For those women who desired bigger profits and large-scale entrepreneurship, however, prostitution was an avenue into the ranks of the capitalists and into the public sphere. Yet, while their sisters labored to gain acceptance in the public sphere, the fancy ladies worked to create a private sphere of normality for themselves within the sexual marketplace. Regardless of their success or failure at enterprise or family or both, Helena's "soiled doves" widened the sphere of legitimate women by segregating "bad women" in one sector of the city and leaving the rest of Helena, including public spaces, open to other women and their aspirations.

Less well-known than the Samuel Hausers, T. C. Powers, and C. A. Broadwaters of the city, Helena's fancy ladies affected the development of the community and the lives of its citizens from the beginning. First among the fancy ladies at Last Chance Gulch, Fanny Bird, a black woman, appeared officially in the records on June 14, 1865. Soon Belle Robinson, Fanny Clark, and Mary Ann Petch emulated Fanny in Helena and purchased their property with earnings that probably derived from a brisk business during their first summer in the Prickly Pear Valley. After the winter of 1866, more prostitutes settled in Helena: Louisiana Martinez, Juana Torrera, Kate Silvers, Catherine Harrison, Eliza Carico, Henrietta Bischoff Zipp, Louise "Big Lou" Courselle, Nellie Perkins, Eliza Thompson, Eleanor Alphonsine "Madame Mustache" Dumont, and others—thirty-seven in all.[2]

Like many of the merchants who supplied the miners, Helena's "soiled doves" also appear to have migrated from other mining camps or bonanza towns whose best days had passed. Louise Courselle, for example, came north from California, and Carrie Whitney evidently started out in the cattle towns of Kansas.[3] These women arrived with capital, paying between $300 and $1,000 for their property in cash or in "good clean bankable gulch gold dust."[4] Between 1865 and 1870, after the fashion of Helena's small merchants, over $50,000 changed hands as these proprietor prostitutes made their initial investments or exchanged holdings, mostly among themselves.[5]

Helena's thirty-seven proprietor prostitutes made 119, or 44 per cent, of the 265 separate property transactions undertaken by women between 1865 and 1870. By circumstance or preference, the women of the demimonde dealt more with each other rather than with men. They also saw an advantage in dealing with a neutral figure, the probate judge, at public auction where the highest bid regardless of the bidder's gender secured the property.[6] Once situated, they behaved as other entrepreneurs and raised capital by mortgage.

Women in the demimonde accounted for all twenty mortgages made to women during the period; nearly a third of those mortgages were made by women to other women. The most common form was a chattel mortgage that alienated the women's beds, bureaus, pillows, sheets, bolsters, lace curtains, and spittoons to secure a loan. On the average, a prostitute could garner $500 in this manner.[7] When the women could not borrow from each other, they turned to neighboring businessmen. Edward Zimmerman, the Lavenberg brothers, John Mahan, and even respectable men of the stature of the Holter brothers, dealers in hardware and lumber, M. F. Truett, the probate judge, and the Herrmann brothers, furniture manufacturers, financially assisted the "working girls"—sometimes to the merchants' financial dismay.[8]

In the course of business dealings, the "soiled doves" and neighboring entrepreneurs came into conflict. In these disputes, the proprietor prostitutes demonstrated financial astuteness and familiarity with the law. In February of 1871, for example, merchants Selig and Alex Lavenberg sued Henrietta Zipp, also known as Henrietta Bischoff, for nonpayment of a $940 merchandise bill. Henrietta replied in kind. Most of the goods, she claimed, came as gifts from the Lavenbergs "in consideration of her favored affection and personal kindness" and constituted part of an arrangement whereby Henrietta agreed to act as an informal advertiser for the Lavenberg concern. The Lavenbergs pressed their suit, and in early July they threatened further action against her Joliet Street property. Faced with financial disaster, Henrietta retaliated, charging that the Lavenbergs had knowingly sold her the merchandise to furnish a house of prostitution. Because prostitution was contrary to public policy, the Lavenbergs could not legally carry their suit into court. The brothers swiftly denied the accusation and redoubled their efforts. On July 5, 1871, Henrietta countered with a deposition, specifically defining her "personal kindness" toward the Lavenbergs: a summary of receipts that itemized "lodging" at twenty dollars a night and "wine" purchases at five dollars a bottle. Henrietta's bill neatly equaled her dry-goods bill. In late July, the outmaneuvered Lavenbergs discreetly settled with Henrietta out of court.[9]

Using similar tactics, Catherine Harrison sued Thomas E. Pounds for nonpayment of $730 in October of 1870. In her complaint, Catherine alleged that Pounds had defaulted on loans totaling $375 and on a bill for "labor and service" that she estimated at $355. Pounds, a representative to the territorial legislature from Deer Lodge County, had apparently "boarded" at Catherine's from time to time before the legislative session and had departed owing money. For unknown reasons, Catherine left the territory shortly after November of 1870, and the disposition of the suit was never settled. Both Catherine and Henrietta felt free to bring their financial disagreements before the courts.[10]

Disputes between members of the demimonde and the legitimate business community were not an unlikely possibility; both the fancy ladies and respectable merchants occupied the same area of the city.[11] During the 1860s, Helena's houses of prostitution congregated in an entrenched tenderloin district that corresponded to the town's legitimate business section. First located on upper Wood Street with saloons and the Helena Theatre, prostitutes had moved to Bridge and Clore streets by the time major fires in 1869 had destroyed several Main Street businesses and the original tenderloin area. In the aftermath of the destruction, the probate judge sold various properties in the townsite at bargain prices, including many on east Wood Street. The soiled doves moved down the hill to take advantage of the sale.

White prostitutes, who shared the general and pervasive prejudice against Chinese, avoided the Chinatown section at the extreme southern end of the gulch and drifted farther north on Clore Street, establishing an L-shaped district that included Clore Street from Bridge to Wall streets and the east Wood Street and Bridge Street properties. In short, prostitution intruded financially and geographically into Helena's legitimate economy. Juana Torrera purchased property in the rear of the banking house formerly occupied by the Hershfields; Louise Courselle owned property across the street from Mike Reinig's grocery store; and John Denn, another grocer, often opened the back door of his shop late at night to accommodate the "working girls'" late-night Sunday shopping. Still other female entrepreneurs situated themselves adjacent to the district's many saloons.[12]

By 1870, approximately sixty women in Helena engaged in prostitution as madams, "hurdy-gurdy" owners, quasi-saloonkeepers, or common prostitutes.[13] Except for the Chinese prostitutes, these fancy ladies came from parts of the United States in the same proportion as did other Helena residents. Overwhelmingly, they lived alone in single-female households or in households composed entirely of women. At an average of twenty-eight years old, they were older than other women in the community; none were in their teens, but few were older than thirty-five.[14] Prostitutes on the Comstock Lode, the only other comparable mining town for which statistical data are available, were about the same age as Helena's "soiled doves," but the towns' prostitutes differed greatly in ethnicity and wealth.[15] The majority of Helena's prostitutes were native-born and had money. Twelve women, or one-third of the white demimonde population, reported having an average of $2,500 in personal wealth, and fifteen of them owned property. Approximately 60 per cent of the fancy ladies reported either personal wealth or property or both. Catherine Harrison and Mollie Grahm maintained bank accounts. Over half of Helena's prostitutes had sound finances; those who were not entrepreneurs in their own right worked under the purview of other women. Prostitution on Last Chance Gulch was women's business grounded in women's property and capital.[16]

Not immune to the economic vicissitudes that affected the regular business community, prostitution in Helena suffered a local depression in 1871 that thinned the ranks of the proprietor prostitutes. Only Catherine Harrison, Julia Bunker, Henrietta Bischoff, Nellie Perkins, Mollie Grahm, and Louise Courselle remained.[17] Josephine Airey, who had left Helena in 1869 to try her luck elsewhere, returned in 1871 and sensed economic opportunity in the midst of depression. She began building a reorganized tenderloin that in a decade would assume the proportions of an empire.

Sometime in 1858, fourteen-year-old Mary Welch arrived in New York harbor. Born on January 1, 1844, in Ireland, she came to America to escape poverty at home and, presumably, to "better her condition in life." Reportedly, she made her way to Chicago and worked in the red-light district there during the Civil War. After the fashion of the demimonde, she changed her name to one with more elegance, styling herself "Josephine Airey."[18] She came to Helena with capital. On April 5, 1867, Josephine purchased an improved property from Mary Ann Petch, paying $375 down and optimistically promising to pay the remaining $675 within three months.[19] On Valentine's Day in 1869 (the same day Helena's Main Street burned), Joe married another Wood Street habitué, Albert Hankins, a Chicago gambler with a dubious reputation.[20] Two other fires in the spring and fall of 1869 destroyed Main Street again, leaving both legitimate and illegitimate businesses in a precarious position. After two years of plying her trade, Josephine wanted to move closer to the center of activity, and on the morning of June 15, 1869, she spent four dollars for a lot two blocks farther east toward the intersection of Main and Wood streets. Catherine Harrison must have also seen the possibilities of the new location, for later that same afternoon she bought Josephine's newly acquired property for $150.[21] Taking her profit, Josephine and Albert decided that their future was not in Helena.

The Hankinses joined the stampede to White Pine, Nevada, the location of one of the most spectacular examples of boom-and-bust on the mining frontier. Beginning in 1868, the silver excitement in White Pine reached its peak in 1870 and just as quickly died by 1873. By her own account, Joe spent two years near Treasure Hill during its heyday. Perhaps she recognized White Pine's instability, having witnessed a similar phenomenon earlier in Montana. Whatever the reason, she returned to Helena in the fall of 1871, bereft of Albert but with money in her purse.[22]

Josephine came back to a depressed Helena. Reports from the R. G. Dun agent repeated again and again that "business was poor" and that many businessmen had sold out and left the city. Another fire on October 1, 1871, had leveled the Main Street business area, but this time business owners confronted a compounded disaster. The Great Chicago Fire a week later bankrupted dozens of insurance companies, leaving Helena's entrepreneurs with no means to recoup their losses. On October 11, 1871, Josephine bought out Henrietta Bischoff for $2,000, half of which she had at hand. She planned to raise the remainder with a loan from Harriet Truett, wife of the probate judge. Mrs. Truett drove a hard bargain, forcing Joe to mortgage her new property and chattels for $1,000 at 2 per cent interest per month. In addition, Truett guaranteed monthly interest payments and punctual repayment of the principle by holding a legal bill of sale for one dollar. Joe had irrevocably committed herself. On October 19, 1872, Joe satisfied the terms of her bargain, and the cashier of the First National Bank cancelled the note. Joe had a toehold in the demimonde once again.[23]

Situated on the corner of Bridge and Joliet streets, Josephine Airey's establishment—it is unclear whether it was a "hurdy-gurdy," a small saloon, or a simple prostitute proprietorship—provided her with the means for expansion. Six months after she had made good her mortgage, Joe made another purchase. On April 17, 1873, she spent $200 to reclaim the property she had sold two years earlier to Catherine Harrison.[24] A minor investment for Joe, the amount equaled four to five months' wages for the average working woman in Helena. Less than two months later, on July 15, 1873, she began to raise capital, using the property as collateral.

For her next mortgage she approached Selig Lavenberg, a Bridge Street dry-goods merchant in partnership with his brother Alex. The brothers had contracted loans with other prostitutes on several occasions. The R. G. Dun agent described Alex as, "Very hard pay. 'L' lives here with a woman not his wife. He is a very hard case." Undeterred by the Lavenberg character, Joe put herself in jeopardy again by mortgaging all her property and personalty, including her underwear ("three dozen pair under clothes"), for $3,000 at 2 per cent per month.[25]

Although Joe had prospered on the corner of Joliet and Bridge streets and although her inventory of personal effects now included "one gold watch and chain, five diamond rings, one fur cloak, muff, and cuffs, twelve dresses . . . three shawls, [and] one velvet cloak," another fire in January 1874 damaged her property and put her holdings in financial peril. The conflagration, which began in the Chinese residential section near the corner of Wood and Main streets, burned everything for two blocks on both sides of Main Street. Pressed by the Lavenbergs who suffered considerable losses in the fire, Joe drew on a hidden reserve and paid off the mortgage on January 26, 1874, six months before it was due.[26]

Joe suffered damage in the fire, but other proprietor prostitutes—Louise Courselle, Nellie Perkins, and Mollie Grahm—watched their futures in Helena burn up with their houses. They never recovered from losses that totaled nearly $12,000.[27] Coupled with the earlier departures of Catherine Harrison, Julia Bunker, and Henrietta Bischoff, the disaster effectively ended the era of the proprietor prostitute, the first phase in the history of prostitution in Helena.

Along with the other Helena business owners, Joe started over and rebuilt. Eight months later she acquired a lot directly across the street from her holdings, Louise Courselle's scorched and devalued property. Joe had acquired another bargain, paying only $150 for property that before the fire had been valued at $2,000. She made no further purchases over the next four years, but during this period her status changed from proprietor prostitute to quasi-legitimate tavern owner. Joe opened the Red Light Saloon on Wood Street and hired James T. "Black Hawk" Hensley, a local gambling talent, as its manager.[28]

As the economy improved in 1878, Joe re-entered the real estate market, purchasing another property on the south side of Wood Street.[29] One month later, on December 17, 1878, she married Hensley. In marriage, Joe did not entirely give up her financial independence. In February 1874, the Montana legislature had approved a statute allowing women to own and operate businesses in their own right. The "sole trader" law permitted women separate entrepreneurial identities; and, as other women had, Joe engaged in enterprises separate from her husband's concerns. Attentive to detail, she periodically updated her inventory as she acquired new properties; from these listings, it is clear that "Black Hawk" had only marginal involvement in Joe's affairs.[30] From time to time, his name appeared with hers on deeds, but this seems to have been a courteous gesture on Joe's part; she kept her investments securely and legally in her own name.

In 1879 and 1880, Joe added to her portfolio of properties by purchasing nine parcels on the north and south sides of Wood Street. For a total capital investment of $1,800, Joe owned most of the Wood Street demimonde. These properties were inexpensive because the district had acquired an unwholesome reputation and many of the poorer businesses had not rebuilt after the fires. Respectable owners of respectable businesses had moved their businesses farther north on Main Street, and Joe happily bought up their depreciating properties.[31]

By 1880, when Josephine Airey Hensley had gained entrepreneurial control of the demimonde, the character of prostitution in Helena had changed. Just as civic and economic responsibility for the city's future came into the hands of the Helena Board of Trade, so control of Helena's demimonde devolved on Josephine Hensley. The concentration of entrepreneurial power and property in one person limited the possibility of proprietorships and engendered new forms of prostitution in the city.

Symptomatic of the trend away from independent proprietorships was the situation of the Chinese prostitutes. Nearly half of the approximately fifty-three prostitutes in Helena in June of 1880 were Chinese. Their living arrangements and the profile of their ages differed markedly from their white counterparts. The Chinese women were a little older, averaging twenty-eight years, and the range of their ages was greater: there were several women in their teens and several in their forties. Most of them lived with men, identified variously as a servant, a restaurant keeper, a baker, and an acrobat; one Chinese fancy lady lived with seven Chinese cooks. Most often, these women lived with pimps whom the census enumerator described as "loafers." These Cantonese women lived in patterns distinctly different from those in their native country, and it is apparent that men controlled prostitution in Helena's Chinatown. There is no record, for example, of any Chinese woman owning property or appearing in any criminal court action on her own behalf. In the social structure of the sexual marketplace, Helena's Chinese prostitutes were at the bottom.[32]

The demographic character of the white prostitute population changed little between 1870 and 1880. Their ages averaged a little younger—twenty-seven in 1880 compared to twenty-eight in 1870—and they were generally between twenty-one and thirty-five years old. Broadly speaking, the regional origins of the white "working girls" mirrored the origins of their earlier sisters in 1870 and the general population in 1880, although the Midwest provided more "working girls" proportionally than it did legitimate settlers. Unlike the Comstock during the same period, most of Helena's "soiled doves" were from native stock. Generally, prostitutes' economic control and resources diminished during the decade. The prostitutes' wealth in the form of bank accounts declined by 15 per cent, although nearly one-third of them still had some kind of working capital. Property ownership by prostitutes also decreased from 45 to 13 per cent, and their aggregate financial base (property or wealth) decreased by roughly 20 per cent, from 57 to 36 per cent.[33]

The most significant change, however, occurred between 1870 and 1880 in the prostitutes' relative loss of autonomy; they became renters rather than proprietors. This decline in property ownership radically altered the prostitutes' living arrangements. By 1880, exclusively female households in the tenderloin had virtually disappeared, and 50 per cent of women lived in households that included men. Rosa Diamond, for example, lived with co-worker Annie Williams and Percy Joyce and George L. Howard, both unemployed. Blanche Emerson and Anna Southhard shared quarters with William O'Keefe, an actor. Elizabeth Kimbal and Mary Waters occupied the same dwelling as did John Keenan, a house painter. Although it appears that "loafers" might have been part of the white demimonde, the opposite seems to be more likely. The two-story buildings on Wood and Clore streets were multiple-household dwellings. While this does not preclude the possibility of pimps, men and women in the tenderloin probably rented separate quarters in the same dwelling.[34]

As workers, fancy ladies could earn munificent wages, especially during the summer when the mines and building trades were in full operation. Some prostitutes, the "summer women," only worked in Helena from June to September. Particularly during the placer years, winter in Helena for the prostitutes meant an economic drain on their resources; working men who remained in town restrained their spending, and the prostitutes' best customers, the miners, either left for jobs in a warmer climate or economized until the mines re-opened in the spring. In 1880, the monthly earnings of the seven prostitutes who maintained bank accounts in Helena's two major banks, the First National Bank of Helena and the Merchants National Bank, ranged from Belle Crafton's monthly earnings of $179 to Rosa Diamond's $337. A fancy lady plying her trade along Wood Street could expect an impressive average monthly income of $233; bricklayers, stone masons, and carpenters commanded only $90 to $100, and bank clerks earned $125 per month.[35] Compared with the $65 monthly wage the highest paid saleswomen received, prostitutes' compensation was royal.[36] Women in the demimonde had expenses: they paid rent, medical, grocery, and liquor bills; indulged themselves in fine furniture and related household items, furs, expensive clothing, and jewelry; and probably paid bribes to local lawmen.[37] Even so, a typical "summer woman" could make a profit of $500, or not so typically, she could, like Rosa Diamond, leave with $1,000 in her portmanteau.[38]

The women of the demimonde could and did accumulate capital. What they did with it is open to speculation. It would have been easy for them to change their names once again, board the train in Butte, and reappear in another city as a young, respectable widow. They could marry and take up a normal nineteenth century existence. For at least one-third of Helena's demimonde, that was a distinct possibility; and given such an alternative, the fact that these women chose to remain in Wood Street's evening world suggests that they gained a kind of economic and social autonomy by bargaining their sexuality. At the center of this sexual marketplace was Josephine Airey Hensley, who by 1880 had become known as "Chicago Joe."

Chicago Joe added legitimate properties to her holdings as she accumulated more capital. In 1881, she bought a small farm, which she sold two years later at a profit. During the following two years she pursued absentee owners of increasingly expensive property, finding Louis Garcin in Marseilles, France; Leopold Goldberg in Salt Lake City; and the Godfried Stamms in Los Angeles. Persistent in her acquisitiveness, Joe invested $1,400 in the purchase of four additional properties in and around her central holdings.[39] By 1883, Joe had completed the first phase of her career. She had moved beyond actual prostitution to the management of sexual commerce as a landlord and "hurdy-gurdy" owner, and in the purchase of the Stamm property, she had made her first move off Wood Street and into a more legitimate enterprise. Located on Water Street, the Stamm holding included a fair-sized tenement that Joe kept clean of prostitution and operated as quarters for men and women who were comfortable living in Helena's tenderloin.[40] Owning the amount of property she did, Joe effectively controlled the Wood Street district.

Despite Chicago Joe's large real estate holdings and her economic control, other entrepreneurially minded madams acquired real estate and invested in Helena's lucrative red-light district. Bridget Ryan, born in St. Louis, Missouri, in 1837, had changed her name to Lillie McGraw before she arrived in Helena in 1874. She bought a parcel of land from John Denn, a lot that had earlier belonged to proprietor-prostitute Nellie Perkins, and promptly dropped out of sight, perhaps returning to where she likely began her career, in Portland, Oregon, to amass capital. Lillie reappeared in Helena in 1880 to develop the former Denn property and increase her realty. Located on the corner of Cutler and South Warren streets and too far from the center of activity, Lillie's second purchase had little potential. She quickly sold the Cutler Street property to Emma Howard, the wife of a whitewasher who profited by her close connections with the red-light district, and then turned her attention to Wood Street. On October 22, 1882, and March 2, 1883, Lillie bought the lots adjoining her original purchase for $300. By the summer of 1883, she had built two modest plaster-veneered buildings on a sloping hill at the end of Joliet Street. Soon she was depositing between $300 and $500 per month in her bank account.[41]

Joliet Street burrowed into a hill that acted as a natural buffer zone between the tenderloin and the rest of the community, creating a kind of discreet *cul de sac*. Across Joliet Street from Lillie McGraw's establishment on the west side stood Belle Crafton's house. Born Mollie Byrnes in New Orleans, Belle was twenty-two when she arrived in Helena the summer of 1880. She worked through that summer until November, left and returned briefly before Christmas, then disappeared again until the following April when she decided to settle in Helena. During that summer she deposited an average of $500 per month (sometimes $50 a day) in her bank account; she purchased her lot on Joliet Street from John Shober in September 1881 for $200.[42]

An associate of Mollie Byrnes, New Yorker Carrie Patterson was twenty-nine in 1880 when she came to Helena as Blanche Emerson, a prostitute who would work fairly steadily but who would also spend nearly all her earnings. During 1881, Blanche only worked sporadically, mostly in the summer, and by that fall she had left town. The following summer, Blanche returned to Helena to settle. This time she worked steadily, having leased Fannie Spencer's property. By December, she had purchased a lot from John Mason that fronted on Bridge Street in the block where Chicago Joe was the chief property owner.[43]

Before New Year's of 1884 all of the tenderloin's *dramatis personae* had taken their positions, and the outlines of their empire were visible to tenderloin denizen and Main Street citizen alike. From Joliet Street west to

Clore Street, then north on Clore Street to the corner of Wall Street, the demimonde had at its center Chicago Joe with the other female entrepreneurs, the lesser lights, clustered around her. Prostitution had survived as women's business and had created a female community in the city's demimonde where everything was for sale. Women owned a large part of the "half-world," controlled a good portion of its economy, and established the tone of its social relationships. In a few short years, however, Clore Street on the district's western fringe became the sector of the demimonde where two-thirds of the prostitutes—the ones for whom the business held out little promise—sold themselves. The untimely deaths of early proprietors, the successful mobility of some, and the character of the women initially attracted to the neighborhood contributed to the failure of prostitution as business on Clore Street. The lives of Dolores Jarra Stanchfield and Sarah Dubay illustrate the two sides of prostitution: one successful, the other not.

In 1868, during the proprietorship phase of the red-light district's development, Dolores Jarra purchased two lots on Bridge Street in the original red-light district. One of these adjoined Fred White's dance hall, and Dolores probably worked for White as a saloon dancer and occasional prostitute. By 1869, she was financially secure enough to make loans to others in the area and to acquire additional properties: several lots at the intersection of Clore and Bridge streets and the notorious "Twin Cottages" on Wood Street. Dolores also had taken a lover, Lewis Washburn, who clerked for a local transfer firm and fathered her two daughters, Minnie Washburn Jarra and Louisa Washburn Jarra. Although Dolores claimed no legal connection with Washburn, she made certain that her children legally had a father, at least in the eyes of the Catholic Church. When Lewis apparently departed Helena in 1874, Dolores bought his homestead in the Prickly Pear Valley.[44]

The 1870s were not Helena's most promising years; and despite her success, Dolores and her two young daughters moved to Butte sometime between 1874 and 1878. In March 1878, Dolores extended a mortgage to Charles Stanchfield, a bartender *cum* concessionaire, on the bar fixtures in Lober's Opera House to secure his indebtedness to her. This transaction was not uncalculated and aimed at protecting Stanchfield's chattels from execution. On March 20, 1878, during Silver Bow County's drive to curtail dance halls, Butte authorities arrested Stanchfield for "keeping a dancing saloon," found him guilty, and fined him.[45]

Whatever their relationship had been, Dolores Jarra and Charles Stanchfield formalized their commitment to each other by marrying on December 16, 1878, one month before leasing a dance hall on Butte's Park Street a block from Venus Alley, soon to become one of the most notorious tenderloins in the West. Unsuccessful in this venture, the Stanchfields had better luck two doors farther east where they opened another "dancing saloon" with Dolores as the principal attraction. The

Stanchfields prospered and elected to leap into nineteenth century respectability by returning to Dolores's farm near Helena.[46]

Perhaps mindful of Charles's earlier financial debacle at the opera house in Butte, Dolores Stanchfield determined to protect her children's and her own future. In 1881, she transferred all of her Helena property to her minor daughters and appointed Stanchfield their legal guardian; in subsequent years, she also filed a sole tradership declaration testifying to her intent to engage in farming and entered successive separate property declarations. In this fashion, Dolores guaranteed that the courts would safeguard her and her daughters' interests should Stanchfield prove unreliable.[47] The Stanchfields' divestment of holdings in Helena's tenderloin, including the Clore Street property, furthered their separation from the demimonde.[48]

By 1890, the Stanchfields owned property taxed at $12,630 and were among Helena's economic elite. The Stanchfield daughters had attended St. Vincent's Academy, and Minnie, the younger of the two, made a white-collar marriage to a Butte drugstore clerk in 1894. Like others in Helena, the Stanchfields prospered and then suffered during the aftermath of the Panic of 1893 when Charles Stanchfield chose the worst economic moment to begin an ice business. Capitalized by a mortgage on the Stanchfield farm, his small business failed during the Panic of 1893. Like many others, the Stanchfields lost the farm to their mortgagee and left the state, presumably to begin again. If Dolores Jarra Stanchfield had endeavored to improve her own and her children's lot, as the records suggest, she succeeded. What is more, she executed these complex legal maneuvers without benefit of formal training or even education; Dolores Jarra could not write her name.[49]

Unlike Dolores Jarra's steady progress, Sarah Dubay's sojourn in Montana had been an unhappy one from the beginning. Her first marriage to Tobe Bowden ended when Bowden died violently in Bannack in 1876. Two years later, on May 24, 1878, she married Charles Dubay at the singularly isolated community of Iron Rod in Madison County, Montana Territory. In October of 1879, Charles Dubay decamped, leaving her with ten pounds of flour and a little sugar. Pregnant at the time, Sarah miscarried. In 1880, she turned up in Helena, calling herself a widow and working as a servant in the Thomas Reece household. Domestic service did not appeal to Sarah, and by June of 1881 she had purchased three lots at the intersection of Clore and Bridge streets and had firmly ensconced herself on Clore Street. Sarah was a drinking woman and when Sarah drank, she turned quarrelsome. Between 1881 and 1882, Sarah went to court twelve times either as a complainant or a defendant. At her last appearance, the court had tired of Sarah and packed her off to jail for thirty days.[50]

For whatever reason, Sarah ceased to pester the courts and set about putting her life in order. Charles Dubay reappeared in Butte, and Sarah promptly petitioned for divorce on September 15, 1882, on the grounds of extreme cruelty. Although Charles Dubay claimed that Sarah had deserted him on numerous occasions, the court ruled in Sarah's favor and she became a single woman. In both her divorce and in other disputes, Sarah, like the proprietor prostitutes before her, learned to take advantage of the courts on civil matters. She sued Celia Cooper, a black prostitute, for recovery of rent due her on household furnishings and successfully repulsed an attempt by the estate of Alexander Beattie to deprive her of properties on Clore Street. Not quite finished with Charles Dubay, Sarah discovered an irregularity in their divorce decree and threatened him with bigamy until the court rectified the error.[51]

Sarah remarried in 1885, choosing Samuel Stevenson, an illiterate, common laborer who commenced to bilk her of her money and batter her. The marriage had not lasted two years before Sarah divorced Samuel on the grounds of extreme cruelty and drunkenness. Even though Sarah owned a single lot on Clore Street, she declared a sole tradership to become a real estate rental agent and leased her property for several years to the Matere brothers, Clore Street pimps. Sarah retained her toehold on Clore Street but was content to allow others, in this case men, the use of her property. Leasing her property to pimps, Sarah Dubay Stevenson dropped out of sight in 1889.[52]

Sarah Dubay's career in the courts documents the hazards of life in the demimonde, where a woman could be robbed or assaulted or both by her customers and by her sister workers. Likewise, she could beat and steal from her clients and neighbor prostitutes. Between 1873 and 1883, Wood Street and Clore Street regulars were involved in fifty-four separate criminal actions. As defendants in thirty-four of the cases, women complained of other women in half the suits. Chicago Joe, for example, chased Annie Glessner down Wood Street in July 1873 and "did foully beat and bruise" the Glessner woman. Annie applied to the court, and Joe paid a ten dollar fine for assault. In the other seventeen cases in which men, usually law officers, brought complaints against women, the "soiled doves" lost. Belle Crafton pulled a revolver from her reticule on April 6, 1881, and threatened to send C. L. Vawter to his heavenly reward. Vawter promptly complained to the court. Arrested for exhibiting a deadly weapon, Belle soon stood in the dock, pled guilty, and paid her fine. Women complained of men in twenty cases; in half of those, the judge or jury found for the female complainants.[53]

Analysis of these court cases suggests two things. First, there was a singular lack of legal and judicial concern with sexual commerce; officers of the law arrested no women for prostitution or keeping a disorderly house before 1886, even though the police court was located in the red-light district.[54] Second, the demimonde women used the courts to settle petty squabbles among them that could not be resolved by the tenderloin's leaders and to challenge men who assaulted, robbed, or threatened them.

The court cases also disclose three groups of men who associated with prostitutes: working-class transients, unmarried professionals, and middling neighborhood businessmen in occupations allied with prostitution. Most of the demimonde's clientele came from the working class, but the prostitutes maintained both irregular and regular relationships with merchants and professionals. Few of Helena's commercial elite dealt directly as customers with the "soiled doves."[55] Most clients were single men, although some married men certainly patronized houses on Wood and Clore streets. In short, the prostitutes provided an essential social and sexual diversion for Helena's large, single-male population.[56]

Petty crime plagued Helena's demimonde, but the fatal violence or self-inflicted death and debilitation that was characteristic of prostitution in other mining towns was not evident during the city's early days. Not one whore in Helena died by her own hand before 1883.[57] Although there are no reports of prostitutes dying of alcoholism or drug overdose between 1865 and 1883 in Helena, the women were rampant users of alcohol and drugs. Hurdy-gurdy women drank with clients nightly and consumed large amounts of liquor, and they had easy access to opium, morphine, and laudanum.

Helena's demimonde did not grind all its residents in a mill of degradation during the first two decades of its existence. The community of "soiled doves" produced no one comparable to the Comstock's Julia Bulette or Denver's Mattie Silks, who have been glorified by some historians as successful madams. But for every Helena prostitute who had accumulated enough capital and had a chance to leave the profession, there were two who had less of a chance. The biographies of Blanche Emerson, Belle Crafton, Lillie McGraw, Dolores Jarra Stanchfield, and Chicago Joe lend support to the idea of female social mobility via prostitution because they moved out of actual prostitution and up in the tenderloin's hierarchy.[58]

The form of prostitution in Helena during the empire-building phase of its development indicates that Wood Street and Clore Street regulars operated in the mainstream of nineteenth century capitalism and not as exploited "line workers." These female entrepreneurs acted as other frontier capitalists did: aspiring to acquire property, to profit, to move up or out into a better social and economic position. Like other capitalists, some succeeded. After fires had weeded its population during the 1870s, the demimonde had expanded once again by 1883. The proprietor prostitute reappeared, albeit in fewer numbers, and two new forms of prostitution emerged: the limited prostitute proprietorship, a house rented by a woman from another woman; and the *maisons de joie*, the familiar bawdy houses managed and owned by a madam. Also by 1883, the regular business community held the women's entrepreneurial enclave at arm's length. Respectable merchants who earlier had felt free to extend mortgages to the fancy ladies no longer dealt on Wood and Clore streets. The demimonde was becoming a world unto itself. Legitimate business was transacted on Main Street; the skin trade operated in its special place, and in that confine, the women were capitalists with rooms.

After the railroad arrived in 1883, the citizens of Helena began to dream of replacing Denver as the "Queen City of the Rockies." The railroad overcame the isolation that had plagued the community from the beginning. Railroaders, with and without families, poured into the town and trains left with bullion pulled from the mines and smelter in the new ore reduction center. Along with the city, the demimonde dreamed.

Chicago Joe continued to acquire property and add to her demimonde empire: an unimproved lot in the newly platted Capital Hill Addition in September 1884; later the same month, another property farther west on Wood Street, which she used as a house of prostitution and placed under the management of her long-time associate, Nellie Reynolds; an improved lot in the central Wood Street area in October 1886 from another old associate, Mrs. J. E. Aiken, the former Mollie Grahm; the last of Mollie's property in Helena in August 1887; and a final purchase on September 13, 1887, a stone warehouse that Joe probably used as storage for the liquor she sold in the Red Light Saloon. Joe also continued to move toward legitimacy, renaming the Red Light Saloon the Red Star Saloon. She also acquired an interest in the International Hotel and made her first loan to a demimonde newcomer, Anna Muller, through Muller's agent, Sully Buyck.[59]

While Joe extended her holdings on Wood Street, the Joliet Street entrepreneurs did not sit idle. Lillie McGraw sold, purchased, or clarified her title to eight pieces of property between 1884 and 1889, most for small amounts. Belle Crafton, however, expanded her portfolio as she assumed her given name, Mollie Byrnes. In May 1884, she secured the old Kiyus Saloon property, next door to Joe's Red Star Saloon. On November 15, 1884, she went to the county clerk's office with David Marks, a lawyer who did much of his business in the Wood Street district. At 3:10 in the afternoon, she conveyed the property to Marks as Belle Crafton; five minutes later she repurchased it as Mollie Byrnes. This was the first step in Mollie's larger plan to move up in the district's hierarchy and from there into respectability.[60]

Between 1886 and 1889, Mollie made several property transactions that changed her position in the demimonde. On February 26, 1886, Mollie sold her original holding on the north side of Wood Street to newcomer Lottie Cole. The next day she bought the end of a block that fronted on Joliet from Michael and Matilda Reinig, who had operated a grocery store on Joliet for many years. In 1887, she purchased a parcel on State Street between South Warren and South Ewing streets in a residential area that twenty years before had been the original red-light district. On August 27, 1888, she sold the Kiyus Saloon property for $5,000 and bought two residential lots in a newly platted city addition. Finally, in 1889, she acquired another residential property. In the space of a few years, Mollie had reduced her holdings in the demimonde to a single piece of property and had invested her money in residential properties in other parts of the city. But her single Joliet Street holding was important. By the end of 1886 she had built a dwelling there called "The Castle," a tasteful *maison de joie*, and with it the prostitutes' empire was complete.[61]

The spring of 1886 still marked the eve of what would be the brief tenure of prostitution's empire in Helena. At that time, fifty-two white prostitutes lived on Clore Street or in the Wood Street vicinity. Twelve per cent owned their own places of business and 22 per cent had bank accounts. Despite prostitution's growth in Helena as women's business, it rested on a narrow economic base. Seventy-three per cent of the "soiled doves" rented from or worked for 12 per cent of the women; one-quarter of the prostitute population rented from male landlords on Clore and Jackson streets. Should one of the landed prostitutes fail, prostitution as women's business would be in jeopardy.[62]

Joining in the optimism that pervaded Helena in the mid 1880s and fueled a building boom, Lillie McGraw, Mollie Byrnes, and Chicago Joe Hensley refurbished or added on to their establishments. Their customers, they realized, desired more sophisticated and elegant entertainment. Mollie built "The Castle" by mortgaging all her property for $6,000 and adding her considerable income to finance the $12,000 in construction costs. Simultaneously, Lillie expanded her Joliet Street operation. In 1888, she built a $5,000, two-story, brick, tin-roofed dwelling diagonally across from "The Castle" to handle the overflow from her main establishments. She also remodeled her existing houses nearby and had them connected by an elevated walkway.[63]

Not to be outdone, Joe refurbished the Red Star Saloon in 1887. She also opened the Coliseum, a small variety theater; and in 1888, she built "a two and one half story brick building, tin roof, 31 x 32 feet; estimated cost $5000" on Bridge Street. Joe realized that her highly successful Coliseum Theatre could bring even greater profits if she enlarged the operation. Accordingly, Joe built a theater of brick and stone at a cost of $23,000 just to the east of the Red Star Saloon at 16 Wood Street. The new Coliseum opened to a full house on July 4, 1888, achieved immediate success, and soon boasted a weekly payroll of $1,000.[64]

Between the legitimate theater acts at the Coliseum, Joe's employees circulated through the crowd selling beer at a dollar a bottle and champagne at five dollars a pint.[65] Heavily curtained private boxes for the discreet allowed the women to conduct private business with the Coliseum's predominantly male clientele. Convenient in its arrangement for Joe and her employees, the Coliseum drew criticism from many of Helena's citizens. The advent of the Coliseum, however, was not the first time when doings in the tenderloin had raised comment.

In a face-to-face community such as Helena, other women in the town could scarcely avoid coming into contact with the fancy ladies. Helena's middling women may not have liked the situation, but they reserved their disapproval more for the men who visited Wood Street than for the women who worked there. Writing to her sister in 1871, Elizabeth Chester Fisk noted with dismay when a "young man who used to sing and dance in a hurdy house and was an especial favorite with Daisey Dean (a low, bad woman who keeps a saloon) read a sort of sermon, prayed, exhorted and sung" at the Methodist Church. Later, in 1873, Elizabeth related an incident that had preceded the wedding of Mr. B., an aging, alcoholic roué. "I have heard," wrote Elizabeth, "of a charming little tableau down in the greenhouse when Mr. B.'s old Wood St. mistress drew a revolver on his future bride and threatened to kill her." Since Elizabeth lived near Helena's tenderloin, she had ample opportunity to have knowledge, if only superficial knowledge, of events on Wood Street. In a letter home in 1890, she expressed her disapproval of Joe's theater, and her trailing ellipsis hinted at the nefarious possibilities inherent in wine, women, and song:

> We have today in Helena licensed gambling houses to say nothing of the saloons open all the time. The Coliseum, a low theatre, I hardly know how to describe it where girls serve the drinks in booths and lure men in. . . .[66]

Elizabeth Fisk's misgivings reflected a broader and growing concern for moral improvement among Helenans, a decided change from the laissez-faire attitude of earlier years. After the city incorporated in 1881, public profanity, vagrancy, opium use, habitual drunkenness, and especially prostitution came under scrutiny. In addition to providing the cynosure for the town's program of municipal reform, the controversy over whether or not to eliminate, tax, or tolerate the vice district revealed social cleavages and ideological differences that often characterized frontier communities in transit between small town and city, between frontier and settlement.

Two groups personified the divergent attitudes toward reform and were instrumental in changing Helena's urban identity: the town's merchant pioneers, those who arrived in the city before 1870 and endured through Helena's depression years, and the prosperous *arrivistes*, those with little frontier experience who settled in Helena during the post-railroad period. Between 1884 and 1890, the men of these two dominant elites tried to transform public morality.

On August 14, 1884, the *Daily Independent* reported that the paper had received numerous complaints against Ming's Opera House, charging the house with the indiscriminate seating of members of the demimonde in the dress circle and parquette. In response, theater manager John Maguire notified the vendors of reserved tickets that, while he had no wish to bar the "soiled doves," their tickets would hereafter be limited and their seating confined to a less conspicuous area. The Wood Street regulars did not let the slight go without remark. Five of them stole habits from the Sisters of Charity and, so disguised, presented themselves and tickets for the five demimonde seats at an evening performance. Even though manager Maguire quickly had the "sisters" thrown out, the brazen prostitutes' prank outraged Helena's citizenry.[67]

The initial impetus for moral reform, however, did not come immediately from local politicians. The "first wave of moral reform that [had] struck Montana," as one citizen pointed out, came in the 1885 Montana legislature. In 1885, Montana lawmakers considered several moral reform measures: an anti-gambling statute, an age-of-consent bill, an anti-hurdy-gurdy house bill, and an act to prevent wife beating. Only the dance-hall proposition became law, but the anti-gambling proposal provoked the most discussion and identified the two sides of the reform debate. On one side, some legislators were reluctant to forego the considerable benefit derived from gambling license fees; on the other side, some lawmakers placed the common good, the safety of future generations, and the purity of the community treasuries above monetary gain. The legislative discussion also exposed the reformers' various strategies and the difficulties they faced in framing legal and enforceable social control statutes.[68]

When the legislature finished its business, Helena's aldermen quickly followed the legislature's example and initiated a moral reform program of their own. In June 1885, the city council considered an amended version of Ordinance No. 7, a lengthy rule that covered offenses against good order and morals. Section seventeen of the revision dealt specifically with prostitution:

> Any prostitute, courtesan, or lewd woman who shall by words, signs, or action ply her avocation upon the streets, at doors, windows . . . [or make] any meretricious display of herself upon the streets in any loud or lewd dress or manner calculated to draw attention to her avocation or shall appear on any public street after 9 p.m. except in case of necessity [shall be fined]. . . .

Mayor James Sullivan vetoed the proposal, pointing out that it was unnecessary, unconstitutional, ill-defined, and generally subject to misuse. "Just to what extent," Sullivan said, "you feared these persons might 'ply their avocation . . . at windows,' I do not know, but I do think the present ordinance, sustained by the community not entirely devoid of decency, will protect us from the supposed evils."[69]

With Sullivan's veto, any further discussion of the social evil abated until October 8, 1885, when the city council approved an ordinance excluding women from any employment on Main Street.[70] Designed to protect legitimate business interests rather than to attack the skin trade, the rule effectively created a *de facto* red-light district on Wood, Bridge, and Clore streets. Comfortable with this solution, the council turned its attention to other municipal matters and did not bother with the tenderloin or moral affairs until the following year when Joseph E. Hendry became city editor of the *Daily Independent*.

A self-confessed "pilgrim, even of the pin-head type," Hendry was a brash newcomer to the fraternity of Helena journalists. Having arrived in Montana with the railroad, Hendry followed the creation of Northern Pacific rail towns and their newspapers from Billings to Livingston to Butte and finally to Helena, where he took over management of Montana's largest daily. Editor Hendry knew his business, and immediately the *Independent* changed from a bland hodge-podge of reportage to an aggressive daily. Two of Hendry's innovations were detailed listings of police court proceedings and investigative pieces on Helena's various vice problems.[71]

In enumerating police court appearances, Hendry gleefully praised the swift justice of the police magistrate, detailed the moral turpitude of the defendants, and joyfully tallied the fines accruing to the city. From time to time, Hendry bolstered these daily tabulations with sensational investigative columns. Although the *Independent* had always maintained an interest in reform, Hendry brought a new fervor to its vice reportage and articulated the views of the newcomers to Helena, whom he felt shared his perception of civic life and his concern for moral reform. These newcomers, like Hendry himself, had little previous frontier experience.[72]

Not only did Hendry keep up a steady drumbeat for moral reform by treating *Independent* readers to daily recitals of their city's public disgrace, but he also touted the cause of the Democratic party. Despite the *Independent*'s enthusiastic support of a balanced Democratic ticket, Helena followed its tradition of fickle politics. Voters turned out the Democrats and ushered in the veteran, merchant Republicans. Immediately, Mayor Albert Kleinschmidt and his aldermen responded to the *Independent*'s social criticism by passing an ordinance to suppress opium dens and their habitués. The ordinance was a public success as the police raided the joints and arrested their managers, owners, and clients. The *Independent* was overjoyed and totalled the fines as they dropped into the city treasury.[73]

Spurred on by the raid's success, council members mounted an attack on another group of moral delinquents—the "soiled doves." In June 1886, Mayor Kleinschmidt directed the ordinance committee to prepare a regulation for the purpose of confining the activities of women of questionable character. The committee dutifully undertook the task but could not agree on an acceptable bawdy-house measure. The council was more successful; it hammered out a sweeping anti-prostitution ordinance that banned prostitution from the city in uncompromising terms. Under the headline, "Wood Street Shaken to Its Core," the *Independent* noted the moral triumph, but its editorial column recognized the difficulty in enforcing such a law. "It is at least well," the *Independent* remarked, "to have such an ordinance ready for use in case the social evil becomes too bold and intrusive in its demeanor." To the *Independent*, the intent of the ordinance was not to eradicate prostitution but to make it less conspicuous and economically advantageous for the city. In July, the *Independent* noted: "The ordinance against prostitution, besides returning a considerable sum in fines to the city, has a pronounced effect in quieting down the social evil—making it less obtrusive and offensive." What the city council meant by its own regulation was unclear, but the aldermen did not have enforcement in mind. The *Independent*'s claims for a fattened treasury aside, few arrests for prostitution appeared in police court notices.[74] Later that summer, the city's and the *Independent*'s reform program suffered a severe setback. On August 21, 1886, Helena police went to the Red Star Saloon and ordered Chicago Joe to close on the grounds that the Red Star was a "hurdy-gurdy." Joe refused and had the officers thrown out, but they returned with a warrant and arrested her along with two of her girls. Joe's attorney was former Territorial Secretary Isaac D. McCutcheon, a man renowned for his ability to extricate, with legal legerdemain, the guilty from the hands of the law. McCutcheon defended the Red Star owner before Judge Joseph Davis and a jury on August 30. After some difficulty, the attorneys agreed on a jury of five: George T. White, a brick and stone mason; C. P. Van Wart, a dry-goods merchant; Martin B. Moran, a contractor; John A. Quirk, a police officer; and Fred Favor, occupation unknown. None of the jurors could be numbered among the pillars of the community and all lived on the fringes of the demimonde.[75]

Elbert D. Weed's opening argument for the prosecution described "hurdies," and specifically the Red Star, as immoral "establishments wherein men's souls are lured to the shores of sin by the combined seductive influences of wine, women and dance. . . ." Weed called the arresting officers to the stand as witnesses to the lethal combination of wine, women, and dance or what people normally took to be the pleasures of a "hurdy-gurdy" house. In his cross-examination, McCutcheon asked if the officers had actually seen a hurdy-gurdy being played; none of the men had the faintest idea what the instrument was. After McCutcheon tutored each with the help of a *Webster's Dictionary*, they admitted that no such instrument was played at the Red Star Saloon. McCutcheon did not call his clients to the stand, although a reporter noted that Joe and her girls were taking the proceedings cavalierly. In his closing remarks, McCutcheon argued that a violin, a piano, and a cornet provided music in Joe's saloon; and, given that statutes must conform to the commonly accepted definitions of words, the Red Star could not be considered a "hurdy-gurdy" house. The jury retired with a dictionary and a copy of the original complaint; they returned at seven-thirty that evening, deadlocked. Judge Davis would have none of that and returned the jurors to their deliberations, although he later permitted them to adjourn for supper. At nine o'clock the jury returned a verdict of "not guilty."[76]

Aghast, Helena's journalists scored the verdict and the trial's legal flummery. The *Helena Independent* headlined its article covering the trial, "An Inning for Sin." With tongue in cheek an editorial writer observed that Joe's case was ". . . based upon a unique technical defense, and a lack of musical education on the part of the witnesses for the prosecution." The outraged *Helena Herald* implied a complicity by the jurors with Wood Street interests and predicted a renaissance of "hurdy-gurdies" now that the statute had been found faulty.[77]

The tenderloin's respite did not last long. By January 1887, the Montana legislature opened a new moral offensive against another demimonde institution, the variety theater. Early in the session, legislators worked on a statute to prohibit the sale of liquor and the employment of women in variety houses. Because variety theaters specialized in bawdy entertainment and, like hurdy-gurdies, often fronted for forms of prostitution, the bill threatened the sexual marketplace by removing one of its central clearinghouses. More to the point, the bill was aimed at three establishments, and one of them was Josephine Hensley's Coliseum Theatre. The bill passed, and the *Independent* confidently predicted the Coliseum's doom.[78]

But Joe Hensley was moving toward social legitimacy; she simply turned the Coliseum into an extraordinarily successful operation by changing the bill of fare to vaudeville, providing temperance beverages, and eliminating her female employees. In a short while, the *Independent* was mentioning the Coliseum's attractions in its columns.[79]

With the legislature concluded, the *Independent* turned its attention to local politics and the annual city election. Once again the Republicans were successful: only two Democrats won council seats. One of them was John Worth, a Main Street saloonkeeper who represented, among other constituencies, the red-light district. The election also broke the exclusive control of the council by the pioneer merchants, as four relative newcomers gained aldermen's seats. Foremost among them was Richard Howey.[80]

Educator, lawyer, minister, and businessman, Howey arrived in Helena in 1880 to be superintendent of schools. The following year, he was appointed superintendent of public instruction for the territory, and by 1884 he had become business manager of the Independent Publishing Company. He shared with his wife, Laura Spencer Howey, a number of reform interests: temperance, women's education, women's rights, and work among the poor.[81] Howey provided the council with a new perspective, not only on the financing of municipal improvements but also on the improvement of the city's morals.

An incident soon tested Howey's position and liberal opinions. On June 4, 1887, police arrested sixty-five white and Chinese prostitutes in the city's two red-light districts. According to the *Independent*, "the present onslaught shall be the first of a quarterly raid to be hereafter made and the fines so collected to be considered as a license for the privilege of conducting such institutions, as efforts to totally suppress the practice are considered useless, the evil being one, like gambling, ungovernable by either legal, social, or moral laws."[82] The subsequent discussion in the city council chambers revealed a range of opinion regarding the "social evil," the differences in perspective between old-timers and *arrivistes*, and the extent to which behind-the-scenes arrangements governed public policy.

A few weeks after the roundup, concern about bawdy houses monopolized city council debate. William Lorey, a wallpaper dealer and a relative newcomer to Helena, began the exchange by protesting the presence of houses of prostitution on Water and Cutler streets "contrary to the tacit understanding had between members of that locality and the city council. . . . it was understood that they [prostitutes] should confine themselves to Wood, Clore and Bridge streets." Lorey's solution: remove the women from Water and Cutler streets. Robert Wallace, a grocer, suggested that the soiled doves be moved to a different area in the city and be licensed, thereby bringing the city additional revenue. Richard Howey was dismayed. He "did not want to derive revenue from houses of that kind; did not want to take a cent in any shape or manner from houses of ill-fame; that source of revenue was disreputable and objectionable to the best people of Helena." Wallace reiterated his plea for licensing, but Archer O. Simons, Singer Sewing Machine parvenu, was of the opinion that it could not be done. Yes, it could, replied Richard Hoback, pioneer real estate broker, arguing that prostitution was a trade and occupation under the language of the revenue ordinance. Marcus Lissner, veteran proprietor of the International Hotel, argued that the doves should go because the prostitutes' presence depreciated property values in the area. City Marshal John Read presented the lawman's point of view: "Who would be the prosecuting witness in case I made the arrest?" he asked. "There are plenty of witnesses," snapped Howey, "if you can only find them." With that the council agreed to refer the issue to an *ad hoc* committee on public morals and deal with the issue at the next meeting.[83]

Council discussion continued on June 24, 1887. Reassured by the city attorney that the bawdy-house ordinance was sufficient and enforceable against any and all establishments, council members wrestled with the question of interpretation. According to the *Independent*, ". . . the feeling prevailed, apparently, that the scarlet women should not be entirely suppressed, but rather confined to Wood, Bridge and Clore streets, the places originally intended where they should reside." Whereupon the council ordered that the prostitutes be forced from Cutler, Water, and West Main streets. But Howey was not finished. In an impassioned speech, he suggested yet another consideration:

> All the sin and fault is laid at the doors of the women; no charity is expressed for them and no consideration given as to the cause or reason for being inmates of such places; they are there not through choice, but by force of the grinding heel of destiny or fate. Some mercy should be shown them; they should not be driven out from every quarter; the hand of reform should be held out to them; it was the evil arising from the vile passions of men that made them what they are, consequently they should not be the more degraded. . . . Tacitly prescribe certain limits where they shall dwell as done heretofore by the council, thereby exercising our charity by permitting them to remain there unmolested.

When he had finished, Howey moved that the council adopt a resolution preventing the execution of Ordinance No. 86 for the purpose of raising revenue. The resolution passed unanimously, and the *Independent* quickly protested. "The council," wailed the editor, "is compromising its own ordinance and, worse still, is compromising with the houses of ill-fame."[84]

On October 7, 1887, the *Independent* reported the arrests of approximately one hundred women under the provisions of Ordinance No. 86. The arrests, editor Hendry explained, constituted a quarterly fine in lieu of licenses. The incident immediately occasioned a clash of authority between the city attorney, who refused to prosecute the women because of Howey's resolution, and the police magistrate, who fined them under the ordinance. The doves themselves were willing to pay the quarterly assessment; they considered the arrangement cheap compared with that in other cities. The city fathers once again found themselves discussing prostitution.[85]

Howey reminded the council of its resolution and presented an amended version that would guarantee a refund of the fines to the offenders. Howey's motion engendered considerable debate over the propriety of the raids in general; but, when the council voted on his amended resolution, the pioneers, the council's majority, agreed with him while the newcomers, a vocal minority, did not.[86] The city council had reached a compromise between the partisans of tolerance and the supporters of unyielding moral reform. The city would accommodate prostitution within bounds, but local government would not profit from it.

The city council meetings during October 1887 fairly settled its challenge to Wood Street and the issue of the suppression of prostitution in Helena. But afterward, a sporadically enforced informal licensing system apparently went into effect. Annual police reports included arrests for "keeping a bawdy house" commensurate with the established number of women in Helena engaged in prostitution. In May and December of 1890, for example, authorities briefly jailed ninety women (the estimated number of women working in the demimonde). On another front, the Helena Board of Trade took pains to portray Helena's tenderloin as a relatively benign neighborhood. Summing up his description of the saloons and gambling houses in the district, the Board's secretary wrote: "There is no disorder, no excitement, and nothing that is in the least dramatic. You look in vain for characters such as inspired Bret Harte's tales of the California mining camps."[87]

Despite the secretary's reassuring prose, it was business as usual in the demimonde, although the "life" was becoming increasingly debilitating and lethal. The fast life with its attendant hazards—alcoholism, alienation, drugs—had begun to take its toll. Blanche Mitchell shot herself; Kitty Williams committed suicide by taking an overdose of morphine; Lillie Fillmore died of syphilis at age thirty; and Nellie Summers, a black prostitute on Clore Street, ended her life with whiskey laced with arnica.[88] Beginning in the mid 1880s, this trend continued through the 1890s and into the twentieth century. One incident in 1896 is particularly illustrative of both the change in the demimonde's atmosphere and the social organization of prostitution in Helena.

On September 16, 1896, Dora Forrest and Madge Dowd left Lillie McGraw's bordello to go downtown. Despite the housekeeper's admonition "not to get full," their trip eventually turned into a drinking spree as they went from saloon to saloon ordering hot whiskeys. Sometime after midnight they ended up in a drugstore on Jackson Street. Dora attempted to buy morphine on the pretext that she needed something to help her sleep. Reluctant to dispense the drug, the druggist refused and made up a less potent preparation. Dora and Madge made a few inconsequential purchases of combs, small baskets, and boxes decorated with seashells. When Dora became sick in the store, the druggist pushed them into a waiting hack. In the wee hours of the morning, they returned to Lillie's Joliet Street house, where the housekeeper let them in. According to testimony, both Madge and Dora were drunk but not unsteady enough to need assistance up the stairs. They ordered another drink from the bordello bar, chatted with the house's other inmates, and displayed their purchases. As was the custom in bawdy houses, Dora invited Madge to share her bed. When the housekeeper looked in on them later, Madge and Dora were sitting up in bed talking. Sometime during the night, Dora substituted morphine for the druggist's soporific, and both women drank the preparation. In the morning, Dora Forrest was dead and Madge Dowd was barely alive.[89]

Called to the stand during the coroner's inquest, Lillie McGraw stated that the women had arrived only two weeks before. As evidence she produced a telegram that the two women had sent from Portland, Oregon, asking about possible employment and guaranteeing their rail fare. Lillie had two openings, and the women had come. In terse sentences, Lillie testified that both women had a history of drug abuse and suicidal incidents. After some questioning, Madge Dowd corroborated Dora's interest in suicide; Dora had spoken of taking her life on several occasions but had wanted to wait until they returned to Chicago to do the deed. About her own intention, Madge was deliberately vague, ascribing her need for morphine to a fall. All of this was enough for the coroner's jury; they returned a verdict of death by self-administered poison.[90]

This and other inquisitions give us a glimpse of the internal organization and social relationships of a Helena bawdy house.[91] Apparently, the madams ruled their *maisons* with considerable authority. The evidence in court records suggests that these queens of the demimonde wanted no more public exposure than necessary. In an effort to distance herself from Dora and Madge, Lillie McGraw claimed in effect that the women had been just passing through and that her bawdy-house was little more than a hotel for women. From Lillie's point of view, these transients had caused her trouble by bringing her business into the limelight.

There is also some evidence to suggest that Helena madams had connections with houses of prostitution in other western cities and that a communications network linked one red-light district with another. The "working girls" traveled from one city to the next, wherever their services were in demand. Mediating between the transient prostitutes and the madam was the housekeeper, who was responsible for the day-to-day operation of the house and for maintaining some control over the women's lives. It fell to Lillie's housekeeper, for example, to control the girls' out-of-house drinking, to assure that the house's furnishings were not damaged, and to preside over the kitchen and bar staff and their services. Only when it became necessary to deal with an outsider did the housekeeper go to the madam.

Desperation and ennui infused the prostitutes' lives. Although their workdays ran from early evening until four o'clock in the morning, the coroner's inquests suggest that their schedule was more flexible. Some took occasional nights off only to drink themselves into oblivion. By the mid 1890s, the stay of prostitutes in Helena, which a decade before had been counted in years and months, was measured in weeks. The railroads permitted these women even greater geographical mobility—a few weeks in Portland, a few in Helena, and then on to Chicago. All this movement, it seems, was an effort to escape the emptiness of their existence and to meet the madams' demand for variety. The optimism that had characterized Helena's demimonde, as evidenced by its active entrepreneurial behavior and feisty litigation, had given way to sadness. Whoring no longer held out even the illusion of opportunity. For those who occupied the few places at the top of Wood Street's hierarchy, the possibility of escape into a better life dimmed. One of those who tried was Mollie Byrnes.

After building "The Castle," Mollie made her bid for respectability. For her consort she chose Thomas Butler Eddingfield, a salesman at Feldberg's clothing store. Mollie was thirty-two and Eddingfield twenty-eight when they married in 1890.[92] The next year, Mollie leased "The Castle" to demimonde parvenu Lillie Ashton, and she and Thomas moved to her new residence at 212 State Street.[93] For three years Mollie found the respectability she desired, but Thomas Butler Eddingfield proved to be a poor matrimonial choice. On July 9, 1898, Mollie petitioned the district court for a divorce, charging that Eddingfield was, among other things,

> . . . guilty of extreme cruelty in that he has repeatedly applied to her vile and opprobrious epithets, calling her "low shanty Irish" and reflecting upon her chastity as a wife. . . . That he has repeatedly used personal violence to her. That on the 3rd day of July 1898 he struck her a violent blow upon the head, which blow she is informed by her physician will result in permanent injury.[94]

What bothered Mollie the most was Eddingfield's lack of ambition and business sense. Mollie further charged

> that the said defendant has during the past years been habitually intemperate, using intoxicating drinks to such an excess as to be disqualified thereby the greater part of the time from properly attending to business. That during said time he has secured from her large sums of money on the pretense of going into business, which he has consumed in dissipation and riotous living, and that he has dissipated all her property.[95]

No doubt Eddingfield knew of his wife's past and had anticipated an easy and indulgent life. For the sake of respectability, Mollie had stayed with a man who abused and humiliated her. But after several years, Mollie, who had once threatened C. L. Vawter with a revolver, had had enough. On August 31, 1898, the court declared the Eddingfield marriage dissolved. Thomas Eddingfield did not appear at the proceedings.

Mollie, however, did not easily relinquish her goals of marriage and nineteenth century, middle-class normality. Less than a month after her divorce on September 24, 1898, she married William Weinsheimer of Marysville, a nearby mining camp. Despite her divorce and remarriage, Mollie continued to see Eddington. One evening in February of 1899, Mollie and Thomas got drunk together, and Mollie conveyed an undivided one-half interest in the State Street property to him for a dollar. A few weeks later, Eddingfield filed the bill of sale at the county clerk's office. When Mollie discovered what had happened, she brought suit against Eddingfield to void the deed. She complained that "the defendant induced the plaintiff to drink of drugged or intoxicating beverages until she became utterly incapable of doing business" and that while she was indisposed Eddingfield had fraudulently persuaded her to sell her property. The court found that Eddingfield's payment was grossly inadequate and ordered him to restore the property to Mollie.[96]

In another real estate transaction, this one designed to further separate her from the tenderloin, Mollie disposed of her flagship property. On December 11, 1899, Mollie sold "The Castle" to John Steinbrenner, the owner of the Cosmopolitan Hotel, for $7,000 subject to her lease to Lillie Ashton. The property had provided the bulk of Mollie's income in the preceding years, and Weinsheimer saw it all slipping away from him. On December 9, 1900, Mollie made a will designating Weinsheimer as her sole heir. Three days later she was dead of acute alcoholism, and Willie Weinsheimer was a rich man. Mollie's estate was valued at $20,000.[97]

Mollie Byrnes left a half-brother, James Byrnes, and two minor nieces in New Orleans. The terms of her will did not satisfy them, and James Byrnes contested the will, claiming that Mollie had been coerced into signing the document. He charged that Weinsheimer had encouraged Mollie's alcoholism so that he might more easily exercise his influence over her and that he had often threatened to kill her. Weinsheimer had done these things, Byrnes alleged, to acquire Mollie's money and property. Byrnes went on to accuse Weinsheimer, whom he characterized as "a shiftless worthless adventurer," of planning Mollie's demise from the beginning of the couple's marriage. Correct or not about Weinsheimer's mercenary motives, Byrnes had rightly pointed out that Mollie was so weak physically at the time she made her will that she could not sign her name. Although Mollie was literate, she had signed the document with an "X." In further support of the family's contestment, Byrnes's attorney, A. E. Carleton, introduced witnesses who testified to the existence of a second will that entirely excluded Weinsheimer and bequeathed her estate to her nieces.[98]

The trial lasted an entire week. In the end, the jury upheld Willie Weinsheimer's claim. Byrnes's case rested on a subtle point of law and he was an outsider; Weinsheimer was a local resident. Yet, the dispute was still not resolved. Byrnes's attorney moved for a new trial, citing the discovery of new evidence. He presented several affidavits to the court in which one deponent claimed that she had been intimidated by Weinsheimer; a second hinted that Weinsheimer had bribed witnesses; and the last intimated that Mollie Weinsheimer might have been murdered. Even on the basis of these statements, the case was not retried. Weinsheimer and Byrnes settled out of court for $750.[99]

Both of Mollie's attempts to attain middle-class respectability had failed. She had moved up within the demimonde's hierarchy but had been unable to move out. An alcoholic and tied to Helena by her business interests, she tried too late to leave for greener pastures. Cities were settling down, and it was no longer so easy to blend into the West's transient population. That Mollie tried so desperately to marry and surround herself with the paraphernalia of middle-class existence attests to both her and other prostitutes' efforts to use the skin trade as a springboard into legitimacy. The mercenary men who had courted Mollie and her associates were not attracted to Mollie but to the profits to be made in the tenderloin.

Mollie Byrnes's relationships with Eddingfield and Weinsheimer allude to a fancy lady's desire for normality and to the growing presence of men in the demimonde. Although pimps and their fellow travelers had not been unknown in the Wood Street district, their influence had been muted.[100] In contrast, pimps' control of prostitution on Clore Street became normal.[101] Beginning in the mid 1880s, men realized that there were economic benefits to be derived from involvement in the skin trade. The career of Anna Muller illustrated the reorganization of management in the sexual marketplace that transferred control from madams to pimps.

In 1885, Anna Muller and Sully Buyck arrived in Helena. Anna and Sully had met in a bawdy house in New York City sometime in 1880 or 1881. At the time, Buyck was so financially embarrassed that Anna had to redeem his trunk from a neighboring bordello. They became attached to one another, and Buyck followed Anna when she opened her own establishment. Taking out legal title of the house in Buyck's name, Muller turned over the profits to him. In 1884, she opened another house of ill fame in Chicago. Again she placed the property in Buyck's name and gave him the receipts. She also advanced Buyck the capital for a saloon, but the venture collapsed, and Anna soon departed for Helena.[102]

On her arrival in 1885, Anna immediately acquired several houses of prostitution on Wood and Clore streets, this time in her own name. Buyck appeared shortly afterward with the proceeds from the sale of the Chicago property. Anna and Sully resumed their relationship with Sully chiefly responsible for marketing and rent collection.[103]

Their relationship disintegrated in the fall of 1889. Buyck returned from a frolic on the shores of France—financed by Anna—to inform her that he had found another woman and that he intended to leave her. But Buyck required signature deeds to Muller's property to assure his sole ownership, and he embarked on a program of abuse and intimidation to obtain them. On November 21, 1889, Anna surrendered; she conveyed property worth $8,000 to Buyck for the sum of $3,000 in the hope that this gesture would keep him by her side. Ironically, Buyck used Anna's own money to "purchase" her property. He had simply retained the profits from the summer months and augmented the amount by mortgaging Anna's Wood Street lots to Chicago Joe Hensley.[104]

Two years later, Anna Muller sued Buyck for the recovery of her property, charging that he had obtained it fraudulently. With the aid of an aspiring young lawyer, Thomas J. Walsh, Anna won a judgment against her former consort in the lower court. But Buyck was not so easily defeated, and in company with Massena Bullard, one of Helena's more unscrupulous lawyers, Buyck appealed the judgment to the Supreme Court of Montana.[105]

The learned justices found themselves wrestling with the definition of pimp and pondering the nature of the business relationship between a madam and a pimp. Writing for the entire court, Justice Robert Harwood ruled that there was no rule of law that allowed a pimp, by virtue of his employment alone, to seize any title to the proceeds from bawdy houses. Justice Harwood, moreover, noted sarcastically that Buyck had operated under the erroneous assumption that he was entitled to leave Anna in the same condition in which she had found Buyck—with only a trunk. This kind of thinking, according to the court, was entirely misguided and underpinned Buyck's fraud. Justice Harwood also had a few words for Massena Bullard concerning the attorney's clumsy reminder to the court to avoid any moral or sympathetic gestures toward Anna. In uncharacteristic fashion, Justice Harwood admonished Buyck's counsel that the decision had been rendered purely on its legal merit and added his opinion of the parties involved. "From a moral stand-point," Harwood wrote, "there may not be much room for comparison between the parties to this action. But if such comparison was necessary, we have no doubt, considering the condition and advantages of the respective parties, that the defendant [Sully Buyck] would be awarded the superlative degree for depravity of conduct." With that the court ordered Buyck to restore the property and to pay a cash settlement to Anna, who left the city a few years later.[106]

During the 1890s, prostitution was no longer even a dubious opportunity, although many women on Wood Street were still optimistic. In 1890, there were eight land-owning demimonde women who held property with an assessed value of $102,560. They contributed nearly $1,000 to city coffers in personal and property taxes in addition to the "fines" levied by the city's informal licensing system. Only the railroads and a few of Helena's most successful entrepreneurs paid more taxes than the demimonde.

Prostitute landowners and other female investors controlled the property in Helena's tenderloin. Catherine Richardson, Sarah Deegan, Deborah M. Hoyt, and Emma Howard, who kept their distance from Wood and Clore streets but rented to the fancy ladies, provided housing or work places for approximately one hundred white prostitutes who worked out of nearly thirty-five houses in the area. Most of these women lived alone, in pairs along Clore Street in the "cribs," or in the better houses on both sides of Wood Street. Lillie McGraw's *maison de joie* could accommodate as many as ten women, and Lillie Ashton at "The Castle" employed between five and seven "working girls." But even at its height, the empire was cracking apart.[107]

Beginning in 1890, Chicago Joe ran into financial difficulties, and she approached Thomas Cruse for assistance. Cruse, an Irish immigrant who had discovered the bonanza Drum Lummon mine at Marysville in 1876, had a solid bank and a familiarity with the demimonde. Joe mortgaged several of her properties to Thomas Cruse Savings Bank for $6,000.[108] Again in difficulty in 1892, Joe went to Jacob Switzer, a wholesale liquor dealer who had done business with her over the years. Switzer loaned Joe $10,000 on most of her Wood Street property. On August 5, 1893, Joe returned to the liquor dealer and mortgaged the rest of her holdings for $5,194.50. For three years Joe held her mortgagees at bay; but on March 14, 1896, she sold all of her property to Jacob Switzer for $21,119.23, an amount almost equal to the sum of her mortgages. Gambling that the financial squeeze after the Panic of 1893 might take down the Cruse bank, Joe and Switzer ignored Joe's previous mortgages to Cruse. The bank, which neither folded nor forgot Joe's mortgage, took Joe Hensley, her husband, and Switzer to court, charging that part of the property sale was illegal because Switzer's claim to the property was subordinate to the bank's lien.[109]

Switzer and the Hensleys had taken a calculated risk. A financial conservative, Cruse had not invested heavily in enterprises outside Montana, and he had maintained a large capital reserve. When the Panic of 1893 came and several Helena banks suspended operations, the Drum Lummon's bullion carried the day and kept the bank's doors open. Switzer, Chicago Joe, and her consort saw that they held a losing hand and admitted their defeat by simply not appearing in court.[110] The disputed property went into receivership, and with Chicago Joe Hensley's financial collapse two-thirds of the demimonde had passed out of women's control by the spring of 1896.

Lillie McGraw and Mollie Byrnes had also brushed with financial calamity. In January of 1889, Lillie had borrowed $3,000 from the Cruse bank, using her Wood Street property as collateral. Unaccountably, nine months later, Cruse canceled and released the lien against Lillie's property, although she had not paid the principal. Mollie Byrnes also felt the press of her creditors. Along with mortgages she had made during the late 1880s to finance construction of "The Castle," Mollie found it necessary in July 1888 to consolidate part of an earlier loan from John Shober with a $5,000 loan from the Cruse bank. This mortgage, although it matured in a year, went unpaid until 1895. In 1888, Mollie borrowed again on her unimproved property from the Cruse firm. Finally, in 1895, she mortgaged 212 State Street to Florence Gates for $1,000; she satisfied this last indenture within the year.[111]

All this suggests that the Wood Street regulars had overextended themselves in the building boom of the late 1880s. When recession struck Helena, the female entrepreneurs, like their male capitalist counterparts, were in a precarious position. Two of the women were able to weather the depressions, but Chicago Joe, whose enterprises were the most ambitious, went under.

What economic reverses did not do the years did. On July 17, 1898, sixty-one-year-old Lillie McGraw died in her Joliet Street house of cirrhosis of the liver. Five days earlier, doctors had surgically opened her abdomen only long enough to discern that Lillie's liver was irreparably damaged. Her property was leased for a time to Allie Carleton, an enterprising young madam from Butte, but Lillie's heirs could not pay the property tax and saw the lots go on the sheriff's block in 1900.[112] On October 23, 1899, Josephine "Chicago Joe" Hensley died of pneumonia in her home on Wood Street. At fifty-six, Joe left the world as she had come into it—poor, illiterate, and honorable. Three months before her death she had satisfied her mortgages to Jacob Switzer. On December 12, 1900, Mollie "Belle Crafton" Byrnes died at the age of forty-two.[113]

All the dowager queens of the demimonde were dead at the opening of the twentieth century. With their passing, prostitution fell into men's hands and ceased to be women's business. Lillie Ashton continued to operate "The Castle" and other leaseholders continued to ply their trade on Wood Street, but the entrepreneurial power was not theirs. Neither Switzer nor the Cruse bank's receiver had an interest in maintaining the demimonde as the women had.[114] Except for "The Castle" and one of Chicago Joe's old houses, the marginal "cribs" on Clore Street became the center of the district; the elegance of the empire had faded.

The lives of others who figured in the women's empire also changed by 1900, but in different ways. Thomas Butler Eddingfield moved to the edges of Wood Street society and ended his Helena career as a commercial agent in a seedy rooming house. Without his lady, James T. "Black Hawk" Hensley was set adrift. After Joe's death he moved into the old Stamm tenement on Water Street and worked as a bartender. From there he went to Reeder's Alley and worked as a common laborer before he disappeared from Helena in 1902. Albert Hankins, Joe's first consort, died in a folding-bed accident in Chicago. Allie Carleton managed Lillie's house for two years before she moved on, and Willie Weinsheimer remarried less than a year after Mollie died and lived a comfortable life until his death in 1951. Lillie Ashton operated "The Castle" until 1904 when, it was said, she left for Chicago to marry a wealthy man.[115]

When the census enumerator made his rounds in 1900, his tabulations reflected the changes in the demimonde. Between 1890 and 1900, Helena lost nearly one-quarter of its population, and the number of prostitutes had decreased accordingly. There were fifty-five fancy ladies in 1900, six of whom were Asian. As Helena had grown older, so had the "soiled doves." Their average age in 1900 was twenty-nine, although most of the white prostitutes tended to be in their early twenties. The majority of these women—94 per cent—lived by themselves or in exclusively female households. In this respect they had returned to living arrangements that had dominated the demimonde thirty years before. More immigrant women than ever before had taken up the "life," accounting for 38 per cent of prostitutes; the Midwest continued to supply more "soiled doves" than it did regular members of the community. Economically, too, much had changed since 1870. Not one prostitute owned property nor did any fancy lady maintain a bank account in the firms that had succeeded the failed banks of the 1890s. Suicide and violent death became commonplace. Ida Reed was shot to death by her fancy man. Sarah Golden and Lillie Moran committed suicide. And any number of Clore Street and Wood Street women died of alcoholism, tuberculosis, Bright's disease, and pneumonia. By the turn of the century, Helena's red-light district had much of the sadness, desperation, and death commonly associated with the descriptions of prostitution in reform tracts.[116]

The social and economic structure of the nineteenth century, which limited women to the most menial and lowest-paying work and made material wealth available only to a limited number of them, created an environment conducive to prostitution. For a young woman alone, overworked, poor, or ambitious, prostitution provided a means for survival and a way to acquire luxuries. Nevertheless, it has been argued that achieving success through prostitution was, at best, a pyrrhic victory; prosperity in the demimonde exacted equal social cost from its workers. The history of women in the nineteenth century is littered with comparable hollow triumphs. Sexually vulnerable, nineteenth century women embraced the ideology of "passionlessness"; in doing so they traded their sexuality for elevation to moral and intellectual beings. Catharine Beecher sought to enlarge women's influence by turning the home into a female domain and domesticity into a science. Instead, the home became a prison and domesticity, destiny. Similarly, the frontier provided some women with the opportunity to capitalize on an unfortunate situation. Nineteenth century capitalism depended, in part, on the exploitation of women's sexuality, but the fancy ladies of the urban, mining frontier in some measure controlled the terms of their exploitation and profited accordingly. Moving into the marketplace, they forfeited a private life. As public women they faced the problem of creating a private, domestic existence for themselves—precisely the opposite dilemma facing legitimate women who wished to carve out a place in the public sphere.[117]

Only so long as the social structure of the frontier remained loose and the West's population continued to be transient was this possible. Once the social structures tightened and settled, prostitution became another circumscribed role for women. Prostitution's history in Helena illustrates this process. Between 1865 and 1883, the fancy ladies achieved the economic means for upward and outward mobility. Helena's demimonde expanded spatially and economically during the following years, but ownership consolidated into the hands of a few women. In 1890, the same year that the U.S. Census Bureau could no longer draw a frontier line, Helena's Wood Street empire began to topple.

Despite the demimonde's growing geographical and social isolation from the larger community and its eventual economic decline, the fancy ladies influenced the development of the city and its legitimate citizens.

Helena's anti-prostitution campaign illustrated the further development of the community's identity and the differences between *arriviste* and pioneer perspectives. Although a moral imperative to remove prostitution from the body politic underlay their efforts, the newcomers developed a more pragmatic approach to the problem. They argued that if the city was to harbor prostitution, first it should be made unobtrusive; second, it should be made economically onerous to the women to encourage their departure; and third, the city should be financially compensated for its public embarrassment.

The pioneer merchants were more concerned with economics. On the one hand, they worried about depreciating property values and the threat that conspicuous, expanding prostitution posed to the growth of the city and to their entrepreneurial futures. On the other hand, they understood that prostitution was an important contributor to the business community as an employer and customer. The tenderloin required groceries, liquor, insurance, and construction. The pioneer aldermen, uncomfortable with a formal licensing system that would bestow a civic blessing on the skin trade, did not want the fancy ladies and their profits to disappear. They desired some measure of social control, but its form was problematic.

In sum, the debate over prostitution involved competing visions of the city's identity. The town's survival depended on its entrepreneurial good health, but a capital city also had to provide a wholesome atmosphere, display some sophistication, and maintain a semblance of culture. Although both newcomers and old-timers seemingly shared this vision, they were often motivated by different conceptions of urban life and civic responsibility. The newcomers advocated relatively uncompromising reform measures aimed at emulating eastern society; the pioneers were more willing to reconcile the moral laxity of frontier society with a new moral stringency. In effect, the newcomers established a new standard for behavior in western society, but it was one that would often be leavened by an older liberality.

The history of prostitution in Helena also suggests something less easily documented. Although the prostitutes' empire lasted only a brief time, it left a legacy for other women in the community that has continued into the twentieth century. Responding to a social investigator's questions, a Helena bartender in 1953 said: "This is Montana . . . Women have a right to sit in bars. . . . Nobody thinks anything of it around here. . . . They're all good fellows. . . . Not a hustler among them. . . . We got houses for that."[118] Implicit in the investigator's question was a common assumption: unescorted women who frequented saloons were by definition available for commercial sex. Intrinsic in the barkeep's answer was a different attitude, one that did not develop overnight. Aside from expressing a nineteenth century attitude about prostitution's role in deflecting male sexuality away from respectable women, the bartender's remarks suggested that the city's physical and social arrangements had been altered with respect to women. For the barkeep, a woman's presence in a public tavern did not mean sexual sale. Montana women, according to the barroom overseer, had social rights unavailable to women elsewhere. Women outside the demimonde had acquired the freedom to come and go as they pleased in all manner of public places without fear of censure. From the barkeep's point of view, prostitution had something to do with this redefinition of social space. He was probably correct. Because prostitution removed the threat of male sexuality and confined illicit sexuality and its purveyors to a particular geographic area, other women were free to move through other parts of the city. In short, respectable women profited from other women's willingness to trade with their bodies; Helena's fancy ladies had helped redraw the boundaries of the public sphere for Helena's middling women.

The demimonde was only a part of Helena's female community. Other women may have changed their names as the prostitutes had, but they changed them because they married to raise families. These married, middling women represented the majority of Helena's female population. Up on the hills on either side of the gulch away from Wood Street, the mothers and daughters of Helena worked out their destinies in different ways, compromising with the frontier in the same manner as the city fathers had with the "soiled doves" of Wood Street.

CHAPTER THREE

Mothers and Daughters of Eldorado

The Generations of Helena's Middling Women

LIKE SO MANY OTHER MINING TOWNS along the Rocky Mountain cordillera, Helena represented a kind of Eldorado for its settlers. Whether they came to prospect or to profit from supplying the miners, as businessmen, artisans, or professionals they anticipated "bettering their condition in life," to use a popular nineteenth century phrase. But there was more to the settlement of these Eldorados than townspeople raising cities out of the wilderness; the frontier also worked on its inhabitants, especially the women, as they tried to fashion homes reminiscent of the ones they had left behind. In a number of ways, both the unsettled nature of the community and its special demographic circumstances affected middling, married women and brought them to new perceptions of themselves.

Helena's frontier conditions transformed these women as profoundly as they had the Wood Street regulars, but the transformation took very different forms. First, middling, married women in Helena faced a visible conflict between their prescribed nineteenth century female role and their experiences as capable, independent individuals in a young mining town. Second, Helena's rough social environment, combined with the town's civic pretensions, undermined churches and schools, the institutions in which nineteenth century women normally anchored their power, and countenanced gambling, prostitution, and cronyism, community activities that were frankly antithetical. Consequently, married women entered into community betterment work for their own and their children's benefit with a purposeful energy. Third, women maintained the community's social welfare systems, effectively contributing to Helena's economic and political stability. Fourth, Helena's matrons engaged in significant economic activities that often escaped the census taker's notice. Fifth, the frontier eroded women's informal networks, the web of friendships that underpinned nineteenth century women's lives, and cast women back into the home and domesticity. And sixth, the peculiar demography of the frontier, especially the disproportionate number of men to women, created a scarcity of domestic help that increased the burdens of managing a household for middling women, encouraging women's critique of domesticity and the inequity of the relations between husbands and wives.

The majority of Helena's women were wives and mothers engaged in what the census enumerator termed "keeping house." Imbued with the ideal of "true womanhood" and touched by the "cult of domesticity" —the nineteenth century cultural ideals that defined women as submissive, self-sacrificing, moral, and devoted to home, hearth, and husband—Helena's matrons came to the urban mining frontier directly from their homes and families in the States.[1] They resumed their lives in a rough-and-tumble mining camp, accepting the nineteenth century women's mission: to provide a home for their husbands, to rear their children, and to re-create the genteel domestic world—that is, to "keep house."

While management of a household normally connoted unpaid labor, "keeping house" in Helena masked a variety of economic activities. Foremost among these was keeping boarders. In 1870, 20 per cent of Helena's women managed to find space for an extra miner, clerk, laborer, or spouse's employee.[2] By 1880, 27 per cent of the town's women provided for both their families and additional paying guests. With boarding rates of between five and seven dollars a week, keeping boarders represented a healthy monetary contribution to the household, especially if a housekeeper could manage two or three lodgers.[3]

Women also went into business for themselves. Married women could enter business by declaring themselves sole traders, a complicated process with capital limitations. Although women did not overrun the county clerk's office with declarations, between 1870 and 1883 twenty-six availed themselves of the territory's legal provision for married women's entrepreneurship; by 1898, the number had grown to 119.[4] The women's businesses were equally divided among mining and commercial brokerage, saloon operation, farming and livestock raising, and small retail operations. On the whole, the businesses were modest with little capital investment, and their owners were women whom the Dun Company man described as "good for small engagements." Whereas a businessman's familial obligations moderately influenced the R. G. Dun agent's recommendation for credit, women's household responsibilities were decisive. Mrs. Conway, for example, paid her bills, but the Dun man could not recommend her because she had too many children and a worthless husband to support.[5]

There were a few startling business successes among Helena's middling women.[6] The R. G. Dun agent estimated that Mary Aaron, a Jewish businesswoman who operated a branch of her husband's millinery business to be worth between $5,000 and $7,000. Hannah James moved from retail furniture sales to being a railroad construction contractor. By

1883, four women had formalized their intention to become accomplished capitalists. As their sole tradership declarations announced, Deborah M. Hoyt, Catharine Ming, Josephine Totten, and Jeanette Cole designated themselves real estate and mining property brokers. While some wives legalized their participation in the marketplace, others engaged in informal, sporadic work for cash payment. In letters home, Elizabeth Chester Fisk referred to her employment as a teacher, seamstress, and bookbinder. "I prefer," she wrote on one occasion, "to work for money rather than sew for Mrs. Fisk [her sister-in-law]. There is no necessity for my doing either. I followed my own inclination."[7]

Many of Helena's married women, however, cared a good deal about securing ownership of their possessions as a protection against misfortune. Over the years, a steady stream of wives paraded through the clerk and recorder's office to file separate property declarations. Often these statements were uncomplicated affairs that legally protected a woman's household furniture or her piano from execution. More numerous were declarations that involved business fixtures or livestock, detailing the number, kind, and color of ducks and cows. By 1883, 10 per cent of Helena's wives had taken precautions to separate their property from that of their husbands; the majority of these inventories represented considerable assets.[8]

While formal and informal businesses were also important elements in women's economic lives, property ownership underpinned Helena female entrepreneurship. In 1867, a handful of women, most of them with dubious reputations, had purchased property. Three years later, nearly one-quarter of the community's adult women owned real estate; by 1880, 40 per cent of Helena's women were property owners.[9] Besides representing considerable capital investment, property ownership implied the receipt of rents, lease income, and collateral to finance other investments. Many women earned income by helping young families into their first home. Helena's propertied matrons privately financed a healthy one-quarter of the mortgages made between 1886 and 1893 and profited from the accrued interest.[10]

For the town's women, property ownership meant more than economic gain. The territorial constitution and statutes permitted all property owners to vote on property taxes and school trusteeship issues.[11] In the spring of 1887, when voter registration for general elections became mandatory in the city, a group of Helena women, seeing that the registration provision included no reference to gender, attempted to extend their franchise by registering. "The judges, however, took a different view of the matter," the *Herald* observed, "and turned the fair ones away." Nevertheless, on more than one occasion, women flexed their political muscle. On April 7, 1888, for example, they elected temperance advocate Richard Howey to the school board over perennial Board of Trade-supported candidates, H. M. Parchen and Richard Lockey.

Attributing Howey's success to the female vote, the *Herald* reported that the ladies had been out in force.[12]

On another front, Helena women became active county workers, if only on a volunteer basis as the Poor Relief Committee. The winter of 1886-1887 was particularly severe, and with Helena's sudden growth in population the number of the city's poor increased beyond the capacity of individual charity. Whether because of the city council's inability to provide relief on a case-by-case basis or because of the city's reluctance to hire additional personnel, Mayor T. H. Kleinschmidt and the council abrogated their responsibility for the care of the city's indigent. In an open letter in the city's newspapers Kleinschmidt asked representatives from each ward to meet with him to determine the best course. Thereafter, the city council surrendered almost complete care of the city's destitute to the Poor Relief Committee. Although the committee was accountable to the city budget, Helena's women acted in the same manner as a modern welfare department. Between 1887 and 1891, they determined eligible cases, arranged for supplies from local merchants, disbursed the funds allocated to the committee by the city fathers, and kept financial records of their activities.[13]

Politically experienced and economically powerful, Helena's women helped create social divisions within the community by serving as hostesses to the parties and receptions that punctuated the lives of Helena's upper and middle classes. "True womanhood" had fallen on hard days in the mining camp. Newspapers failed to mention women's activities, and early divorce cases made no special pleas on the basis of "true womanhood." Elizabeth Chester Fisk, a staunch supporter of the standard, also noted its eclipse during her first decade in Helena. Commencing in the mid 1880s, the mistresses of Helena reinstated the ideology in a grander but perhaps more superficial form.[14] With the guidance of local society columnists and under the influence of *arriviste* women, Helena wives set the standards for and the style of social intercourse. They learned to forego their hats while dancing, to disclose engagements promptly, and to persuade their gentlemen to more genteel conduct. Sometimes the columnists' advice to Helena society approached the ridiculous. To circumvent the strictures of Lent, one columnist suggested that Helena socialites employ liveried, silver-buttoned black boys as personal messengers during the penitential season. The buttons, the etiquette authority stipulated, should bear the family crest (if one could be resurrected); in the absence of heraldry, the lady's initials would suffice.[15]

Besides acting as arbiters of the town's social circles, Helena wives served as visible indicators of their husbands' wealth and position in the social hierarchy. The Thomas Cruse wedding in 1886, for example, set the tone for future social gatherings in Helena and their reportage. Henceforth, newspaper accounts of weddings included detailed descriptions of ladies' dress and long lists of the wedding gifts and their donors. Helena citizens calculated the number of their "best people" by the number of fish forks and Worcester china plates. Helena's elite and middling wives were the masters of this delicate social accounting.[16]

As purveyors of a revamped "true womanhood" and as the principal watchdogs of the traditional family and its values, wives in Helena exerted a conservative influence on the community. To safeguard their children and to fulfill their own expectations of urban life, during the mid 1880s they took the lead in defining proper education, correct moral behavior, and the town's cultural life. Weaving themselves into special interest organizations, religious societies, sororal orders, and cultural clubs of all kinds, Helena women sought to curb the town's excesses by providing antidotes to the effects of saloons, faro parlors, bordellos, and hotel lobbies.

In some instances, they departed from their service orientation to plead women's causes or to defend men who represented their interests. When the Reverend F. D. Kelsey preached against the dangers of morphine use at the funeral of a local physician, the medical fraternity, particularly Dr. William Steele, criticized his remarks as erroneous and inappropriate. Helena's matrons rallied to Kelsey's defense and proposed a boycott of Steele's practice unless he moderated his behavior. On another occasion, they supported the hiring of a female librarian when the male incumbent proved inimical to the sensibilities of the library's female patrons. In the press, they advocated the cause of equal and practical education for women.[17]

Despite their advocacy and social calculus, most women lived less public and more prosaic lives. The average middle-class woman living in Helena in 1870 was from the Northeast, twenty-two years old, married, nine years younger than her husband, and "kept house" in a nuclear family household composed of four persons: husband, wife, child, and either a boarder or a servant.[18] Women between the ages of twenty and thirty numerically dominated the female population in Helena. Although there were approximately two hundred women who corresponded to this description in 1870, only fifty-four women who fit the 1870 age cohort remained to be counted in 1880. Thirty to forty years old in 1880, these women shared a common experience: more than a decade on the urban mining frontier. A composite portrait of them suggests some of the ways in which their frontier sojourn set them apart from other nineteenth century women.

Those women who came and stayed in Helena during its first decade were white and members of the middle and upper classes; they were the wives of men who had prospered on the frontier as professionals and businessmen. The group also included the wives of artisans, several working widows, two proprietor prostitutes, and a black woman. Like their husbands, these pioneer women capitalized on the possibilities engendered by the frontier. Two-thirds of them owned property, and 20 per cent of them were engaged in some kind of business.[19]

Pioneer women comprised the backbone of the female cultural, benevolent, and political organizations in Helena. Fifty per cent of these women engaged in some kind of community reform or betterment activity. Isabella Kirkendall, Hannah Rumsey, Elizabeth Fisk, and Catharine Ming all served terms on the Poor Relief Committee. In 1894, Catherine Cannon, Elizabeth Fisk, Matilda Reinig, Jeanette Loeb, and Norma Chadwick put their efforts into the "Helena for the Capital" campaign. Writing to the club's president, Emma S. Cannon alluded to the whistle-stop team's special background: ". . . you chose your *Pioneer* Women Campaigners of the State of Montana *well* for we have really *had* to have *some* courage and independence of spirit. . . ."[20]

For some women of the pioneer group, independence was often not a matter of choice. Because of widowhood or divorce, 15 per cent of the pioneer women were without a spouse in 1880.[21] Survival for women alone on the frontier meant entering the labor force, and many of them found employment or filed sole traderships. But a marriage unbroken by divorce or death did not guarantee a pioneer woman the company of her husband. Helena's isolation assured wives of businessmen that their husbands would be absent for long periods when they went on extended business trips to the States or other parts of the territory.[22] In either case, marital disruption was a hallmark of the pioneer women cohort. The biographies of Mary Coleau Lavanash, Fannie Spencer, Catharine Ming, and Mary Ann Eckert are variations on the theme of bereft women and show how a husband's absence often pushed women into new roles.

Mary Coleau arrived in Montana sometime before 1870. Her marriage to Frank Coleau was brief; Frank Coleau simply abandoned his wife. Divorcing her husband on the grounds of desertion in 1872, Mary stayed on the ranch that Frank had left behind and in 1873 declared herself a sole trader engaged in the business of raising livestock. Less than a year later she married Augustus Lavanash, a farmer and quarryman, but her alliance with him had unfortunate consequences. In July 1879, she accused Paul Lavanash, her brother-in-law, of rape. Although the rape case never came to trial, Mary appeared before the court in March 1880, petitioning for a divorce from Augustus Lavanash on the grounds of desertion and cruelty and asking that the Lavanash property be set aside for her. The court obliged. At thirty-six years old, Mary was twice divorced with three children. Between June 1880 and May 1884, Mary manipulated her small real estate holdings to stave off financial disaster but to little advantage. Apparently, members of the Coleau family, who had stayed behind after her first husband's departure, undermined her efforts. In May 1884, one of their number, Bessie Coleau, tried to gain by larceny what she could not obtain from Mary legally. Even after she had charged the Coleau woman with theft, Mary apparently avoided the confrontation and left Helena, presumably to try her fortunes elsewhere.[23]

Fannie Spencer Fordonski, one of two fancy ladies who remained continuously in Helena during the depressed 1870s, lived by deception. She lied consistently and irreverently about her age, her place of birth, and her marital status. Born in Nauvoo, Illinois, on July 11, 1845, to Hyrum and Elizabeth Spencer, Fannie came west with her family two years later. Hyrum Spencer, who had attained some status among the Latter-Day Saints and was among the first of those whom Brigham Young directed to join the exodus to Salt Lake City, died on the Mormon Trail. His brother, Daniel, who would soon become one of Mormonism's great spokesmen and advocates of polygamy, cared for the family's welfare and married Elizabeth. Although Elizabeth Spencer refused Daniel's first call to polygamy, she offered no opposition when he married three women in 1854. By the mid 1850s, Fannie was a member of a sprawling polygamous household that had its share of tension and jealousies. On May 25, 1865, Fannie married Isaac Fordonski, a Gentile, and the couple departed Utah Territory for Virginia City, Montana. At Virginia City the Fordonski marriage foundered. Fannie found the charms of Barney Hughes irresistible, and witnesses in a subsequent divorce action testified that Fannie had been criminally intimate with him in September of 1867. Charging Fannie with adultery, Isaac finally divorced her in 1871. By then, according to one witness, Fannie had become a "public woman in Helena."[24]

Louise Courselle, one of Helena's early proprietor prostitutes, and soon to be Bozeman, Montana's madam *par excellence,* helped Fannie get a start in Helena's demimonde by loaning her money on Fannie's small amount of personal property. Like many proprietor prostitutes, Fannie had a checkered but successful financial career. In 1880, after adding to property she had purchased six years earlier, Fannie optimistically looked forward to expanding her domain on Clore Street. But on December 18, 1881, Fannie Spencer suddenly died. Her Clore Street property and personal effects were sold at a sheriff's sale to satisfy her creditors.[25]

Absence, not divorce, unsettled Catharine Ming's life. John Ming's far-flung business interests required his vigilance and absence from the Ming household in Helena. His stock operation in Miles City, Montana, especially demanded his attention. Because he could not attend to the minutiae of his business transactions, Catharine became his agent and learned the intricacies of management. John Ming shared all of his business affairs with his wife and frankly advised her on one occasion to go slowly: "don't depend on me for some time to do much up there." Catharine took his advice. In December 1883, Catharine and her mother, Jeanette Cole, filed sole traderships as commercial brokers, while Catharine continued to supervise the Ming family affairs in John Ming's absence.[26]

John Ming died in December 1887, leaving Catharine and their two sons an estate valued at $150,000. Catharine continued to manage the Mings' fortunes, dealing with damage suits and ownership disputes as deftly as her husband had. Catharine was not above manipulating the law to gain an advantage. In the wake of the 1893 panic, for example, Catharine and her sons conspired in a complex trustee incompetency litigation to fend off the First National Bank's attempt to foreclose a mortgage and the city's clumsy effort to assume control of the Ming estate. The Ming offspring charged their mother with mismanagement of their father's estate, thereby negating a large mortgage transacted by Catharine Ming. By the time Catharine Ming died in 1920, she had made financial forays into Alaska and California.[27]

A businesswoman in her own right, Mary Ann Eckert operated a successful photography studio on Main Street. Like Fannie Fordonski, Mary Ann Eckert bore an unsavory reputation: She owned considerable property in the tenderloin, maintained her residence there, and located her business on the edge of the red-light district. The R. G. Dun agent accorded her a guarded recommendation on the basis of her prompt repayment of debts, even as he reported that she was not known for her "A-1" character.[28]

The Dun agent had good reason to question Mary Ann's character. On her deathbed in 1888, she confessed to the 1879 ax murder of grocer John Denn. In the flurry of journalism that followed her revelation, there were allegations that Eckert had begun her frontier career as a hurdy-gurdy dancer and that she had maintained dubious alliances with several men to move up the social ladder. Aside from these allegations, she was adept at protecting her interests, both personal and economic. Mary Ann, for example, filed a divorce petition in 1873, claiming that her husband had deserted her in 1871. The divorce proceedings were never completed, and Mary Ann was later reported to have said that she "did a bunk on him." Perhaps Mary Ann kept the divorce petition as insurance against her husband's untimely appearance. Despite problems in her personal life, Mary Ann succeeded in business and provided a sizable estate to her daughter, "Jessie" Eckert Schwabe.[29]

Mortality and movement thinned the ranks of the pioneer women between 1880 and 1890. Mollie Kemp's suicide was an unusual case. Becoming increasingly despondent over her daughter Anne's death from spinal meningitis, Mollie attempted to take her own life in 1886. When her surviving daughter, Ella, intervened, the gun went off and killed daughter instead of mother. Several years later, Mollie Kemp was found drowned, her death labeled a suicide and attributed to long-standing melancholy. Those who did not depart their lives in Helena simply departed Helena. Bridget Allen, for example, divorced her husband and disappeared; the Abraham Sand family moved to Salt Lake City; and the Woolfolks went on to Chicago.[30]

For those who stayed and survived, the age difference between husbands and wives among the pioneer cohort had made itself felt by 1890. By then, Helena had a coterie of rich widows. "An interesting feature of this list of taxpayers," a Helena newswriter commented on a tabulation of citizens with taxable assets above $10,000, "is the large number of women who are comfortably 'fixed' and who as a rule are widows."[31] With few exceptions, women holding taxable property with an assessed value of $10,000 or more were bereft of their spouses. These "well-fixed" women, most of whom were of the pioneer cohort, comprised 16 per cent of the elite tax bracket.[32] By 1900, twelve women proudly called themselves capitalists, and half of them were among Helena's pioneer women.[33] Even as the pioneer cohort prospered through shrewd investment of inheritance, its number declined. Of the fifty-six women who resided in Helena from 1870 to 1880, only eighteen remained in 1900.

The narratives of the pioneer cohort women—women who lived out their young womanhood on the frontier—suggest several common themes. First, their backgrounds and their activities in Helena reveal that they shared a vision of genteel society, an ideal of true womanhood, and a concept of woman's role within an upright and sophisticated milieu. Second, they intensely involved themselves in reform activity aimed at the social and moral improvement of the community. Third, they lived for long periods of time apart from their helpmates and had to depend on their own resources. Finally, and most important, they evinced a high level of economic activity predicated on property ownership, investment, and the manipulation of capital. Certainly, most of these attributes were hallmarks of womanhood nationally during the same period; in Helena, the difference was a matter of degree and economic activity. Nonetheless, the degree was significant and economic activity was sophisticated and widespread.

In pioneer women's biographies there is no clear evidence that the influences of the frontier transformed women's lives and set them apart from their late-arriving contemporaries and from other nineteenth century American women. Yet, there are suggestions that the peculiar demography of the frontier created significant differences in these women's lives. Helena's isolation and the delay of rail transportation, for example, necessitated their husbands' absences for long periods of time. The age difference between husbands and wives and the ubiquity of divorce intensified the chances that frontier women would be cast upon their own resources far more than women elsewhere. Similarly, the town's corruption, especially the men's saloon-centered society, made reform more necessary, immediate, and intense than elsewhere. Pioneer women's high degree of economic activity and property ownership can be explained by the availability of inexpensive or depreciated property in Helena. This circumstance, in turn, conferred limited electoral franchise on a sizable group of women, giving them practice in politics and some political power.

The women of the pioneer cohort only superficially resembled the "true woman" of the nineteenth century. Behind their facade of refinement and conformity lurked small-time tycoons in petticoats, tough administrators, school board kingmakers, and social cartographers of class lines. Many of these women would live on into the twentieth century, but by 1900 they had handed over their tasks to the next generation, the daughters of the frontier.

The pioneer women bore sixty-nine female children; of this number four died before 1900. Fifty-five per cent can be accounted for at the turn of the century. Of these, 35 per cent worked in some capacity for most of their lives. Seventeen per cent experienced divorce, and 19 per cent never married. One-quarter participated in community life through political, cultural, and leadership organizations. Benefiting from their parents' investments and property ownership and their own advantageous marriages, few among the pioneers' female children had financial problems.[34] Not only do their biographies reflect exaggerations of traits found in the women of the first generation, but their biographies also suggest that the pioneers' daughters differed from their twentieth century counterparts in other regions.

Lottie Rumsey, the daughter of Hannah and William Rumsey, was born in Helena on June 13, 1867. Eccentric to the point of saving a severed finger to accompany his burial, William Rumsey had fled the Civil War to try his luck in the Colorado and Montana mining frontiers where he prospered as a miner and mercantile store owner. Lottie led a leisurely life, punctuated by visits to Illinois relatives, music lessons, and educational dilettantism. Before 1890, however, in partnership with the Episcopal Church, she had also opened a school for the children of Chinese laborers; she continued her work with the city's Asian residents well into the twentieth century.[35]

Lottie Rumsey was well past forty years old in January 1913 when she married Evan D. Owen, a middle-aged widower from Butte. In March 1913, Owen struck Lottie and made false accusations against her chastity. Not about to endure Owen's violence, Lottie appeared in court in September and secured a divorce on the grounds of cruelty. Thereafter, Lottie pleased herself and according to her family became engagingly eccentric, hanging calendars in her living room like portraits and evincing a total indifference to domestic amenities like running water and indoor plumbing. For many years Lottie was secretary for the Sons and Daughters of Montana Pioneers, a position that required considerable organizational talent and time. In her sixties, she married dentist George Willett, with whom she spent her last years.[36]

If eccentricity touched Lottie Rumsey's life, Marie Kleinschmidt's represented an early twentieth century equivalent of a counter-culture existence. Forsaking her parents' opulent lifestyle, she married telegrapher Thomas Southworth in 1906, moving out of Helena to a log cabin in

Unionville that Southworth had built for his bride. Although the couple furnished the cabin with several grand pieces from her parents' fashionable home, Marie Southworth led a life of simplicity and community service. In addition to being a Republican committeewoman, a member of the board of election judges and clerks, a Women's Club member, and secretary of the Sons and Daughters of Montana Pioneers, she was also a self-taught botanist. Her will contained a final gesture of community interest: she bequeathed her property to the Florence Crittenden Home, a home for unwed mothers.[37]

Community activism also marked the life of Helen Lehman. Born in 1871, Helen had come to Montana from New York with her mother who had returned east to give birth to Helen. Educated in the public schools of Helena and in Washington, D.C., Helen returned to Helena, working first in her father's grocery and bakery business and later as the society reporter for the *Helena Independent*. When her father, Charles Lehman, moved his business to Lewistown, Montana, in 1893, Helen closed the Helena store, remaining for some months to tidy up the Lehman interests before rejoining her father's business in Lewistown. In 1895, Helen Lehman married Austin Warr, a successful Lewistown businessman and assistant cashier of the Bank of Fergus County.[38]

After her marriage, Helen Lehman Warr directed her energies toward her family and community betterment. In addition to raising four children, she became secretary of the Lewistown library, president of the Women's Club, a member of the school board, head of local Red Cross activities, and an active promoter of plays, concerts, and cultural events. After her husband died suddenly in 1917, Helen Warr added the management of his business affairs to her community work. In her obituary in 1930, the *Lewistown Democrat News* commented that Helen Lehman Warr had created a place all her own in Lewistown society; the writer might have added that she very nearly created Lewistown society.[39]

Noting both the business skills and the sense of public service evinced by the pioneer daughters, one Montana historian wrote of Mary Lockey: "[She] presents a rare combination of the successful educator and the successful business woman." Born in 1874 and raised in Helena, Mary Lockey was in her thirties before she found her calling. Living with her parents, who had retired in Palo Alto, California, Mary taught in the local high school where she became involved in informal discussions of pedagogy and educational policy. In 1906, at the suggestion of Stanford University President David Starr Jordan, Mary Lockey founded Castilleja School, a women's college preparatory school. She had inherited not only her mother's capital but also her parents' business acumen; she incorporated her school, while she retained ownership, the presidency of the corporation, and the headship of the school itself. By 1910, Mary Lockey had purchased property, had erected five buildings, and had assets valued at $100,000. A single woman throughout her life, Mary pioneered a tradition of professionalism and scholarship for women in northern California. She died in 1939.[40]

The Kirkendall sisters—Nettie, Bessie, and Clara—all exhibited various characteristics that were typical of second-generation frontier women. Nettie, the oldest of the three and a kindred spirit to her activist mother, Isabella Kirkendall, assumed the position of clerk with the county water department, a position commensurate with other county department managers. During the early twentieth century, she joined her mother as an active supporter of the suffrage campaign and participated in community activities as much as her employment would permit. Clara, the only one of the three sisters to marry, divorced her husband in 1905 on grounds of cruelty. In 1934, she married a childhood sweetheart, Harry Shepard, and the couple went off to live in Alaska. Very much in charge of her life, Clara stubbornly and successfully at one point brought suit against the federal government for recovery of damages suffered when Indians stole mules from one of her father's wagon trains. Bessie, the youngest sister, worked as a milliner and sales clerk for most of her life. Unable to find a satisfactory niche, according to her family, Bessie remained single and generally indulged herself with shopping and travel.[41]

Clara Holter, the daughter of Mary Pauline and Anton M. Holter, reveled in the lifestyle her father's wealth produced. Clara was no beauty, but her status and her family's money assured her of invitations to Helena's social events. Among those who attended the same parties as she did was Percy Kennett, capitalist Samuel Hauser's stepson. Handsome and self-confident, Kennett cut a figure in Helena society that distracted most of the city's belles at one time or another. When Kennett singled out Clara and courted her, she was delighted, but her brothers and parents had misgivings. From their point of view, Percy Kennett lacked substance and was not what they had in mind for their only daughter and sister. When Clara and Percy eloped in 1888, the family hid its disappointment and braved the community's energetic gossips.[42]

For Clara, the romance soon evaporated. Percy Kennett turned out to be a shallow, undependable, sometimes drinking man who failed to manage the enterprises the Holters provided for him. When he accidentally shot himself to death in 1900, Clara was left with two small boys, both of whom died of tuberculosis in early adulthood. In the 1920s, she met Harry Gray, who charmed, flattered, and persuaded her to marry him. Unfortunately, Gray proved to be a fortune hunter of considerable cunning. Once married, he informed Clara that he was not a U.S. citizen, that he expected her to "dance to his tune," and that he had married her for her money. Devastated, Clara consulted her brothers and with their support she obtained a divorce—for a price. From an arrogant girl who had been a society pacesetter, Clara Holter Kennett matured into a women of quiet charity. Perhaps in memory of her sons, she financially assisted young men through law school and young women in nurse's training.[43]

Several patterns run through the stories of the frontier daughters that differentiate them from their mothers and from the majority of American women in 1900: their marked inclination to make a life for themselves apart from marriages; their greater propensity toward employment; their dedication to community involvement characterized by activism but also by leadership; and their indifference to traditional lifestyles, which gave them the freedom, within bounds, to live as they chose.

During its frontier and immediate post-frontier period, Helena influenced the attitudes of its second-generation women. The unbalanced sex ratio occasioned by the depletion of the male population in the aftermath of the Panic of 1893 affected marriage prospects for the daughters of the frontier. Whereas 46 per cent of the city's female population between the ages of twenty-one and thirty were unmarried in 1900, 55 per cent of the frontier daughters were unmarried.[44] Frontier daughters also continued the tradition of frequent divorce that characterized the frontier, and especially Montana. Twenty-seven per cent of Helena's female population worked in 1900 and 25 per cent of American women were in the work force by 1910. More than one-third of the frontier daughters worked in both decennial years.[45] Following in their pioneer mothers' footsteps, the pioneer daughters were involved in community affairs and, in instances, became civic leaders, creating or supporting institutions that assisted both women and the community. Finally, the frontier daughters eschewed traditional female lifestyles and created lives marked by self-fulfillment and individuality. Although not all of them decorated their homes with calendars like Lottie Rumsey or lived in a cabin in the woods like Marie Kleinschmidt Southworth, most of them chose to live their lives on their own terms.

Most of these pioneer mother and daughter chronicles, however, exist as oral histories or as scattered references in archival miscellaneous files. But at least two of these women left a detailed record behind. The lives of Elizabeth Chester Fisk and her daughter, Grace Fisk Bryan, put these observations in sharper focus, delineate more clearly the differences between the generations, and add to the composite portrait of the mothers and daughters of Eldorado. Their narratives exhibit the process of change on the frontier.

Elizabeth Chester Fisk was among those women of the pioneer cohort of middling women who participated in Helena's history and was a particularly reliable witness to the process of women's transformation on the frontier. In addition to exhibiting the hallmarks of the pioneer women, Elizabeth's story reveals the other dimensions of womanhood on the frontier: the difficulties involved in sustaining female networks;

the pressures placed on mothers to rear their children in an unsettled, worldly environment; and the gradual diminution of the "cult of true womanhood."

Elizabeth Chester Fisk closely corresponded to what might be termed the average, middle-class woman living in Helena between 1870 and 1900.[46] A native of Connecticut, Elizabeth was twenty-four in 1870; her husband, Robert Emmett Fisk of New York, the editor of the *Helena Herald*, was eight years her senior. Nearly duplicating the statistical average household, they lived with their daughter, Grace, and May Bromley, Elizabeth's boarder and future sister-in-law.[47] Elizabeth did not think of herself as one of the elite, but rather viewed herself as solidly middle class. From time to time, she would complain that the Fisks did not have sufficient money to entertain on a scale commensurate with some of her wealthier acquaintances. By Elizabeth's own admission, it "took a long purse" to keep pace with Helena society. Similarly, neither Robert's nor Elizabeth's name appears with any frequency in the long guest lists of the elite during the 1880s.

Elizabeth watched Helena's society with a critical eye. By her own account, she differed in significant ways from the majority of Helena's wives whom she sometimes criticized as frivolous. In comparison with them, Elizabeth observed that she had a greater sense of duty, a steadfastness of purpose, and a more defined set of principles than did the rest of the town's matrons. Elizabeth's story is illustrative of the interaction between women and their environment and with one another. All of this Elizabeth recorded in the hundreds of letters she faithfully wrote to her family in Connecticut, describing nearly three decades of life in Helena.

Born in February of 1846 in Vernon, Connecticut, to Azubah and Asa Chester, a Congregational minister, Elizabeth grew up in an atmosphere of New England piety, gentility, ardent belief in abolitionism, and the Union's cause. Elizabeth helped manufacture blankets for the Union Army during the Civil War, and in one of her bundles of blankets she pinned a patriotic and encouraging note. Captain Robert Fisk received the blankets and was so taken with the sentiments expressed in the note that he commenced a correspondence with Elizabeth that lasted for the remainder of his military service. At the war's end, Fisk traveled to Connecticut to meet his correspondent and benefactor.[48] Well-pleased with each other, Robert and Elizabeth decided to marry after she finished teaching in the spring of 1867. Elizabeth's matrimonial decision betokened even greater changes in her life than leaving the classroom; Captain Fisk planned to settle in the West.

One of six brothers, Robert Fisk came from an up-state New York family that was equally as genteel as Elizabeth's. Robert's elder brothers had early appreciated the promise of the West and had established themselves in St. Paul, Minnesota. During the early 1860s, James Liberty Fisk had led expeditions across the Dakotas to Montana's goldfields, and he subsequently persuaded his brothers, including Robert, to stake their fortunes on Helena. Once the Fisks purchased the presses and inventory of the defunct *Montana Radiator,* Helena's first paper, Robert's journalism experience in Indiana made him the logical choice to edit and manage their Republican newspaper. Robert traveled east in early 1867 to solicit advertising, to purchase printing supplies, and to marry Elizabeth. Elizabeth and Robert boarded the steamer *Little Rock* in late May and headed up the Missouri River to Fort Benton and then overland to Helena, Montana Territory.[49]

Elizabeth suffered none of the physical strain or the conflicts between husbands and wives that had characterized the overland emigrations to Oregon and California. Nonetheless, the fairly relaxed and comfortable journey by steamboat into the Rocky Mountains was still a rite of passage for Elizabeth. It was an opportunity for her to reflect on the contrast between the East and the frontier and on herself, her beliefs, and her place in this new setting.[50]

At the outset of her journey, Elizabeth's letters home reveal a conservative young woman of nineteenth century, middle-class sensibilities from a religious family possessed of abolitionist sympathies and the northeastern "cult of true womanhood." Except for advocating abolitionism, Elizabeth supported the status quo; she despised the South and its culture and believed in the superiority of things Yankee. About the women on the riverboat, Elizabeth observed:

> . . . it is matter of surprise and grief to me to find people so ignorant of the Bible as many of these ladies who are my traveling companions. It may be they are just a slightly acquainted with all other books. This sad ignorance cannot be asserted of the New England women, of whom there are several on the steamer, only of the southern and western women.[51]

Both Elizabeth's devotion to her religion and her allegiance to the "cult of true womanhood" conditioned her well-defined and, on occasion, rigid ideas about the proper conduct of men and women. On the one hand, Elizabeth applauded restrained, lady-like behavior, but on the other hand, she abhorred its excess. Writing to her sister about a near-drowning, she revealed her rejection of frail and frivolous womanhood: "Some of our lady passengers behaved very foolishly on the occasion, clasping their hands frantically and screaming delightfully. The impulse was strong to throw *them* over and wash away some of their would-be ladyism."[52]

Also impatient with over-blown masculinity, Elizabeth criticized a male passenger as "a great swell and brag, and an ignoramus" when he made a spectacle of himself by chasing an antelope to prove his hunting prowess. Each man and woman, Elizabeth believed, had his or her appropriate gender roles, characterized by restraint, purpose, and usefulness. Of Mr. Whitlatch, her husband's business associate, she wrote: "With many excellent traits of character he combines some which would mar the happiness of any true woman." Marriage, family, community service, a superior moral sense, and selflessness defined a woman's duties and sensibility, and Elizabeth judged others according to these measurements. Like most nineteenth century women, Elizabeth set women's superior moral nature against male corruptness and believed women to be more amenable to marriage because of their unselfish, selfless characters. Having grown up under the aegis of the "cult of true womanhood," Elizabeth embraced its tenets fully. Once on the frontier, however, she modified or discarded some of her previously held ideas. First she reordered her "noble savage" image of the plains Indians. Seeing poor, hungry, ragged, or naked people instead of prairie princes, she quickly assumed the prejudices of her fellow passengers. In similar fashion, she dropped her romantic illusions of the frontier. On the middle border, she observed both an idleness that affronted her sense of industry and an inflated sense of self-importance that ran counter to her ideal of moderation. She also noted how work on the land had worn out both men and women. In addition to these disillusionments, Elizabeth saw how other social conventions broke down the farther she traveled from St. Louis. Slang and informality of address became more frequent, and notions of what constituted standards of privacy and cleanliness bowed to necessity. In Boone County, Iowa, for example, Elizabeth found herself sharing a bed with a total stranger and wolfing down food she would have formerly found unsanitary.[53]

Elizabeth's belief that her self-control and restraint set her apart from and above the rest of the women on the steamer, however, remained firm and unshaken. Toward the end of the trip she congratulated herself that she had kept aloof from the quarrels and petty jealousies that had overtaken other women on the *Little Rock*.[54] When Elizabeth arrived in Fort Benton in late July 1867, both her baggage and her fundamental nineteenth century ideology had arrived intact.

Once in Helena, Elizabeth immediately entered into the life and work of the household she and Robert shared with his elder brother, James. And she accepted Helena as her home, a place that held out the promise of personal fulfillment and opportunity.[55] To her sister, she wrote:

> My first impressions of Helena have been generally confirmed. I like the place much; it is not like home, but there is a wide field for usefulness here, and, entering upon the work earnestly and prayerfully one need never be lonely or disheartened. There is *room* here for every one to win a name and an influence that shall be widespread and shall ever be for good on all those around. For these, if for no other reasons I like the place.[56]

In her commitment to Helena, however, she stood apart from other women in the community. Later, in 1867, she wrote to her mother that she was "one of the few ladies who have come to this country that is pleased and expresses the intention of remaining longer than till spring." Yet, dedicated though she was to both her household and the town, Elizabeth still found fault with the minimal role religion played in community and home life. Elizabeth genuinely despaired of the situation and resolved to be otherwise:

> . . . the question will come what can be expected of the community at large, when those who profess to be governed by good motives thus live. I would not, I do not judge them, but only pray that I may not tread in their steps.[57]

Elizabeth's resolution to separate herself from Helena's common, irreligious crowd soon included a similar decision to segregate herself from the legion Fisk family members. Unable to find a satisfactory role in her brother-in-law's home with her lazy sister-in-law and fractious niece and suffering from isolation and loneliness because of her husband's frequent absences, Elizabeth sought congenial female companionship and entrée into Helena's social circles. She put aside nineteenth century social etiquette and, beginning in September, card case in hand, she ventured out on her own to make friends.[58]

Elizabeth faced making friends in Helena's frontier community with ambivalence. The few women in Helena were markedly different from those she had known in the East, and the total female population was heterogeneous in religion, ethnicity, and class. She came into contact with Jews, Catholics, non-believers, and uneducated or socially unrefined women. Elizabeth could overlook her scruples or she could cleave to her principles and remain friendless. She chose to learn a measure of tolerance and accept friendships that cut across the social boundaries so dear to refined nineteenth century society.[59] Her sister-in-law's illness and Elizabeth's added responsibility for the operation of the household coupled with Robert's departure to cut short her foray into Helena society.

Because of their husbands' prolonged absences from the city, Elizabeth and other women of the community shared the experience of isolation and loneliness. In late 1867, Robert determined that the *Herald*'s survival demanded his return to the East to solicit advertising and to purchase supplies.[60] Left alone to cope as best as she could in a household she could barely tolerate, Elizabeth confronted her first Montana winter and a crucial point in her frontier career.

Bereft of Robert and with her role in the household ill-defined, Elizabeth experienced personal freedom. "I am at liberty to go out whenever and wherever I wish," Elizabeth wrote to her sister soon after her husband's departure, "and I have time to manufacture all sorts of pretty things." She immediately set about finding some useful occupation for herself and took up tutoring, work she did for cash. Elizabeth's attitude toward her employment reflected a growing realization of her own autonomy and capabilities. Although reluctant to do so during her first months in Helena, Elizabeth took advantage of the Fisk's prosperity and enjoyed the luxury of a servant. Blessed with household help, Elizabeth seized the opportunity to take walks late at night and to attend the theater by herself.[61]

Part of Elizabeth's new freedom extended to her relationships with men in the community, and Elizabeth tested these social boundaries with her brother-in-law, Van, and with an attractive bachelor, Dr. William M. Bullard. The time she spent with the good doctor became a matter of public concern, and Elizabeth confessed in a letter to her husband: "They tell me I am flirting with the Dr. Do you fear to trust me, Rob?" A month later, writing to her husband about a ride to a nearby mining camp with Dr. Bullard, she revealed something of the ambiguity of her position: "Was there any harm in doing so? This town is so different from my old home that I need one to advise me often. I have always depended so much on mother's judgment in matters of this kind."[62]

Although the "cult of true womanhood" supported women's moral capabilities, Elizabeth also pressed the intellectual boundaries of her female role. She freely discussed scientific and philosophical topics with her gentlemen callers, and she discussed the newspaper's business affairs with the *Herald*'s interim manager: "He seemed to think that a woman was not capable of talking business, but he was forced to change his mind."[63] Within a month of Robert's departure, Elizabeth had realized a sense of herself independent from her husband and marriage:

> I did not think it possible when Rob left me that I could be so happy without him, and especially in this place. I do not call it home. But I have learned, if I knew it not before, that one can be happy independent of externals. I sometimes wonder at the self-contained life I lead. I am dependent on no one for my comfort and serenity of mind, although my friends are kind and serve me in every possible way.[64]

The winter of 1867-1868 served to confirm Elizabeth's commitment to the community and her ideas about women's part in its development. In December 1867, she wrote to her mother, "much as I love you, I can yet happily make my home apart from you, and seek in a new country wider spheres of usefulness." A month later, her sense of participation heightened, and she conceived of herself participating in an enterprise far greater than herself:

A. J. Lawson, photographer

Main Street in Helena looking north from the foot of Broadway during the 1890s

F. J. Haynes photographed Helena, Montana, in 1890 from the south, showing the Main Street commercial district (left), the tenderloin section (center), and the courthouse and Catholic institutions (right).

This photograph, taken after the 1871 fire, shows the Kiyus Saloon, which entrepreneur prostitute Mollie Byrns purchased in 1884.

F. Jay Haynes, photographer, Haynes Foundation Collection

F. Jay Haynes, photographer, Haynes Foundation Collection

The Northern Pacific depot, shown here in 1885, was on the eastern edge of town, three miles from the commercial district.

The interior of Mollie Byrns's house at 212 State Street

Edward M. Reinig, photographer

This ca. 1908 photo of Joliet Street in Helena's tenderloin section shows the Bluestone House (center), Lilli McGraw's *maison de joie* below the Bluestone, Mollie Byrns's ''Castle'' (corner of Wood Street, farthest cross street), and Chicago Joe's Coliseum on State Street (large, dark-roofed building, far left).

C. W. Carter, photographer, Salt Lake City

Known as "Chicago Joe," Irish-born Mary Welch had taken the name Josephine Airey in Chicago's tenderloin before coming to Helena in 1867. She prospered as a madam and entrepreneur, purchasing property in the city's red-light district and reigning over a tenderloin empire during the 1880s, before the hard times of the 1890s brought her financial ruin.

The R. E. Fisk family in 1898 (left to right): Florence McIntyre Fisk, Robert, R. E. Fisk, Grace, Stanley Bryan, Jim, Elizabeth, Florence, Rufus

The R. E. Fisk family in front of their home at 319 Rodney Street in Helena in the early 1880s

Grace Fisk in Helena at about the time she won a contested divorce from hotel clerk Hardy Bryan.

Daughters of Helena's pioneer women in 1885 (left to right): Lottie Rumsey, Alice Crounse, Clara Holter, Pearl Davenport, Bella Sharpe, Nellie Gage, Emma Hedges

E. H. Train, photographer

Ida Wilson, Anna Warfield, and Mary C. Wheeler, the first students to graduate from Helena High School, chose "No Step Backward" as their class motto in 1879.

> . . . each one, often unconsciously is helping to shape the destinies of our common land. You see, mother dear, I am enthusiastic over my new home. And why should I not be, for here are centered all my best hopes for the coming years. I want to stay here, to identify myself so closely with this land that I cannot live elsewhere.

For Elizabeth, women's part in this magnificent destiny consisted of using her good influence to tame the less savory aspects of the mining town. "An earnest woman," she wrote, "wields a vast amount of influence in this community as in any other, but it seems here to be so much more needed and widely felt."[65]

Unfortunately for Elizabeth, her new-found autonomy had brief expression. By March 1868, both the Fisk household and the *Herald* were in an uproar. From her sister-in-law's poor health to ubiquitous mice, Elizabeth again faced chaos at home. The newspaper confronted financial disaster when its Democratic political opponents maneuvered to evict the Fisk clan from their home and to bankrupt the journal. The interim editor folded under the pressure and took to drink, further imperiling the business. Elizabeth, now even more closely confined to home and its tensions, sank into a depression and remarked after a visit to the Catholic cemetery, "I would not wish to die here." Recalled from the East, Robert started back to Helena to take command where the inebriated editor and the other Fisks could not.[66]

Waiting for her husband to return, Elizabeth reflected on her experiences and realized that she had gained some measure of strength,

> . . . and I trust laid the foundations of a glorious, would I might write, a *perfect* womanhood. I never yet fully realized what and how much it is to be a true, whole-souled, woman. Such capacities of doing, being, and suffering, such striving for the good and pure, not only, or chiefly for ourselves, but for those whom we love.[67]

Elizabeth acknowledged the nineteenth century female role of self-sacrifice and selflessness, but she had also experienced its alternative. A few days after she had extolled "true, whole-souled" womanhood, she wrote that if she had had the winter to live over again, she would have been more selfish.[68] A few weeks before her husband's return, she equated independence with selfishness and had

> . . . come to the determination to be independent of any and every one, to seek my own enjoyment where I can best find it, independent of all who would *selfishly* seek to oppose my plans. This listening to and heeding the advice of *all* my friends has caused me much vexation and sorrow during all the winter and independence is the only comfortable plan.[69]

Elizabeth decided that continued residence in the Fisk household had cut her off from society and prevented her from receiving her female friends. Finding "not much congeniality of tastes and pursuits" in the Fisk house, she resolved on Robert's return to make a separate home for herself and her husband.[70]

"Home" had two different meanings for Elizabeth. She defined her home, "The New Northwest," as the larger community and region. Writing of this region in her letters, she began by referring to the working man and slipped from "they" to "we," identifying herself with the public enterprise of settlement. In that sense, "home" connoted a special, public entity of which she was a participating member. But "home" also meant the separate, private, physical and social space she intended to occupy with her husband, a place she would order and command herself. Elizabeth inextricably linked these two "homes," the larger entity a dependent of the smaller, and both necessary to well-being. Two social structures connected these concepts in Elizabeth's mind and provided the means by which the smaller "home" could affect the larger: the church and her social ties with other women.[71]

Nineteenth century, informal, female networks—the web of friendships that connected women to one another—functioned in a variety of ways. Instrumental in establishing cultural institutions and assisting women in their attempts to regulate society, the networks bonded women to each other through the information they shared on topics ranging from health and child care to fashion. These friendships consoled women in their times of trouble, defined the norms for the members, and relieved the tedium, loneliness, and drudgery of women's domestic work. Many nineteenth century women derived more of their emotional sustenance from each other than from the men in their lives.[72] When Elizabeth complained that the demands of the Fisk household denied her access to female friendships and when she claimed she had no "home" in the private sense, she confessed to an existence that was barren and empty.

On Robert's return, Elizabeth first attempted to resurrect the friendships that had slipped away from her and to enter again into Helena's female networks. Earlier she had encountered the diversity of the town's women; this time she confronted another of that population's characteristics: its transiency. In May 1868, she wrote that "every day parties are leaving. . . . Still, as the boats bring to us greater numbers than they carry away, we do not despair or complain." But this constant turnover blunted her attempts to form friendships. Her two close friends, Mrs. Smith and Mrs. Norris, moved away. Referring to Mrs. Smith, Elizabeth wrote, "When I think how much I shall lose in losing her kind friendship and society, I am almost determined never again to make a *warm* friend, a mere passing acquaintance will do. . . ." She also sensed a change in Helena's citizenry from brave pioneers and empire builders to deceitful, petty money-grubbers.[73]

Disillusioned, Elizabeth pondered her dilemma in late May 1868:

> . . . I often ask myself what shall be my course of conduct, how shall I live in such a community. *The temptation is often great to make my home, when I shall gain it, my world, to seek no other companionship outside its little circle* [emphasis added]. . . . Nothing is permanent. One's best friends leave them in a day and pleasant acquaintances prove mere gossips. I have only one lady friend that I could depend on should misfortune or sorrow come. . . . One needs to learn to *stand alone,* to find within one's self the highest delight. . . . Shall I too selfishly address myself to money getting and ignore the claims of society upon me, or shall my influence be used to bring about a better state of things and beget a little public spirit.[74]

Elizabeth quickly decided on her course. A week later, referring to Robert's brief trip to Fort Benton, she wrote, "having given up all my friends for him I cannot well lose him also, even for a few days."[75] The acquisition of their own house in June made Elizabeth's withdrawal from the world of women complete. Now the church functioned as the only connection between her "public" and "private" homes.

Attracted to church life from the outset, Elizabeth found her denominational choice in Helena limited to two: the Catholic or the Methodist churches. A Protestant, she joined the Methodist church and soon organized a Sabbath school for young boys. Although she deplored the poor church attendance and even poorer sermons, she also became secretary of the church women's organization and undertook the planning and fundraising for the church festival in 1868.[76] Elizabeth succeeded in the project, but the rivalries and petty jealousies that she encountered among her co-workers left her disappointed and angry. She vented her bitterness in a letter home, vowing

> both mentally and audibly "never to take part in another affair of the kind should I live to be a thousand years old," and I would say to each and every one who may be influenced by my words, "Shun a Church Festival as you would any other thing which could contaminate you."[77]

Elizabeth's alienation from church work and worship coincided with her increasing estrangement from the community. "I find it impossible," she wrote, "to fully enter into the spirit of this fast-age and faster country." She turned her back on any involvement in either the church or the community and busied herself with her home. "I have," Elizabeth admitted, "scarcely been in the street since the Fourth, and know but little of what is transpiring about town, and don't care very much. I was disgusted with myself and everybody else at the Festival and deemed the life of a recluse wise for a time."[78]

Despite her renewed devotion to home, Elizabeth still displayed flashes of the independence she had found during her first winter in Helena. When her mother asked what would become of Elizabeth should she be deprived of her "natural protector," Elizabeth replied that she would do very well: "I am abundantly able to take care of myself. . . . Every kind of labor, with head or hand, is well-remunerated." She could, Elizabeth continued, do a variety of things: open a school, take in boarders, or operate a washhouse. "The last," Elizabeth added, "would be the most lucrative employment of all, Chinese doing all the work. . . . You see that I do not depend on my *friends* any more than you. . . . I have no little ones to prevent any labors of either kind, and I might add, do not intend to have till we can better afford it."[79]

In the fall and winter of 1868-1869, however, two events pushed Elizabeth further into a domestic existence. In September, when in the best partisan fashion the *Herald* exposed the malfeasance of Mr. Potter, the postmaster, the opposing newspaper and its editor, Mr. Pinney, took up Potter's cause, and the mining town divided over the issue. At the end of the month, the controversy climaxed in violence in Pinney's newspaper office when he shot and killed a member of the anti-Potter faction. Pinney pled self-defense; the *Herald* cried "murder." During the ensuing weeks the opposing factions became warring camps, with Helena's women also taking sides. Part of the minority of *Herald* supporters, Elizabeth found herself ostracized in the worst small-town fashion by other Helena women. Although she put on a brave front, Elizabeth suffered hurt feelings and pride.[80] In September 1868, despite her recent vow to postpone childbearing, she unexpectedly became pregnant. Coincidentally, the Fisk brothers decided to send Robert east again, providing Elizabeth with a convenient excuse to escape her social situation. Shortly after Christmas, Elizabeth and Robert left Helena, he to make his business rounds and she to go to Connecticut, where she remained until the autumn of 1869.[81] Elizabeth gave birth to her first child, Grace Chester, in Connecticut on May 21, 1869.

By the time Elizabeth returned to Helena, the furor over the Pinney shooting had subsided, the lawsuits had been settled, and she re-entered Helena society. This time, the transiency of Helena's citizenry worked in Elizabeth's favor; few remained who remembered the Potter fracas. Still, she remained wary of launching herself into society.[82] At the same time, she came to accept the vagaries of the various Fisk personalities and to make her family her primary circle and the Fisk legion her society, despite the latter's difficult members. The birth of her child served to rationalize further her separation from the community, the church, and the company of other women. As she wrote to her sister, "On the whole, I am pleased with the state of things and feel sufficiently independent of all *outsiders* [emphasis in original] to put up with inevitables. *We are numerous enough as a family to form a community by ourselves*'' [emphasis added].[83]

Elizabeth had responded to the frontier by withdrawing even further into the family and conceiving of women's role in society in an even more conservative fashion. She became more and more concerned with the minutiae of domesticity and child care, creating a self-contained life removed from Helena's women's network, from the church, and from the ever-present Fisk family.[84] She held in abeyance the individualism and autonomy she had learned, and she reacted with impatience when women espoused political positions, especially on women's rights. When Emma Ashley, the territorial governor's wife, came to dinner, Elizabeth observed: ''Everything passed off nicely except that Mrs. Ashley *would* introduce her favorite topic of woman's rights and 'argufy' on the subject till every one was weary.''[85] But in this she also disclosed a hint of vague disturbance at her own abdication.

Although Elizabeth did not venture far outside her domestic circle for more than a decade, she did maintain contact with a few women, and they broadened her toleration of women who were different from her. In Emma Ashley, no paragon of the domestic order that Elizabeth respected, she found much to admire. And Elizabeth thought highly of Mrs. Wiley Scribner, even though she was a devout Catholic. Antisemitism had no place in Elizabeth's world; Helena's Jewish merchants had been generous to her and to Dr. Bullard, her friend. Perhaps to protect his family from future lawsuits and loss of property, Robert conveyed the Rodney Street property to Elizabeth in 1870, and in that gesture Elizabeth acquired a limited franchise.[86] Helena was unincorporated, and Elizabeth was not asked to use her vote until 1874 in the first incorporation election. With her franchise, however, she joined the company of propertied women from different classes.

The years 1871 and 1872 passed peacefully for Elizabeth as she busied herself with domesticity. Because she did not dance or drink, she shunned most of the town's social life. Elizabeth limited her activities to housekeeping, child care, and a literary club. Her sister, her closest friend and confidante, died in October 1871, and Elizabeth plummeted into a black grief for several months. While her sister's death served to remove her further from the social swim, other women were cognizant of her presence. Although she found most women around her to be superficial, a church group voted her Helena's most popular woman in January 1872. Slightly embarrassed by the notoriety and the raffle that had brought her the honor, Elizabeth accepted the award and ascribed it to her moral character and willingness to stand by her principles. On November 28, 1872, Elizabeth gave birth to her second child and first son, Robert Loveland.[87]

Between 1872 and 1875, Elizabeth's placid domestic existence remained undisturbed, save for her criticism and eventual loss of servants and her pique at vagrant pigs on Rodney Street. She continued her church work, contributing fancy needlework, sewing, and baked goods to bazaars and helping Methodist women raise money for a new church building, but she avoided organizing fetes and fairs because, in Elizabeth's mind, they involved gambling. The birth of her third child and second son, Rufus Clark, on May 15, 1875, tied Elizabeth even more closely to Rodney Street. "I devote very little time," Elizabeth wrote, "to outside duties. I do not know that I recognize any duties outside my *home circle*. . . . Some of my friends are disposed to censure my conduct and try to convince me that I ought to get out more." A brief trip to Connecticut between March and July of 1876 was her only respite, but even her devotion to children and home could not mask signs of restlessness. Three small children and the absence of household help taxed her physically and wore her out mentally. More importantly, she continued to feel the lack of women's companionship, advice, and assistance and wished for the "maternal meetings" that had sustained her mother. Her predicament and events in the community and nation led her to begin to re-evaluate how she viewed women.[88]

Elizabeth's attitude toward women's role changed subtly during her domestic sojourn. First, she adopted a quasi-adversarial position with respect to men. "I believe the women of the whole country are becoming demoralized," she wrote concerning a recent divorce, "but they are not alone in the wrong. . . . These things [divorces] are sad. In 'the good time coming' when woman's wrongs are righted how will these social problems be affected?" Discarding her earlier view of women's unrelieved self-sacrifice and service to their husbands, during the mid 1870s Elizabeth vaguely sensed an inequity in the social relations between men and women. Her new perspective, however, remained as undefined as her thinking on politics and women's suffrage.

The year 1876 melted into 1877 for Elizabeth, bound up as she was with domestic activities; but her impatience with the constant demands of motherhood surfaced in October 1877. Pregnant again, she vented her frustration in a letter home:

> I did *not* want any more children, and there have been times in the last few months when I have felt *utterly unreconciled* to the state of affairs, and even now I sometimes think I *cannot* care for any more little ones; but I try to recall the old proverb that "the back is fitted to the burden", and come to believe that strength will [be] given for every duty.[89]

On November 11, 1877, Elizabeth gave birth to her third son and fourth child, Asa Francis.

With four children under eight years old, Elizabeth chafed at the restrictions child care and household duties placed on her in 1878 and finally took action. She dropped all of her outside activities to carve out time for long, rambling walks away from the young Fisks. Except for these stolen moments, motherhood dominated her time. At the same time, her concern over Helena's secular and pernicious influence on her children compelled Elizabeth to make her home a bastion of Christian values and conduct, which meant constant vigilance and unrelieved attendance on the children. Robert's encouragement and expectations of this motherly watchfulness especially exasperated Elizabeth whenever Robert deserted his familial obligations for excursions and jaunts. Elizabeth felt trapped. "I think some days," she wrote, "that I shall either go crazy or run away."[90]

In 1880, Elizabeth began to wonder "when a mother's rest and recreation come." While her need for relief had become critical, she also felt taken for granted. Elizabeth proposed that she and Robert take a trip to White Sulphur Springs, but he demurred, saying she should wait until the entire family could make the trip. That, replied Elizabeth, was not the idea; she pointed out that she had not been away from the children for eight years. Her displeasure at Robert's ability to come and go as he pleased crystallized into resentment: "It does not seem right for them to have all the pleasure while we poor mothers stay at home and take care of the children." Despite Robert's domestic wheedling, off she went for two weeks at the White Sulphur mineral springs. Elizabeth's vacation prompted additional forays outside the home. In 1881, in the face of both her mother's and her husband's subtle objections, she took painting lessons; and during the last four months of 1881 Elizabeth pleased herself by going to Connecticut alone.[91]

Elizabeth was a willing participant in local government, but she remained critical of women's participation in state and national politics, viewing it as potentially damaging to their moral superiority. After visiting the territorial legislature earlier in 1876 with some acquaintances, Elizabeth wrote: "It was a novel experience, . . . but we came home congratulating ourselves that female suffrage had never been extended to Montana, and that nothing compelled us to undergo forty days of law-making."[92]

Although she displayed moments of independence in her personal life, Elizabeth remained politically conservative and firm in her conviction that women should eschew politics. When the city charter finally passed in 1881, Elizabeth accompanied her friends to the polls, claiming, "I must own for myself I am not at all desirous of claiming this privilege but I may perhaps go to gratify some of my lady friends who have no one to do their voting for them."[93] Initially hesitant, Elizabeth soon became a member of a band of conscientious female voters.

Once again, motherhood cut short Elizabeth's independence. Unwillingly pregnant, she wrote despairingly of her condition:

> If I felt really well and like myself I could say many lovely and pleasant things of these fifteen years of my life. But just now, it is a good deal of a burden to live at all and while I know all the "lovely and pleasant things" have been, are still with me, I do not fully appreciate them or feel prepared to say much in their praise.[94]

On April 24, 1882, Elizabeth gave birth prematurely to twins, Florence Rumley and James Kennett, her second daughter and fourth son. With the birth of her fifth and sixth children, Elizabeth's depression became all the greater. She summed up her experience in her second letter of 1883: "I hope the time will come when life will not be so great a burden as it has been for the past year. I have only *existed*. . . ." Her parents' long postponed trip west in 1883 acted as a tonic for Elizabeth; but when she again turned her thoughts to matters outside her domestic circle, she was uncertain. "My responsibility, my accountability," she wrote, "are great in my own household. How far duty extends outside I have not decided."[95]

During the next two decades, Elizabeth would define her relationships with her family and with other women and would set the limits of her duty outside her family. Beginning in late 1883, she entered the public sphere, carrying a long-held private conviction, and attended a Woman's Christian Temperance Union reception. Although the WCTU drew her interest, her involvement in benevolent and reform activities declined during the two years after the birth of the twins; she even came to see her church attendance as a means to avoid domestic obligations. Still, she maintained her interest in temperance, even as she came to recognize that a "church stand" on the issue was a virtual impossibility. By spring 1885, her temperance and church activities occupied different worlds.[96]

As Elizabeth tested the world outside the confines of her home, she noted changes in the women around her. About one of her friends, Harriet Sanders, Elizabeth wrote: "I used to like her but she is another instance (added to the many) of a good woman spoiled by prosperity." Spoiled, perhaps, but it might have been Harriet Sanders's liberal views that affronted Elizabeth. With her sister-in-law, Sarepta Sanders, Harriet was among those women who held political views that were antithetical to Elizabeth's, especially women's participation in politics. Harriet was impatient with the limits placed on women's voting rights, commenting in her diary, ". . . voted for Mr. Howie for trustee. The ladies are allowed that privilege." Other than overseeing the orderly operation of her large household and maintaining a watchful eye over Helena society, Elizabeth joined the Chautaqua Literary Society, although she was reluctant at first because she thought herself too old.[97]

Beset by her own illness and sickness in the family, Elizabeth returned to temperance work in 1886, beginning with a drive to recruit young men and boys to the cause of abstinence from liquor and tobacco. Although Helena's temperance organization had languished from 1883 to 1886, the general mood of reform in the city and the Thomas Cruse wedding put new life in the movement. Liquor had flowed freely at the Irish capitalist's reception, and the numerous drunken incidents after the party spurred the town's women to action. Elizabeth remarked, "It ought to arouse every mother in the city to fight for her boys, her 'God and Home and Native Land.'" Believing that she was one of the few women who unreservedly supported temperance, Elizabeth became increasingly involved. She entertained temperance speakers in her home and participated in many formal temperance activities.[98]

Part of her temperance work involved a shift in the direction of the campaign for abstinence. Instead of devoting its energies toward converting men, the Helena chapter of the WCTU attempted to draw women into the fold by sponsoring colloquia and readings that centered on women's work in the Bible. "Our aim," Elizabeth wrote, "was to show that the curse pronounced on woman at the time of the fall did not exclude her from a share in all that work which tends to ennoble the race." This goal corresponded with Elizabeth's view that wives had not only influence but also power. "So much of a man's future, especially a young man's," she had written in 1868, "depends so much on the choice he makes of a wife. She has almost unlimited power and can make of him what she will." Although these gatherings were intended to mobilize women's influence and were social successes, Elizabeth and her co-workers discovered that Helena's women were reluctant to sign the pledge. Unsuccessful in organizing the city's women, Helena's WCTU became more overtly political and circulated petitions for a local-option liquor law. The membership also worked on specifically women's issues, including a petition and legislative testimony, as Elizabeth wrote, "for the protection of women, changing the age at which a girl may consent to her own ruin from ten to eighteen years."[99]

Elizabeth's temperance work ranged beyond local affairs, which had included the election of school trustees who supported temperance and the arrangement of a non-alcoholic New Year's Day reception for derelict men. In 1886, Elizabeth attended the WCTU's territorial convention in Butte, where she not only read an essay but also won election to the territorial WCTU treasurer's post. Her vote in favor of a resolution advocating the enfranchisement of women indicated how much her views had altered since 1867, when she had criticized Emma Ashley for her position on women's rights.[100] Under the banner of temperance, Elizabeth had moved from informal political activity to formal political activism, from a single issue to a broad-based program of social reform which she shared with like-minded female reformers.

As Elizabeth's political outlook had changed so had her views of child rearing. Grace already had demonstrated that she differed from her mother in significant ways. In 1881, when Elizabeth had asserted her own independence, she had noted a strong independent streak in Grace as well and had remarked on the differences between herself and her daughter:

> She is a fine scholar and spurs the rest on, and as the "big boys" all admire her and listen to what she says, she has a good influence over them. I often wonder at her. She is so fearless and independent and says most unmerciful things to the careless and lazy ones.[101]

Grace went beyond her mother's strength to daring; when Elizabeth remained politely reticent in male company, Grace made her wishes known and had them granted. In the face of these differences in Grace, Elizabeth attempted to cling to her own mother's uncompromising ideas about child rearing. She did not permit Grace to associate with "fast young men," for example; but she had to accommodate some of Grace's differences, admitting that the West forced her to make concessions. "I do not believe," she wrote,

> it is possible in these western towns to bring up a girl in this way without making her feel she is badly used. . . . She is more mature than many girls of eighteen . . . and has been thrown so often on her own resources in the last two years that she has become very womanly and self-reliant.[102]

"Womanly and self-reliant" were not words that Elizabeth had used to describe womanhood during her first years in Helena. Since then, her ideas had changed from identifying womanhood with service to others and with self-sacrifice to self-reliance, a term she had used briefly to describe herself just a decade before. Despite Elizabeth's confidence in her daughter's maturity and judgment, she insisted that Grace return to college, because she believed that higher education was a necessity for both sexes and because she suspected that Grace was becoming caught up in Helena's social scene with all its dangers.[103]

Despite her active work on behalf of the WCTU and her involvement with her growing children, Elizabeth felt isolated. A continued lack of companionship prompted Elizabeth to write: "The other neighbors are good and kind but are occupied with their own affairs and rarely come in for an evening call." Later, she admitted, "I am becoming more and more strongly wedded to home. . . ."[104] The lack of close relationships with kindred spirits outside her family circle helped fuel Elizabeth's need to step up her charitable work.

In February 1887, Elizabeth testified before the territorial assembly in support of stricter rape statutes, even though Elizabeth had always found it difficult to confront sexual issues, much less speak about them. In the interests of this women's cause, she overcame her repugnance. "I cannot tell you," she wrote, "how hard it was to go before this committee one of whom was the *cranky bachelor* and talk about these things." She also continued to visit the Poor Farm, the county home for the indigent; to remain active on the Poor Committee until 1891, when it disbanded; and to campaign for temperance. Her Poor Committee work introduced her to the plight of poor women. "It does seem," she wrote in December 1887, "as if poor women have more than their share of suffering and care in this world." Moved by this insight, she joined the effort to establish a Home for Working Women, a safe stopping place for new arrivals and a retreat for older, single, or widowed women. Elizabeth also continued as WCTU treasurer and as a supporter of the WCTU's political platform, including woman suffrage.[105]

In early 1888, plagued by ill health and unable to find and to retain suitable servants, Elizabeth curtailed her outside activities for a few months. By March 1888, she had rejoined fellow workers on the Home for Working Women project, while she continued working with the WCTU. Elizabeth served on the WCTU's territorial credentials committee, on its finance committee, and as the union's territorial treasurer, while endorsing a strong women's suffrage position, Sunday saloon closure, and temperance candidates in school board elections. Her moderate Republicanism, however, made her flinch at the territorial WCTU's strong prohibitionist position at the 1888 convention. Believing prohibitionism to be as politically unwise and alienating as radical Republicanism, Elizabeth advocated the moderate and more personal approach exemplified by temperance pledges. In addition, delegations from Butte and eastern Montana communities other than Helena had gained greater influence in the organization. For the most part, these women were not Yankees and represented Populist and labor interests. The shift in the WCTU's political strategy and this change in leadership coupled with its membership, prompted Elizabeth to withdraw from the organization. By 1889, Elizabeth had left the ranks of the territorial WCTU and had moderated her local temperance activity.[106]

As she retreated from the WCTU, Elizabeth increased her charitable work, adding the Women's Relief Corps and its administration and activities to her work with the Poor Farm and Poor Committee. Increasingly, she changed her views on women, the domestic circle, and even household help. She concluded that she should have servants to ease her burdens; after all, the time and talent she dedicated to social work was clearly more important than a servant's time or talents. Likewise, Elizabeth questioned the nineteenth century idea of women's innate purity and moral superiority, describing a former servant and her lover: "*Men are so bad*. They seem to care only for their own wishes and the gratification of their passions, and to think women are just the same." Even some of Helena's sophisticated women, who shocked her with their revealing decolletages at a reception in 1889, led her to conclude: "Women are largely to blame for much of the world's wickedness."[107]

Female wickedness aside, Helena's venality began to wear on Elizabeth. During 1889, she contemplated moving to a more congenial city for the children's benefit. Renewed problems with servants also troubled her, but changes in Helena's society disturbed her the most and occasioned another retreat to home and family. Although she retained her membership in the local WCTU and worked for charitable causes, Elizabeth now saw public life and family life as almost mutually exclusive, and she wondered how other women combined the two. Elizabeth was also responding to an important change in Helena's population. The railroads had stimulated a wave of prosperity and had brought a new class of people to Helena. These people invested less in the town and in its activities than did men and women who had lived in Helena from the beginning. Like the membership of the WCTU, the Women's Relief Corps ranks were made up of a different class of women, those who came after completion of the railroad. The Corps disbanded in 1890 and was revived the next year, but Elizabeth resigned her position anyway.[108] She wrote:

> There were none of my friends interested in the work and I was continually coming in contact with a class of women I never met any where else and did not care to be associated with. I had kept along from year to year hoping to induce some of my friends among the better class to join the organization and help to officer and control it but they would not come in because of this other element.[109]

Even as she eased herself out of leadership in her charitable organizations, she remained an active worker and voter. In March 1891, Elizabeth declined to run for school trustee because her Poor Committee work interested her more. She continued to work for the committee until the county assumed management of it in June 1891. In April, she voted against a school bond system she had judged incompetent.[110]

Throughout much of 1890 and 1891, Elizabeth wrestled and contended with her perplexing relationship with her daughter Grace. Beginning in 1888, when Grace had chosen to remain in Helena and not return to college, Elizabeth had expressed her growing concern:

> I have never felt satisfied with Grace's failure to complete the course and graduate. I think the great disappointment was that she herself did not care to make the most of every advantage.

> For I could remember how I longed for such an opportunity when I was a girl. . . .[111]

Although Grace's college decision disappointed Elizabeth, Grace showed signs of increased independence and ability. Grace and her friends became interested in homesteading until her minority status closed that opportunity. She capitalized on her artistic talent, selling several paintings during 1888 and listing herself as an artist in the city directory. Elizabeth preferred that her daughter learn to set type, believing that "every girl, no matter what her circumstances, should be taught some useful trade or calling."[112]

By June 1890, however, Elizabeth was worrying more about Grace's social life than about her acquiring a "useful trade or calling." In a mood of self-congratulation, Robert and Elizabeth presented Grace with a piano because she had delayed getting married. Two months later, despite the gift, Grace announced her intention of marrying Hardy Bryan, a bookkeeper at the Broadwater Hotel. Unimpressed with Bryan, Elizabeth did not take the announcement seriously; he was only one of an endless parade of young men Grace had brought home. Elizabeth hoped that Grace would emulate her daughter's friend, Agnes McLean, of whom Elizabeth wrote: "I do so much honor a woman who makes a name and a career for herself without thinking of settling down to wait for a husband."[113]

Determined to marry Bryan, Grace marshalled her forces. Robert passed the final responsibility to Elizabeth; he would give his consent if she would give hers. Seeing nothing to recommend Hardy Bryan personally, socially, or financially, Elizabeth adamantly refused. Her resolve divided the Fisk family, and Elizabeth soon found herself in the role of authoritarian ogre.[114] It profoundly hurt Elizabeth to be in such contention, and it dismayed her to find that the "female wickedness"—the masculine need to gratify passions—she had recently discovered was in her midst. She always had endeavored to protect her sons from the town's corrupt influences and had counted on Grace's innate moral sense to protect her. Elizabeth had worked hard to build a fortress of Christian values in the home, only to discover she had failed.

Grace sought to please herself instead of adhering to her duty to family, trying to win adherents to her side by openly criticizing her mother's conduct during the preceding years. In letters to her grandmother, Grace charged Elizabeth with encouraging Bryan's suit. Why, she asked, was her mother now reversing her position. In addition, Grace claimed, her mother was away from home so much of the time that she could not know what was happening in her children's lives. Elizabeth defended herself by denying that she had encouraged the relationship in an extraordinary way, but what hurt Elizabeth the most were Grace's accusations about her maternal conduct. Answering her own mother's queries, Elizabeth explained:

> I do not feel that I have ever neglected home or home duties for any outside work or pleasure. I cannot live wholly within that narrow circle nor do I think it any woman's duty to do so. There have been many years of my married life when the children were small that I could not get away from them and then I stayed at home. But I think every mother should have hours of rest and relaxation, of freedom from care, and she must find it out side the home. She has more strength and patience, is better fitted to care for her little ones, if she can sometimes get away from them. . . . In the light of recent events I am sure it is a mistake to deny oneself for the children.[115]

At an impasse with her mother, Grace defended her conduct with Bryan by charging that Elizabeth also went out alone and unchaperoned. Elizabeth rightly pointed out that with her husband away so often and for such long periods on his business trips and pleasure jaunts, her only recourse was to go by herself if she were to enjoy any activity outside the home. A hardened Elizabeth resolved to be less amenable to others' wishes: "The time has passed when I shall attempt to smooth over and make the best of things, when I shall deny myself many things I need. I propose to have my turn at whatever pleasure or profit I can lay hold of for life is fast passing away and all my strength is spent for others."[116] Grace disregarded her mother's obdurateness and married Hardy Bryan on October 1, 1890. Going beyond disapproval, Elizabeth barred Grace from the Fisk house on Rodney Street. That became a topic for Helena's wagging tongues, but it also caused a breach with Robert, who was willing to make the best of things.[117]

Nearly six months after Grace's marriage, Elizabeth relented enough to see her daughter again, although she still refused to meet Mr. Bryan. The affair still rankled Elizabeth and she asked, ". . . why do so many women take leave of their senses when there is a man in the question." By now, however, Grace was pregnant, and Elizabeth regretted that she had not had the opportunity to discuss delaying children with her. When financial reverses struck the Bryan family and Elizabeth found the odious Hardy Bryan under her roof for several months, she met her daughter halfway; but she remained unreconciled to her son-in-law.[118]

By the fall of 1892, Elizabeth and Grace had reached a kind of détente. Grace continued to visit her parents' home without her husband, and from time to time Elizabeth had charge of her grandson, Stanley Fisk Bryan. When Grace fell in with "the latest insane fashion" of dispensing with a petticoat, Elizabeth kept her counsel. But the wounds had not healed. When Hardy Bryan contemplated taking a job away from Helena,

Elizabeth said of Grace and her grandson, "I shall miss them of course, but the sadness of this parting was over two years ago." The gulf between mother and daughter remained unbridgeable.[119]

Home and family continued to absorb Elizabeth. "I think home is about the best place," she wrote in 1892. Her father died that year and her mother, then suffering from a uterine disease, would die the following year. Her mother's death would end an important phase in Elizabeth's life, leaving her without the wise counsel her mother had provided. Elizabeth again withdrew from some of her activities in the community. Worn out from her charity work, Elizabeth complained that the "other element" had taken over the local temperance chapter and that she had lost interest. The organization, she observed, consisted "of women who cannot long conduct such work—any work—successfully." Instead, Elizabeth busied herself sending homeopathic medicines to her mother, and she redoubled her effort on the home front to keep her sons occupied in some useful work. "A boy or young man," she wrote, "is constantly exposed to many temptations in a town like this, and without Christian principles one is never safe."[120]

No longer involved in temperance, Elizabeth returned to the role of political spectator. Although she supported women's suffrage, she remained unalterably opposed to women's political candidacy. After hearing a speech by attorney-general candidate Ella Knowles, Elizabeth wrote: "It was simply disgusting. She swung her arms and opened her mouth and *yelled*. No other word expresses it."[121]

Through 1893, Elizabeth continued in her roles of domestic overseer and political watcher in the statehouse. She attended a joint session of the legislature in February, and in March she watched the balloting for U.S. Senator. When Lee Mantle of Butte won the Senate seat, Elizabeth alluded to the still potent social force of women in the community. "The best women of Butte," she observed, "do not recognize him, so open and notorious are his violations of decency." Hearth and home could not beguile Elizabeth for long, and in 1894 she was the secretary and a member of the executive committee of the Helena chapter of the Women's Helena for Capital Club.[122]

Initially, there seemed to be no contest between Helena and Anaconda for the state capital; but during the summer before the election, Anaconda closed in on its rival. Threatened by Anaconda's frank appeals to the working-class and radical elements in the industrial copper communities, Helena women entered the fray and formed their club to assure electoral victory. Club members, who were primarily married and middle-aged, mounted an efficient and effective campaign by dividing the city into wards for canvassing. With few exceptions the ward coordinators were women who had spent most of their lives in Helena—the pioneers. Organized on the home front, they solicited funds for their group and spread their influence beyond the county. They activated female networks and mobilized men and women who controlled institutions that were largely dominated by women—the churches, the WCTU, and county school superintendent's offices. With a subsidy from the railroads they mounted a whistle-stop tour to argue Helena's case. When the votes were counted, Helena emerged the victor by a narrow margin.[123]

Helena women who worked to make their city the capital had entered into a frankly political contest. They opposed corporate interests of considerable power and artfulness, matching them with their domestic influence and intimate persuasion, powers of organization, and access to private financial resources. These women belonged to the same generation; they had arrived in Helena during the late 1860s or early 1870s. Elizabeth Fisk was at the center of all this, dispatching letters and answering requests with her usual organizational talent.

Back on Rodney Street, Grace's marriage provided the cynosure that put into sharper focus the generational differences between mother and daughter. In 1897, bowing to financial necessity, Hardy Bryan made his way to New York City. Once settled, he expected Grace and his son to join him. Apparently, neither New York nor Bryan appealed to Grace, for she refused him, moved back to her parents' home, and took a job as a telegraph editor with the *Herald*. There she joined her mother who had been employed as a proofreader. In 1898, almost a year to the day Bryan had left Helena, Grace petitioned the court for a divorce, charging her husband with failure to support her during the preceding year and suing for the custody of their son.[124]

Among the twenty-six divorce petitions filed with the court in 1898, *Bryan v. Bryan* was notable in that Hardy Bryan contested the action and brought a cross-bill against his wife, alleging that she had deserted him and was by her conduct during the past three years unfit to have custody of their child. Unlike modern dissolutions where the occasion of "unhappy differences" or "irretrievable break-down" constitute cause for divorce, nineteenth century Montana divorce law required assignment of fault or blame when the parties disagreed. In a contested proceedings, a jury heard testimony and by a three-quarters vote determined the guilty party.[125]

In September of 1898, Hardy Bryan returned to Helena to appear in court and to see his son. Grace had apparently arrived at her mother's estimation of Bryan. Not only did she not speak to Bryan herself, but she also refused Bryan permission to see his son. To that end, she and the Fisk clan resorted to a variety of transparent subterfuges. Menaced from the outside, the Fisk family closed ranks behind Grace. A spate of court orders on Bryan's part produced an equal number of delaying tactics on the Fisks' part. Nonetheless, the jury heard the case in October 1898.[126]

Bryan's lawyer's arguments rested on a strict interpretation of the law concerning the duties of wives to husbands; namely, that a wife who lived apart from her husband's abode risked legal censure and loss of his financial support. Grace's attorney stressed that a husband's choice of home must be a reasonable one, clearly a liberal view of the law. Free to deny or sustain either lawyer's recommendations, the judge chose to emphasize the liberal interpretation of a married woman's duty. Twelve male jurors voted eight to four to award a divorce to Grace Fisk Bryan. It might easily have gone the other way; one juror joined the majority at the last minute because the hour was late and he was getting sick.[127]

The court may have given Hardy Bryan reasonable access to his son, but the Fisks had other plans. Although she risked contempt of court, Grace immediately raced off to California with Stanley in tow for health reasons. Bryan tried again a year later to see his son, but the Fisks once again outwitted him.[128]

Grace and her mother found themselves in the same place in 1898 and 1899—the *Helena Herald*. After Grace joined the staff, Elizabeth worked intermittently as a proofreader with considerable enjoyment: "I always enjoy the work of proof reading and Grace much prefers the telegraph editor's place. So we were both suited." Grace continued to work as an editor or as a reporter until 1902. In that year, following disputes between the corporation and Fisk family members, the Fisks disposed of their interest in the paper and, except for two sons, moved *en masse* to Berkeley, California. Elizabeth had finally gotten her wish—a house with a decent furnace and a community where her children could be properly educated without leaving home. Shed of Hardy Bryan, Grace remarried and settled near her parents in Berkeley. Six years later, in 1908, Robert Emmett Fisk died. Elizabeth outlived him by nearly twenty years, dying on April 22, 1927, at the age of eighty-two.[129]

In *Angle of Repose*, his novel of the mining frontier, Wallace Stegner observed of his heroine: ". . . every drop, indistinguishable from every other, left a little deposit of sensation, experience, feeling. In thirty or forty years the accumulated deposits would turn my cultivated, ladylike, lively, talkative, talented, innocently snobbish grandmother into a Western woman in spite of herself." Stegner might have been describing Elizabeth Chester Fisk and what happened to her during her Helena years. Elizabeth herself more mundanely said, "Truly, this is a world of change." But just as Elizabeth's urban frontier had been altered over three decades, so had she been transformed in the process of adapting to the conditions of a world different from that of her girlhood.[130]

Elizabeth Chester Fisk's biography does not depict the events of a feminist epiphany or even a woman's gradual conversion to the cause of women's rights on the frontier. Elizabeth successfully transferred her conception of women's role as civilizers, mothers, and embodiments of purity, selflessness, and Christian morality from New England to Montana. She arrived in Montana prepared to replicate Connecticut society in a mountain setting, at first through female networks.

Born in 1846, Elizabeth was a member of the last age cohort that had any real experience with the female network system that had sustained her mother's generation, with its maternal societies, band of friends, and coterie of female relatives. Even the number of Elizabeth's letters home testifies to her attempt to maintain a supportive female group within her own family. Her effort to gain entry into a similar female group in Helena failed, not because she lacked initiative but because the transient nature of frontier populations affected the membership of groups. In a world where men dominated women's social gatherings and partisan allegiances determined a man's success, political differences touched women's lives and divided them along with the men, further disrupting the formation of informal, cohesive women's groups. In this milieu and before the birth of her first child, Elizabeth consciously retreated to the most stable and congenial group in her changing environment—the family. The frontier church, with its concessions to gaming and dancing and the poor quality of its preaching, alienated Elizabeth. In the end, Elizabeth effectively walked into her kitchen and nursery, slammed the doors, and remained outside community affairs for more than a decade.

This is only half of Elizabeth's story. Her experience on the mining frontier set up an ideology in competition with the nineteenth century "cult of true womanhood." Left home and to her own devices when her husband traveled, Elizabeth realized her own capabilities and concluded that she could survive without a husband and independent of her role in a marriage. In sum, the frontier promoted Elizabeth's sense of self-reliance. With its numerous moral failings and propinquity of vice, the frontier also gave substance and special meaning to Elizabeth's ideal of a "public" home—the idea that women were housekeepers to the city and mothers to its citizens—and it became increasingly important to Elizabeth as her children matured and as the differences between what they learned in the Rodney Street house and what they learned on Helena's streets became apparent. She contemplated sending them away from Helena's profane influences but opted instead to influence the community by participating in local government to improve sanitation, health, safety, and schooling. The proper and upright training and education of children would not proceed, she believed, unless she took immediate action to ameliorate the quality of Helena's life.

The scarcity of suitable servants placed the full weight of household maintenance on Elizabeth, intensifying her familial responsibilities and her confinement to the home. By 1881, she had tired of the unrelieved domestic burden; motherhood had lost its charm. Elizabeth's nagging unease and quiet complaints about her husband's freedom from domestic responsibilities had turned into frank discontent. Moreover, she realized that such inequity existed not only in her own marriage but also for mothers as a class. Her questioning of the status quo and her actions proceeding out of it were hardly revolutionary events. But her questions were signs of Elizabeth's re-evaluation of the accepted nineteenth century role for women and hinted at a profound critique of the social relationships in the family.

Between 1883 and 1900, Elizabeth's ideas about women's proper role in the home and in society became less ambiguous and conflicting. Sane motherhood and domestic well-being, Elizabeth came to believe, required that women be involved in the world beyond the home. Elizabeth had critically examined motherhood and unrelieved domesticity, and her contemplation had resulted in a dim, half-formed sense of the inequity between the sexes and an identification with other women. For Elizabeth, this vague realization meant a lack of personal fulfillment and time for herself. Her need for time apart from her children and her sense of duty sent Elizabeth into benevolent work that aimed at improving the environment for family.

Elizabeth's involvement in charitable organizations quickly shaded into reform activity with the WCTU. As a WCTU member, she was drawn into women's suffrage and other specifically women's issues. This transition also marked a change in her political activity from informal participation in local politics to formal involvement as lobbyist, witness, and petitioner. But Elizabeth, whose politics grew out of her experience as a mother, remained essentially conservative. Although she was willing to make use of the ballot in local elections and to support women's suffrage under the auspices of the WCTU, Elizabeth drew the line at women becoming political candidates.

Elizabeth's benevolent work, especially with the Poor Committee, also led her to change her attitude toward women's employment. Helena's post-railroad prosperity had created more millionaires per capita than any other town of its size; it had also contributed to the numbers of Helena's abject poor. On her welfare rounds, Elizabeth encountered destitute women without skills or other means to improve their condition. What had begun for Elizabeth as a vague idea of work providing a desirable discipline and alternative to loneliness had turned into a firm conviction that all young women needed a useful skill. She also carried the belief that work underpinned self-reliance and independence. Finally, Elizabeth's experiences with her daughter and other Helena women persuaded her that women's natural inclination toward purity, duty, and self-sacrifice was illusory.

The place Elizabeth arrived at after thirty years on the mining frontier was the place from which her daughter started out. Elizabeth had lived out most of her adulthood in Helena; Grace had grown up there. The crisis between mother and daughter highlighted the changes that had overtaken Elizabeth and illuminated the differences between the generations. For Elizabeth, "whole-souled" womanhood had become an ideological relic, and for Grace the ideals embodied in the concept never had substance. Grace's independence cut across all social relationships, even those of her family and marriage.

This difference between the generations may be best illustrated in Elizabeth's and Grace's attitudes toward their husbands and marriages. When Elizabeth endured and rationalized the shortcomings in her marriage, Grace refused to make the best of her marital disappointments, contriving the dissolution of her own marriage. Implicit in her action was a rejection of woman's dependency on her husband and an equal, self-confident commitment to personal and economic autonomy. When the opportunity arose in the year of separation from her husband, Grace went to work and found herself physically, if not ideologically, beside her mother. By fits and starts Elizabeth came to value self-reliance and moderate her willingness to sacrifice herself wholly for others; Grace had early resolved that independence was the best course. The generations of Eldorado mothers and daughters, while they had taken different paths, had converged.

One historian of women's experience on the frontier wrote, "My original perspective was feminist; I hoped to find that pioneer women used the frontier as a means of liberating themselves from stereotypes and behaviors which I found constricting and sexist. I discovered that they did not."[131] A chronicle of Helena's women suggests a more complex interpretation. On the one hand, it seems clear that first generation westering women did not use the frontier as a springboard to self-fulfillment; on the other hand, it is evident that the frontier thrust these women into situations that fundamentally altered their lives. Frontier women, in short, redefined womanhood, but they did it reluctantly and only when confronted with an environment antithetical to their sensibilities. To look for liberation is to look to the second generation of the frontier.

Catharine Ming, Mary Ann Eckert, Fanny Spencer, Helen Lehman, Lottie Rumsey, and Elizabeth and Grace Fisk are examples of many women who shared the experience of the frontier. As representative women, their lives suggest some of the ways in which the frontier redefined womanhood and altered women's social relationships. Of all the attributes that distinguished the daughters from their mothers, however, the most salient was the daughters' willingness to dispense with an unhappy marriage, to divorce. In this they benefited from a legacy bequeathed to them by their foremothers. Over the years, the women of Helena, although unconsciously, contributed to the terms that would delimit state divorce law in Montana.

CHAPTER FOUR

Occasions of Unhappy Differences

Divorce in Helena, 1865-1907

"DIVORCES ARE COMMON HERE," Elizabeth Chester Fisk wrote to her mother in February 1868, "and it is a common comment that a man in the mountains cannot keep his wife."[1] Elizabeth's remark alluded to the ubiquity of divorce on the frontier and foreshadowed her own experience with marital discord in her daughter's life. The Bryan litigation and other divorce suits in Lewis and Clark County not only reveal some of the pressures exerted on marriages by circumstances peculiar to the frontier, but they also document one way in which women translated their private criticisms of the social relationships between husbands and wives into changes in public policy. Divorce cases in Lewis and Clark County, moreover, describe the erosion of the "cult of true womanhood" between 1865 and 1880, its reacceptance between 1880 and 1885, and the confirmation of the "companionate marriage"—marriage based on mutual affection, respect, and duties—in law by 1895.[2] Women did not set out to reform divorce statutes; rather, the courts responded to women whose appearance in court in part resulted from frontier living conditions. Similarly, when Helena women emulated traditional nineteenth century mores and demanded higher standards of marital conduct as Helena society matured, magistrates reacted by granting them divorces on the basis of a broad interpretation of extreme cruelty. The partnership between the courts and female petitioners, in sum, transformed divorce law in the early twentieth century to include a liberal provision for mental cruelty, which would provide an avenue out of unhappy unions for women in Montana.

Helena's newspapers commented on the numbers of couples seeking divorce, but the writers evinced no particular anxiety as they compared the divorce rolls in Helena with other parts of the country.[3] Outside Montana, however, the increasing divorce rate triggered alarm. In the East, those concerned with the perceived disintegration of marriage formed the New England Divorce Reform League in 1881. The league's membership, laced with leading intellectuals, politicians, and educators, secured passage of a bill that provided for a thorough statistical investigation of marriage and divorce.

The investigation resulted in *A Report on Marriage and Divorce in the United States*, a massive digest published by the Bureau of Labor in 1891. The first of its kind, the bureau report produced a careful county-by-county tabulation of the circumstances of divorce and marriage. Although Montana and the other territories did not capture the compilators' attention (one was moved to write, "The figures for this territory require no comment, there being nothing in them to excite study"), the bureau's report was the first source for statistics on divorce and marriage in the nation. Bureau researchers, however, failed to perceive the regional bias of the skyrocketing divorce rate. Although impetus for reforming marriage and divorce law was an eastern phenomenon, Montana and other western territories set the pace in marital dissolution from the late nineteenth century into the twentieth century. In Montana, Lewis and Clark County led the state in the number of divorces until Silver Bow County and its industrial center, Butte, captured the honor in the 1890s.[4]

Despite the bureau's statistical insouciance, its report provided a catalog of legal grounds for divorce. From the outset, Montana civil law explicitly and in unyielding terms defined the just causes and grounds for divorce: impotency, bigamy, adultery, abandonment for one year, willful desertion, habitual drunkenness, extreme cruelty, or conviction of a felony or infamous crime. Conspicuously absent from this list was neglect or a husband's failure to provide for his wife, a unique oversight among the states and territories comprising the Rocky Mountain mining frontier.[5]

The bureau's report indicated the general nature of divorce on Montana's frontier. First, the rate of divorce in Montana and especially in Lewis and Clark County was extraordinarily high. Between 1865 and 1870, there was one divorce for every three marriages in the county; in 1867, divorces actually exceeded marriages. Compared with a marriage-to-divorce ratio of twenty-six to one in Los Angeles County, California, during the same period, Lewis and Clark County's divorce rate approximated modern figures.[6] Second, wives in Lewis and Clark County had less patience with marital infelicity, regardless of the grounds cited, than did their counterparts in California and in the nation as a whole.[7] Third, although detailed information about the nationality, race, religion, and occupation of the divorcing parties could only "be ascertained by a detective system utterly impossible on any extended scale," the report's compilers gathered enough information to ascertain that desertion ranked as the most common reason for divorce, followed by adultery, cruelty, and drunkenness.[8] Lewis and Clark County conformed to this generalization.

Between 1865 and 1870, forty-seven marriages foundered in Lewis and Clark County; in 60 per cent of these separations one spouse, usually the husband, deserted the other. Thomas and Elizabeth Fortune had been married five years when Thomas abandoned his wife and their three children. He wrote from Salt Lake City to say he would not return. Theodore Steiger abruptly left his wife, Mata, in Virginia City, Nevada, on September 10, 1864. Mata migrated to Montana, opened a stage house, and divorced her husband. After less than a month of marital bliss, H. B. Smith, who apparently harbored dishonorable intentions from the beginning, deserted his wife, Lizzie, in Virginia City, Montana. Lizzie claimed that Smith had enticed her into marriage with false tales of his wealth and his social standing in the community. Charging desertion and fraud, Lizzie won speedy relief. Much more infrequently, wives deserted their husbands. Belle Pixley who associated with a disreputable set in Placerville, Idaho, refused to accompany her husband, Walter, when he departed for Helena shortly after their marriage. In several cases, wives simply refused to come west.[9]

The percentage of marriages terminated because of abandonment reached its peak in Helena during the 1870s, when a national depression, the depletion of nearby surface gold deposits, and the continued lack of rail transportation affected the city. The actual number of divorces, however, declined precipitously during this period of economic hardship; the Clerk of Court recorded three divorces in 1875 and only two in 1876.[10] Evidently, both men and women hesitated to try their fortunes alone.

In those cases where the promise of the frontier proved illusory and the hard times strained their marriages to the breaking point, one partner, usually the husband, took the easiest way out of the marriage and departed. Sumner and Mary Frost had been married for nearly nine years when Sumner decided to leave. Mary testified that his parting words were, in effect, that he was going to have a good time and be gone a long time. Similarly, on Christmas Day 1875, Charles Cox informed his wife of twelve years that "he was tired of staying in Montana" and that he was taking himself and their son to Nebraska. Elizabeth Cox testified, "He told me to look out for myself, that he was never coming back to live with me anymore." Fannie Addis echoed Elizabeth Cox's words in testimony about her husband, adding: "He said that [I] and the children might take care of ourselves." For some wives there were not even parting words.[11]

During the 1880s, with few exceptions, the nature of abandonment remained fairly predictable; spouses, mainly husbands, simply disappeared. Sometimes these disappearances had an aura of calculation and fraud about them. Humphrey Healey left for Deadwood, Dakota Territory, on the pretense of taking a load of wood from Helena to Fort Benton in 1876. He left his illiterate wife, Lucy, and six children behind, although he sent money to Lucy and his children from time to time. Lucy had heard rumors that Humphrey had been living in Deadwood with a lewd woman and that they had departed for Colorado. Convinced that Humphrey would not return, Lucy filed for divorce in 1881. Anna and Harry West were married in Cherokee, Iowa, on April 9, 1884. On April 15, Harry took a team, Anna's money, and her gold watch to Keokuk. He sent the team back. Believing that Harry had family living near Bozeman, Anna set out to track him down only to discover that he had lied. The completion of the railroad into Helena in 1883 made abandonment easier. Thomas and Carrie Finn were married in Glyndon, Minnesota, on June 9, 1883. Thomas did not stay with Carrie long enough to celebrate their sixth wedding anniversary; he left on June 1, 1889, and headed to Dillon, where he wrote Carrie that he "was going south on the Union Pacific Railroad."[12]

The Healey case is illustrative of the long intervals between desertion and formal legal action. In several cases, men and women filed divorce petitions and never bothered to complete them. Mary Ann Eckert, for example, began proceedings against her husband, John, but never brought them to conclusion. Similarly, the Healey case demonstrates the confusion surrounding desertion on the frontier. Humphrey was certainly absent, but his periodic remittances kept Lucy from being an abandoned woman.

The advent of the railroad in 1883 significantly changed Helena and Lewis and Clark County. Within three years, Helena's population quadrupled to nearly thirteen thousand. Between 1883 and 1893, the area boomed with prosperity. Beginning in 1885, women began to voice their disillusionment with their husbands' lack of success on the frontier and to express confidence in their own abilities to make a better match or bigger wage. Emma and Nelson Selsby married in Rockland, California, on February 9, 1876, and remained husband and wife for nearly a decade before Emma decamped for California. Witnesses testified on Nelson's behalf that Emma had often spoken of her intention of marrying a richer man. *Picot v. Picot* illustrated a variation on this theme. Eugene Picot had left his new wife, Mary, in St. Louis for a bookkeeping position at the smelter in Wickes, Montana, claiming that he could not support Mary on his salary. Deciding as well that St. Louis was not for her, Mary went to Wickes, where her unladylike conduct caused Eugene to lose his job. Eugene's attempts to persuade her to more acceptable behavior went for naught. Mary replied "that she wanted to sleep with other men and that she [could] make a living otherwise than by working." Witnesses testified in *Draper v. Draper* that Emma Draper "would rather work out than live at home." Her mother-in-law surmised that Emma had finally abandoned her husband because "she could not have gentleman company enough when she was . . . living with her husband."[13]

The absence of a neglect clause confirmed that women could not rely on their husbands' support, and women's response to abandonment or a husband's failure to provide a good life reflected women's willingness to support themselves. Stunned and bewildered as they often were when abandoned, most women in Helena did not collapse or fall back on the charity of friends, neighbors, or family.[14] Many immediately took up employment or continued in jobs that had occupied them before they divorced. Mary Thomson, who was deserted at the Magnolia Hotel, took a position there; and Mary Picot and Sarah Stevenson had prospects, although not of the legitimate sort. Drusilla Turman became a nurse, and Melissa Waldron continued her work as a dressmaker. Fannie Addis, Adelia Punches, Sarah Sheriff, and others kept boardinghouses. Elizabeth Hill continued as a cook at ranches in the Prickly Pear Valley, and Margaret Shroyer declared that if she were going to work she would prefer to work for herself. Forty per cent of the deserted women testified that they had supported themselves during the required year between their abandonment and their first court appearance.[15] In a few cases, men capitalized on the expectation that women would work. Augustus Reitting, for example, told the court that he had no intention of working when he had a wife. Alben Hill also had expectations of a working wife. Elizabeth Hill testified that Alben was accustomed to sitting in the house with his cigar while she performed the majority of the ranch chores.[16]

Whereas women were more likely to complain of their husband's desertion, women were far more vulnerable to charges of adultery, which accounted for a quarter of the divorces between 1865 and 1870. Elizabeth Greenish, for example, saw a better opportunity in N. D. Johnson, left her husband, and moved in with Johnson. Both her husband, Peter, and the court interpreted Elizabeth's action as adultery. Sometimes adulterous events antecedent to westward migration culminated in a frontier divorce. Elizabeth and James Orten, who had married in Allegheny, Pennsylvania, in 1848, lived together until James committed adultery with F. Horn, with whom he continued to cohabit. Elizabeth and her children traveled to Montana where the court granted her a divorce in 1866. In other cases, the lure of the frontier's fancy ladies proved too much. Ester and Thomas McNally had been married less than a year when Thomas fell from grace into the arms of Blanche Alexander in August 1866. Ester generously forgave all, and the couple moved from Virginia City to Helena. Thomas, however, again proved susceptible to other feminine charms. Carrie Whitney testified in the subsequent divorce proceedings that she had witnessed Thomas in bed with Mary Caspy. Disgusted with her husband's philandering, Ester quickly put Thomas aside. But in the majority of cases, husbands or witnesses caught wives in their lovers' arms. Marital bliss lasted for only one year for John and Ermetta Orem when she accused her husband of infidelity, being a "low down whore-house pimp" and a "lying son-of-a-bitch." Ermetta threatened to sleep with other men, and witnesses testified that John Harrison soon became a frequent visitor in the Orem house and a regular in Ermetta's bed during June and July of 1866. When confronted by her husband, Ermetta declared in effect that she cared more for Harrison's little finger than she did for her husband's whole body.[17]

In *Ornn v. Ornn*, a simple case soon became a more complex and intriguing affair. Initially, Lewis Ornn accused Nancy Ann, his wife of four years, of having criminal connections with Jacob Rickard at the Young American Hotel over a period of two months in 1867. Two days after she received the summons, Nancy Ann countered with charges of her own. Besides accusing her husband of appropriating $3,000 of her money, she claimed that Lewis "was addicted to the indecent practice of self-pollution and would frequently, in the presence of the defendant, indulge in the foul and outrageous practice of masturbation and when spoken to about it by [the] defendant, would reply that he had always been used to it and that it answered every purpose." Nancy Ann declared that Lewis's indulgences had "impaired his mental powers" and made him "unfit for . . . the marriage relation." The jury, however, forgave Lewis's habit and overlooked Nancy Ann's financial claims. The court granted Lewis his divorce and left Nancy Ann free, presumably to take up with Jacob.[18]

Like the Ornn and Orem suits, in which the availability of other men broke a marriage, the promise of opportunity on the frontier played a large part in the Van Valkenberg divorce. Married in Chicago on December 29, 1850, Alonzo and Marcia Ann Van Valkenberg moved to Indiana, where they enjoyed four years of contented marriage until slanders involving Marcia Ann and Garrett Seeger undermined it. In a display of earnestness and trust that would characterize Alonzo's attitude toward their marriage, he dismissed the rumors out of hand. But he could not easily ignore the next episode. Two months after Alonzo left his farm in March 1855 to work on the Illinois Canal, Marcia Ann traveled to Wisconsin with Samuel Childs, passing herself off as Childs's wife—or so the town gossips alleged. Returning home in July, Alonzo discovered that his wife was pregnant. When Marcia Ann bore a full-term baby on February 18, 1856, some quick arithmetic and town talk convinced Alonzo to question Marcia Ann closely. Apparently, Marcia Ann adequately defended herself; Alonzo forgave her everything as he "did have a high regard and affection for the said Marcia Ann at that time."[19]

Six years later, in March 1862, Alonzo left again, this time for Montana's goldfields "in hopes of bettering his condition in life." Before his departure, he rented his property to James Downing and charged him with his family's well-being. By April 1864, impatience with her midwestern life had overcome Marcia Ann, and she sold the Indiana farm and set off in the company of James Downing for Montana and Alonzo. Alonzo met the new arrivals at Junction, Madison County, in July 1864. Sensing that Downing had taken his responsibilities to heart, Alonzo quickly contrived to get Downing employment at a distance, but Marcia Ann had plans of her own. With her connivance, Downing soon became a member of the household—so much so that Marcia Ann began giving Downing her husband's shirts and remaking her undergarments to furnish him with additional clothing. Hoping to dislodge Downing, Alonzo moved his family to Helena, where he had built a house. Despite Alonzo's maneuvering, Downing accompanied them.

On the way to Helena the wagon party camped. While Alonzo pastured the stock, "the said Marcia Ann and the said James Downing went into the covered wagon and after a reasonable time to have connection with each other were seen to come out of the same and by the jarring or motion of the bed of said wagon during the time it was thus occupied, it was believed by one Petersen who occupied a place under the wagon unbeknown to the said James Downing and Marcia Ann . . . that they did then and there have connection with one another."[20] Again at the village of "Beaver Town," Charles Sellick and John Sutes witnessed another act of illicit connection when the motion of the wagon once more betrayed James and Marcia Ann. Roused to action by these reports, Alonzo drove Downing away, although not for long. Once in Helena, Marcia Ann clandestinely invited Downing to the Van Valkenberg house in her husband's absence; soon Downing had insinuated himself into the household, assuming a role for himself in its daily routine.

During the first days of February 1865, events hurried to a close. Marcia Ann, pleading hospitality, convinced Alonzo that Downing should spend the night. On February 1, Marcia Ann made up the beds on the floor in such a manner that aroused Alonzo's suspicions and made him "mortified, chagrined, and exercised in mind." He settled on a ruse. He pretended to sleep and feigned wakefulness at the lightest untoward movement or rustle. The next night, Downing took leave on business, but the next afternoon he was back. That evening Marcia Ann arranged the bedding in the same manner as she had the first night. Alonzo continued to be watchful as before and was aware "when the said Marcia Ann and the said James Downing believing your said complainant asleep did then and there crawl toward each other, the said Marcia Ann slyly slipping down near the bed of the said James Downing when your complainant suddenly roused caught the said James Downing feeling the privates of the said wife, the said Marcia Ann." At last, fully convinced of "utter infidelity, wantonness, and abandonment" of his wife, Alonzo sprang up determined to put the interloper out of his house, but Downing threatened Alonzo with a loaded gun. Alonzo, "broken in spirit and heartsick, and having no loaded arms in the house," found himself standing in the snow in the early hours of the morning.[21]

In a subsequent cross-bill, Marcia provided convincing evidence of Alonzo's numerous absences and of his consequent failure to support herself and their child. In petitioning for her divorce on the grounds of desertion, Marcia Ann omitted any mention of the events of February 1865. The court was at a loss to disentangle the testimonies, but the jury awarded Alonzo a divorce on the grounds of his wife's adultery and gave Marcia Ann a divorce on the basis of her husband's desertion. A few days after her divorce decree, Marcia Ann and James Downing married.[22]

Marcia Ann saw an opportunity on the frontier to "better her condition in life" by exchanging one mate for another in an environment that paid scant attention to marital disintegration.

During the 1870s, suits predicated on sexual transgression subsided. Adultery became an act perpetrated by women who, in nineteenth century parlance, were "public women"; adultery for them was not an isolated incident. Lucy Bassett, wife of Lemon Bassett, had carnal connection with Charles Bixby, John Anderson, James Simpson, and an unknown man. Bassett concluded his testimony with the assertion that Lucy was a common prostitute. In another case, Mary Teats, who had married her husband, Philip, in Madison County on October 31, 1868, disported herself with diverse men between September 1870 and January 1871 and then took residence in a house of ill-fame. Francis Bill began his relationship with the full knowledge of his beloved's profession. He found Caroline Mills in a Salt Lake City whorehouse, moved her to a better bawdy establishment, married her on May 20, 1876, and then filed for divorce in January 1877 on the grounds of adultery. He claimed that Caroline had left him and returned to her trade.[23]

The incidence of divorce suits citing adultery between 1880 and 1890 remained constant, accounting for 9 per cent of the dissolutions in Lewis and Clark County.[24] The pattern of adultery replicated that of a previous decade: Men married fancy ladies and later regretted their choice in marriage partners; or, in a handful of cases, husbands surprised their wayward wives in parlors, kitchens, or bedrooms of working- and middle-class homes.[25] Toward the end of the century, as Helena's citizenry became more self-conscious about respectability, adultery became either less of a temptation or a more discreet undertaking. The temptations of the flesh sundered marriages, but allegations of cruelty soon outnumbered those of adultery in divorce proceedings. In the process of sorting out the merits of these new and varied claims, Helena courts grappled with the definition of extreme cruelty.

Between 1865 and 1880, district judges had no doubt about the legal construction of extreme cruelty. Extreme cruelty referred to physical, life-threatening violence over a period of time; a single, isolated incident was insufficient. The court usually required women to detail at least three occasions of domestic brutality, the last of which demonstrated that the woman's life had been definitely imperiled and her home rendered unsafe. The only deviation from this pattern occurred in cases citing desertion/abandonment and cruelty as primary causes, when one episode of violence was deemed sufficient. Women were entitled to immediate relief in situations that involved cruelty, whereas they were required to wait a year to sustain abandonment/desertion. Adding cruelty to abandonment could accelerate the proceedings considerably. Once a husband had decamped and was unable to speak in his own defense, it was a simple matter to allege the second cause and to secure a quick divorce. Either lawyers or women or both had found a means of effectively circumventing the law.[26]

Fredericka Verges complained that her husband, John, had repeatedly beaten her with a club. Elizabeth Kruger cataloged events of increasing cruelty, beginning with beatings and accusations of infidelity and ending with her husband pitching her into the snow with the intention of freezing her to death. Minnie Coady Wormal's husband finished their quarrels by repeatedly thwacking his wife over the head with a frying pan. George Hinkler on separate occasions nearly choked his wife, Mary, to death and pistol whipped her. Later, George struck a recalcitrant cow across the spine with an ax. When Mary criticized his ill-treatment of the animal, George turned the ax on her.[27]

The travail of Lizette Davis most fully documents the nature of domestic cruelty and women's response in nineteenth century Helena. Lizette, who had married her husband in Helena on July 20, 1868, detailed in her complaint two years of increasingly frequent batterings and petty cruelties. On November 5, 1878, for example, Davis had forced his wife out into the snow after having kicked and beaten her. Barefoot and clad only in her nightgown, Lizette had managed to re-enter the house before morning, but Davis had assaulted her again and forced her out of the house, this time harrying her across the street until she took refuge with neighbors. That same day, Davis had tossed his wife's wash in the hog pen. A month later, Davis had struck his wife, thrown scalding water on her, attacked her with a bootjack, and beat her head against a nail. In her frantic scramble to escape his brutality, Lizette had fallen, causing her to miscarry. On March 15, 1879, Davis had forced Lizette from their bed and threatened her with a knife. That same day, Davis had rolled up his blankets and left.[28]

When asked by the court's referee why she had endured her husband's violence for so long, Lizette articulated her own and no doubt other wives' reasons for staying when she said, ". . . the men had been talking about putting him in jail for mistreating me, and he was crying. I knew he was my man. I got ashamed for him and thought it was best to make it up." In her testimony, Lizette explained that she sought relief in the courts only after she had been publicly abused. "I have," she said, "always done for him everything I could. I have tried to be a good wife, but he abused me so much and I took it so hard I haven't had much health. I have always tried to conceal his treatment of me and cried it out by myself until after he abused me publicly."[29]

Between 1880 and 1890, the number of divorce cases citing extreme cruelty more than doubled; by 1890, nearly one-third of the women petitioning for divorce related episodes of cruelty. But it was cruelty of a different kind. Although battering had by no means disappeared, 42 per cent of the divorce actions filed between 1881 and 1890 mentioned incidents of cruelty that did not entail physical abuse.[30] Meanwhile, following the lead of the Montana Supreme Court, the Lewis and Clark County courts had dispensed with the "three incident" requirement, deeming a single incident of physical abuse sufficient to warrant divorce. In January 1885, Decius Wade wrote for a unanimous court in *Albert v. Albert*:

> We think one beating or whipping of a wife by her husband sufficient to establish the charge of extreme cruelty. Such an act could not be accidental or by mistake; and if not, the probabilities would be that it might be repeated again and again, subjecting the wife to constant fear and rendering her life miserable. *It is extremely cruel for a husband to beat or whip his wife, even once. Mere words can never afford any provocation or excuse for such an act; no words can justify an assault* . . . [emphasis added].[31]

Even as the justices seemingly settled the question of extreme cruelty, the lower courts were granting divorces on the grounds of mental cruelty, preparing the way for yet another elaboration of the statute. Mental anguish took several forms, including sexual abuse. The courts recognized that venereal disease and excessive sexual demands, although they did not comprise a separate category of legal action, could contribute to psychological as well as physical distress. Randall Kemp forced his wife, Hattie, to submit to sexual intercourse in a hut in their yard a week after she had delivered a stillborn child. The court sustained Hattie Kemp's claim that her husband's insensitivity constituted cruelty. More general in nature was Maggie Spencer's complaint against her husband, Silvera. She charged that she was "compelled against her will to submit to sexual intercourse with the defendant with a frequency and to an extent and in a manner that was excessive, unreasonable, indecent and degrading. . . . [and that she] had yielded to his embraces more frequently than any man ought to have demanded."[32]

More numerous were cases that unambiguously specified mental cruelty. Mary Hope and Ella Trunk accused their spouses of treating them in an overbearing manner and of engaging in tyrannical persecutions. Richard Punches contrived such demanding tests of faithfulness for his wife, Adelia, that he destroyed his wife's peace of mind and imperiled her position as manager of the St. Louis Hotel. Although Emil Lilliedahl never physically assaulted his wife, Emma, he whispered from time to time in her ear in the presence of guests that he intended to shoot her after the company departed. Emil also ripped the door off its hinges and shot the clock off the mantle. Mell Keith, displeased with his wife, Ella, castigated her, wished their children dead, and threw his meals on the floor.[33]

Although women tended to tolerate these private insensitivities, abuses, and excesses over a period of years, public humiliation was another matter. In *Monroe v. Monroe,* Mary Monroe sued her husband for divorce on the grounds of extreme cruelty. Mary charged in her petition that she was

> . . . sensitively appreciative of the virtue and honor of her sex which was well-known to the defendant, and knowing of her care for this gem above all price, he has and did on or about the 14th day of March . . . escort a woman of bad fame and a notoriously lewd woman from her place of vice in Helena to a public gathering of ladies and gentlemen. . . . He has been associating publicly and privately with one or more lewd women residents upon or about Wood Street . . . and has carried them out riding with him.

Mary probably had sufficient complaint of adultery to have been successful in her suit, but the public affronts to "the gem above all price" satisfied the court's definition of cruelty. Mary Russell suffered similar shame because of her husband's conduct. Not only was M. N. Russell discovered in a Miles City bawdy house, but he was also found in bed with a man who had been mysteriously murdered during the night. The scandal stemming from the subsequent trial sorely embarrassed Mary but not as much as his later arrest for grand larceny. The court decided that both public disgraces were adequate for relief.[34]

In a few cases, a spouse's failure to perform the nineteenth century's definition of fundamental duties met the court's test of extreme cruelty. Husbands were obliged to provide the necessities of life for their wives and children, and wives were bound to maintain a comfortable home. Both sexes were required to conform to an acceptable code of behavior—at least publicly. Nellie Carleton complained of ill-treatment because she was compelled to earn her own living. James McCameron's wife adamantly refused to perform the most basic domestic tasks for him and added insult by throwing a dirty diaper in his face. James Stranahan's petition for divorce rested primarily on his wife's repeated unladylike behavior. Genishia Stranahan, James claimed, called him a "whoremaster" and a "son-of-a-bitch" on a public street on a number of occasions.[35]

Even as the courts began to recognize and rule on complaints of mental cruelty, divorce continued to follow established patterns. During the 1890s, a steady stream of husbands and a few wives abandoned their spouses, children, and homes in Helena; desertion remained the precipitating cause in approximately 50 per cent of the divorce suits.[36] Like women before them, deserted wives worked to make ends meet. Although during the 1890s women's families often eased their financial burdens and supported them during the pendency of a divorce, the number of pauper declarations increased.[37] Adultery continued to account for 10 per cent of successful divorce petitions. In many of these cases,

Helena was a convenient place to resolve an episode of adultery that had occurred elsewhere years before or to remedy an unfortunate marital choice in the tenderloin. Intemperance also claimed its share of marriages and, like *Davis v. Davis,* illustrated the sharp demarcation between acceptable public and private behavior. Grace Priel, for example, served notice on her husband, Michael, the day after he lay drunk in the street in front of their home shouting abusive commentary.[38]

The courts' policies toward alimony and child custody confirmed the tenacity of some legal attitudes. In 1887, the legislature made provision for granting alimony and then extended the court's jurisdiction in 1895 to include alimony during the pendency of an action.[39] The high rate of desertion and women's eagerness to extricate themselves from bad marriages, however, left the statute generally ignored or unenforced. The number of women who received any form of financial support for themselves or for their children was insignificant and was confined to women willing to do battle with husbands of means.[40]

Children made only shadowy appearances in Lewis and Clark County divorce petitions except as the record noted their names and sometimes their ages. The disposition of children was such a minor issue that few custody battles ensued. Not until 1887 did the legislature take any interest in or grant the courts any authority over child custody matters, and even then the courts permitted custom and circumstance to dictate that the children usually be left in the care of the mother. Exceptions occurred in cases involving a wife's moral misconduct, her desertion of both husband and children, or her self-confessed inability to support the children. From time to time, a divorcing wife underscored the severity of a husband's verbal or physical abuse by indicating that the incidents occurred in the presence of children, but no sense prevailed that such actions threatened the children's tender sensibilities. If children witnessed a domestic donnybrook, the incident seemed only to augment a wife's embarrassment or shame. Between 1865 and 1900, the disposition of children appeared to be of little consequence and custody, a result of circumstance.[41]

While the proportion of divorces, alimony decisions, and child custody policy remained relatively unchanged, the lower courts' interpretation of extreme cruelty underwent another revision. Following the precedent set in 1885 by the Supreme Court, Helena judges reaffirmed the high court's "single incident ruling." A slap, a pummeling, a thrown dish, an accurate boot, or a carefully aimed cake became sufficient cause for divorce. The court also elaborated on its own tradition, begun in the late 1880s, and continued to count verbal abuse, insults to a woman's chastity, and angry threats as acceptable grounds for divorce.[42] Thirty-two per cent of the suits predicated on cruelty filed during the 1890s fell into the category of mental cruelty. For the first time such phrases as "grievous mental pain and anguish," "great mental fear and anguish," and "utter want of affection" appeared in successful divorce suits. Petitions in cases of physical abuse also bolstered their arguments with mention of psychological cruelties.[43] *Lenhart v. Lenhart*, although notable for the severity of its domestic violence, also cataloged commensurate episodes of mental abuse. John Lenhart taunted his wife, Ida, with references to his intimate knowledge of his paramour: "Well, I can get all I want from Jennie Glenn"; "Jennie Glenn is sick with her monthlies now"; "Jennie Glenn has lace trimmings on her drawers"; and "Jennie had on red stockings today."[44] These mental cruelty cases hint at a developing view of nineteenth century marriage that included the companionate ideal and its expectations of mutual affection, respect, consideration, and responsibilities.

More difficult to document is the transformation that occurred in women's expectations regarding marriage. Elizabeth Chester Fisk perceived a certain superficiality, an offensive dereliction of duty, and an inability to carry out social responsibility in the new class of women who arrived in Helena during the 1890s. In Elizabeth's words, women's social service organizations were dominated by "women who cannot long conduct such work—any work—successfully." Women's cavalier approach to divorce during the decade and their seeming disregard for its consequences reflected this ideological shift. Judging from the number of divorce actions dismissed for lack of prosecution by a female petitioner or on a motion from a female plaintiff, women appear to have used the threat of divorce as a domestic lever to pry their wayward mates away from improper behavior of all kinds. Women employing this tactic ran the risk of their husbands' indifference to the prospect of divorce.[45]

Some women held a romanticized view of their role, overestimated the authority of the companionate marriage ideal, and confidently expected the standards of public respectability to shield them from the consequences of their private frivolity and indiscretion. Louis Kaufmann, one of Helena's original, successful entrepreneurs, had spent his young adulthood consolidating his business in the city. A middle-aged man of considerable means when he married in 1886, he anticipated a happy union with his wife, Mattie. His wife disabused him of this notion in a few years. In his complaint in 1892, Louis charged that Mattie had called him "an old hulk of a man" and had twitted him with the declaration that "she had no affection for him, that her love was for another person, and that she did not care for him in any way whatever." To avoid the scandal of a separation and to protect the reputation of his only son, Louis tolerated Mattie's petty cruelties. Mattie initially joined him in this strategy. Louis purchased a horse and buggy for her as a gesture of his good will, although she refused to be seen riding with him. Louis maintained his composure until he returned one evening to find Harry Brown, the object of Mattie's affections, cowering in a closet. The insult stung too much, and Louis left the next morning. Expecting that Louis would overlook even this indiscretion, Mattie was dismayed when Louis filed a petition for divorce within the week on the grounds of extreme cruelty. Even in the throes of divorce, Louis upheld his obligations; he provided generous sums for his son and for Mattie, noting that the amount was "a fair and liberal sum of maintenance, if she is entitled to any at all."[46]

If the dissolution of the Kaufmann marriage indicated a dedication of frontier men and women to the nineteenth century ideal of companionate marriage, the Edgarton divorce highlighted women's misapprehensions about the positive strength of the ideal. Married in 1879 in Watkins Glen, New York, Erastus and Kate Edgarton lived in Helena from 1882 to 1886 where Erastus was president of the Second National Bank. According to Erastus, his wife was a silly and frivolous creature whose conduct had vexed him "to a greater or lesser extent throughout their entire married life." Just how foolish Kate was is documented in her written confession to adultery. In a note to Erastus, she wrote: "I repeat on paper what I said last night. Without going over the matter am willing to say that I was fond of [name deleted] and often while at his office under treatment submitted to his wishes and sexual intercourse." In words reminiscent of a romantic novel, in a second note Kate alluded to being drugged but cavalierly encouraged Erastus to "use this if you choose against me in any way if that is your motive. I care not." Erastus used the notes as evidence for a divorce. To avoid the publicity of a local divorce, Kate and Erastus agreed that Kate would "desert" her husband. She would go to New York, and Erastus would arrange a divorce in Yellowstone County in 1887. Like Mattie Kaufmann, Kate Edgarton underestimated her husband's depth of feeling, expecting that during her sojourn in New York Erastus would come to his senses. Unfortunately for Kate, Erastus assured her that "everything was done quietly as it could be and not have it fraudulent. Please say nothing to anyone in Helena one way or another, and I will do the same, and doing so we will avoid disgrace."[47]

After two years, the life of the gay divorcee became less attractive to Kate. The $100 per month Erastus provided her was not enough. Claiming that she knew nothing of the Yellowstone County divorce, Kate filed for divorce and requested a sizable alimony. Erastus believed that Kate's action betrayed their agreement and promptly discontinued his financial support, arguing that his wife had forfeited any additional consideration. Despite the preponderance of evidence in Erastus's favor, Kate continued to deny any knowledge of or responsibility for her divorce. When the Supreme Court sustained the judgment of the lower court in favor of Erastus and denied her demand for alimony, Kate Edgarton discovered that she had overplayed her hand. The Edgarton case, besides reinforcing some aspects of the companionate ideal, also rendered alimony awards to women more difficult to obtain.[48]

After statehood in 1889 Montana considered organizing its confusing and often contradictory laws in understandable and coherent form. Under the direction of Decius Wade, the author of the *Albert* decision, the state patterned compilation of its domestic law codes after those proposed by legal revisionist David Dudley Field. When the legislature adopted the new code in 1895, the new civil compilation added welfare neglect, a husband's failure to provide the necessaries of life, to the list of acceptable grounds for divorce. In the glossary to the statute, however, compilators, citing a California case, exempted husbands whose wives' earnings obviated the need for support.[49] The law effectively incorporated the judicial practices of the previous decade in a slightly altered form by including both the fulfillment of traditional gender roles and the tenets of the companionate marriage in domestic law by adding "threat of bodily injury" to extreme cruelty. The 1895 civil code established companionate marriage in Montana law, and in the Edgarton decision the high court abandoned its propensity toward broad interpretation in favor of a strict reading of the law supported by precedent.

For the next decade, Montana's lower courts contentedly interpreted the 1895 code in the broadest terms possible, especially the clause referring to the "threat of bodily injury." In 1906, the Supreme Court in *Ryan v. Ryan* set aside the *Albert* decision, which had established the "single incident" interpretation of extreme cruelty. Although the court agreed that Florence Ryan had endured both physical and mental pain, the justices questioned whether Ryan's injuries were "grievous enough" or a threat to her life. In bold language, Justice Holloway wrote:

> In the view of the legislature, a husband may beat or otherwise maltreat his wife, and even so in a brutal manner, without giving rise to an action for divorce, provided only that his mistreatment does not produce grievous bodily injury and be repeated, or if it occurs but once, that it does not produce bodily injury dangerous to life.

Justice Holloway added that the court's proper business stopped short of tinkering with legal definitions and legitimately adhered to the law mandated by the legislature.[50]

In 1907, the Montana legislature responded to the Supreme Court's decision and again considered amending the civil code regarding divorce. Perhaps encouraged by the progressive political opinion in the state, Republican representative and lawyer H. J. Miller introduced an extraordinarily liberal bill proposing "incompatibility of temper" as acceptable grounds for divorce. The measure passed the house but failed in the Senate Judicial Committee. Subsequently resurrected and substantially changed, the bill lost the "incompatibility of temper" phrase only to have it replaced by "mental cruelty." In this form, the measure sailed through both houses. While the legislators broadly defined mental cruelty, they stipulated that physical or mental cruelty had to have existed for a year before commencement of a divorce suit. Even as the state provided the courts with less Draconian guidelines for cruelty, it placed its legal blessing of domestic violence of both kinds for at least one year.[51]

From the outset, Montana civil law undermined nineteenth century concepts of gender roles that were proper for husbands and wives. The omission of "willful neglect" from the legal canon until 1895 was a significant departure from nineteenth century ideology. As a result, Montana courts only slowly recognized the domestic ideal of the companionate marriage, especially the concept of mutual duties, as part of the definition of marriage in Montana. While this legal lacuna suggests an abrogation of male familial responsibilities, it also hints that women were more than household guardians. This observation is borne out by the large proportion of women who were employed both before and after marriage and also by the addendum to the 1895 code that referred to the sufficiency of a woman's earnings as mitigating a charge of "willful neglect." Montana husbands and wives demanded conformity to Victorian sex-role expectations only in the final years of the 1880s, at precisely the time when observers noted that Helena society had assumed new attitudes toward mining camp customs. Taken together, the divorce cases from Lewis and Clark County at the very least reflect both legal and societal confusion about traditional gender roles between 1865 and 1880. At the most, these cases indicate an utter rearrangement of gender roles during the same period and their reinstatement between 1880 and 1885. This is best exemplified by the development of Montana's definition of "extreme cruelty."

Beginning with the Supreme Court's "single incident" ruling in 1885, divorce cases predicated on "extreme cruelty" demonstrate that the courts had begun to accept a definition of male and female conduct in line with the fundamental principles on which nineteenth century marriage rested. Husbands and wives were obliged to comport themselves decently both publicly and privately, but especially publicly. Indecent public behavior often became the critical event in a husband's or wife's decision to sue for divorce. To be guilty of cruelty, moreover, was to violate the boundaries of respect and consideration that husbands and wives demanded of each other. Without benefit of statute, the courts began to recognize mental cruelty as acceptable grounds for divorce. Although there were early indications that failure to fulfill marital responsibilities was an issue, men's obligations were not firmly established until 1895 in the willful neglect clause. In comparison, California had fixed neglect as grounds for divorce nearly forty years earlier, and in California husbands and wives agreed that affection, respect, and reciprocal duties were part of the marriage contract. At the least, the development of "extreme cruelty" in Montana represents part of a national trend, a hesitation to move too quickly away from the comfortable practices of the past; at the most, the

Montana case suggests that the adaptation of the "cult of true womanhood" to frontier social conditions forced new perspectives on "extreme cruelty"—positions that eastern states would ultimately adopt.[52]

Similarly, adultery cases in Lewis and Clark County provide evidence for the ambiguous character of sex roles. To be sure, the double standard and ideology of passionlessness so central to Victorian thinking rendered women more liable to male allegations of misconduct, but adultery suits, especially in the early years of settlement, argue *both* for the tenacity of women's roles as wife, mother, and homemaker and for women's desire to be free from these traditional expectations. Women in the sexual marketplace anticipated that they would marry and assume domestic normality; those outside the tenderloin did not hesitate to seize the chance to better their condition in life, even if their opportunism risked sexual transgression and divorce. Certainly, the frontier, with its far greater number of men, provided an ideal situation for women who dared to select a more suitable husband, and women like Elizabeth Greenish and Marcia Ann Van Valkenburg boldly capitalized on the opportunity.

Divorce records from Lewis and Clark County and the divorce-marriage ratio also indicate that the acceptance in Helena of the companionate marriage ideal coincided with the influx of new settlers after the completion of the railroad in 1883. These *arrivistes* brought with them different social standards that included the demands for urban improvement, the acceptance of a reform ideology, and the companionate marriage ideal.[53] The companionate ideal had its greatest influence between 1886 and 1895, precisely the period that is notable for Helena's boosterism and its imitation of urban sophistication. As Helena's middle-class women elaborated "the cult of true womanhood" in their own fashion and affirmed the companionate marriage, the courts transformed the traditional interpretation of extreme cruelty into a definition of mental cruelty tantamount, in some instances, to incompatibility.

Whether they were pioneers or *arrivistes*, divorcing women were engaged in an almost exclusively female enterprise. In 80 per cent of the divorce cases, district judges were responding to women in circumstances aggravated by the social conditions of the frontier.[54] Lewis and Clark County courts perceived that Helena lacked the welfare machinery to deal with abandoned, battered, or emotionally abused wives, that their city was surfeited with single men, and that the community was infused with a new spirit. When the opportunity arose to resolve a domestic problem, to create the possibility for a new, more stable household, and to stay in step with Helena's societal expectations, Helena magistrates obliged. As G. Edward White observed, late nineteenth century judicial interpretation was a matter of accommodating existing judicial decisions to new factual circumstances; the resulting judicial innovation often represented a clear departure from established practice.[55] The *Albert* decision is illustrative of this evolutionary process.

For Helena's women, the frontier meant a brief suspension of gender roles that lasted less than a decade. The effect of this disruption was neither to victimize nor to benefit women but to effect a re-evaluation of marriage and divorce. Between 1885 and 1895, both couples and the courts were busily restoring and affirming gender roles that sustained nineteenth century marriage and created the lineaments of the companionate marriage. At the same time, these women were becoming accustomed to marital dissolution. If divorce was primarily women's affair, then it was also the community's affair. The high rate of divorce guaranteed that each family would either directly or indirectly have some experience with divorce; consequently, Helena citizens accepted divorce as an unfortunate eventuality. Prominent as agents in both processes were the women of Helena. Indirectly and unconsciously, women contributed to laws that assisted them in their struggle to rearrange—for better or worse, for richer or poorer—the social relationships within the family.

When women next undertook to change the laws that governed their existence in their struggle to win the vote, their actions would be deliberately designed to change the constitution, and their victory would be the result of conscious public intervention in the political process. Montana women would not win suffrage merely by appearing in court in the guise of supplicant.

CHAPTER FIVE

Generation Upon Generation

Woman Suffrage in Montana

LIKE WOMEN'S FASHIONS, woman suffrage came west from the Northeast. But once transplanted, the movement flourished on the western frontier, where it achieved its first successes. By 1871, seven western legislatures had debated the issue, and two—Wyoming and Utah—had granted women the right to vote. Before ratification of the Nineteenth Amendment in 1920, ten states had enacted suffrage legislation, Montana among them.[1] In 1914, the Montana electorate approved a woman suffrage constitutional amendment, and in 1916 the state's voters carried the political process one step further by electing Jeannette Rankin as the first woman to serve in the U.S. House of Representatives.

Despite the region's innovation, woman suffrage in the West stood on conservative, not liberal or radical, legs. Rather than calling for natural political rights, economic equality, or personal growth, suffrage advocates "argued that women should vote because their moral perspective and domestic responsibilities allied them with those anxious to ameliorate the problems of an increasingly complex world"; the suffrage victories in the West "stemmed from the conservatism of these arguments buttressed by Western experience."[2] In addition, the insurgent politics of Populism and Progressivism boosted women's political aspirations and provided an environment receptive to expanded political rights and participation. At the same time, suffragists played to nativist and racist fears and promised a sure corrective to the growing number of foreign-born voters.

Much of Montana's historical record supports this interpretation; it also highlights several anomalies. Woman suffrage organizations formed in Montana during the mid 1890s, long after woman suffrage had been introduced in the territory. Similarly, woman suffrage failed during the Populist insurgency in Montana and succeeded in the hands of the Progressives some twenty years later. Finally, while eastern suffragists laid claim to women's role as "civilizer" and "civic housekeeper" by virtue of female moral superiority, their arguments failed to convince the eastern electorate or its representatives. In contrast, the same conservative, sometimes racist and nativist, arguments made sense to Montana voters.

The success of woman suffrage in Montana, therefore, cannot be attributed entirely to the maneuverings of Populist or Progressive politicos or to the general population's realization of women's contributions to settlement or to a designing male electorate's attempts to counter growing immigrant political clout. The best explanation takes into account Helena's pioneer women—and those who followed them—and their role in influencing women's progress toward full citizenship. The circumstances of women's lives on the frontier, especially the region's sex ratio and skewed age structure, dictated the course of the campaigns for woman suffrage, accounted for their early defeats, and finally set the stage for their victory. Central to this process were the differentiated experiences of three generations of Montana women. Each generation contended with the frontier's exigencies in its own manner and with different attitudes and expectations.

Although the frontier modified the elder pioneer mothers' view of themselves and undercut conventional nineteenth century definitions of women's proper sphere, it also created a further modification in the successive generations of frontier daughters. Women of all ages came to believe that the vote validated their civic aspirations and underpinned their personal autonomy. The accumulation of these generations of like-minded women produced sufficient numbers to use persuasion as an effective political tool.

Even as the shift in generational attitudes assisted the cause of suffrage, other women-related factors contributed to its eventual success. The revival of the "cult of true womanhood" set the backdrop for political activism, legitimizing women's forays into the public sphere as municipal housekeepers. In addition, Montana's population shifted from an urban mining to an agricultural base, as homesteading families poured into the state during the early twentieth century, augmenting the state's female population. Above all, however, women's interest in securing the vote precipitated the suffrage movement, and women's life cycles influenced the movement's uneven pattern of activity and quiescence. As the suffrage movement's principal protagonists and beneficiaries, women were the catalysts that welded the disparate elements of reform into a successful campaign for full admission to citizenship. From the beginning, Helena's mothers and daughters were the critical element in this process.

The Revolution, Susan B. Anthony's suffrage weekly, made its first reference to Montana on September 30, 1869. Noting that Mrs. James M. Ashley, wife of Montana's new territorial governor and president of the Toledo, Ohio, woman suffrage club, would shortly join her husband, the paper happily looked forward to hearing of Mrs. Ashley's and the governor's good work. *The Revolution* could not have anticipated the vicissitudes of Montana politics or the problems Emma Ashley would face in Helena. Governor Ashley's tenure in office was a spectacularly brief one, and Emma Ashley failed to rouse much interest in women's rights. On Thanksgiving Day in 1869, she irritated her hostess, Elizabeth Chester Fisk, with her strident advocacy of women's rights. But by February 1870, Elizabeth referred to the declining support of Emma Ashley's cause with satisfaction: "Woman's rights and the like are not so rampant as formerly."[3] At year's end, Emma Ashley had fallen into line with other Helena wives. Coping with the problems of child care and housekeeping—problems that were exacerbated by conditions on the frontier—demanded her attentions just as they did other women's. On one occasion, Elizabeth found Emma sitting in a daze in her partially furnished, unheated house.[4]

Emma Ashley and others sympathetic to the cause, who might have provided leaders and members for the *Revolution*'s prospective suffrage organization, had far too many demands on their time. Between 1870 and 1883, Helena's women were too busy juggling their domestic and work responsibilities to become involved in the cause for women's rights. Most of Helena's wives were young, had small children, and oversaw a household without domestic help. Many single, respectable women worked. Women who plied their trade in the tenderloin had a different concept of women's rights. Helena's adult female population, too, lacked the sheer numbers to sustain any organized political work.[5]

But one organized women's political group was active and played an important role in the woman suffrage movement. The Woman's Christian Temperance Union first introduced woman suffrage as an issue in Montana in 1883 as organizers founded temperance chapters in Helena and other large Montana towns. To give women the means to change their communities, the WCTU necessarily included suffrage in their broad program of social reform. Cast in Victorian rhetoric and consonant with the "cult of true womanhood," the WCTU arguments rationalized women's political participation on the basis of their putative moral superiority, not as a natural right.[6]

Many Helena women joined the WCTU, but mothers who worried about their children's well-being in a city dominated by saloons and tolerant of social vices had special reasons for joining.[7] Women's domestic responsibilities, however, continued to divert their attention and time, thereby limiting the WCTU's effectiveness. The structure of the state organization reflected these problems. In 1887, the organization divided its office of secretary, establishing both recording and corresponding secretary positions, because "the burden was too heavy for the busy housekeeper, as the W.C.T.U. worker usually is."[8]

The WCTU did enroll some members who otherwise might not have supported woman suffrage, and these women pushed the organization toward reforming local conditions that affected families. Consecutive

WCTU conventions endorsed the principle of suffrage, but their agenda aimed specifically at enlisting support for social reforms that were germane to their families' well-being. In the late 1880s, the state WCTU leadership encouraged its membership to elect temperance candidates to school trusteeships and to influence city councils toward curbing hours at saloons and gambling houses.[9] At the 1889 WCTU convention, the membership endorsed the national women's rights and suffrage program, but members were preoccupied with local issues and devoted more discussion and energy to securing the ballot to vote on local liquor licensing.[10] The WCTU had introduced many women to political activism and the suffrage issue, but the concentration of the membership in women of prime child-rearing age and communities' condonation of vice channeled women's interest into local politics at the expense of wider political participation. Curtailing the liquor trade and setting the proper tone in schools became more pressing in light of women's concern with their children's future. Nonetheless, the appearance of the WCTU and its involvement in community affairs underscored the renaissance of the "cult of true womanhood," while it rationalized women's legitimate entry into the public sphere and politics.

Concomitant with the WCTU's initial organizing efforts was the territory's push for statehood. The Montana Constitutional Convention of 1884 raised the issue of equal suffrage but dismissed any further consideration of it on the suffrage committee's curt recommendation that "it was not expedient to grant to women general sufferage [*sic*]."[11] Believing that they had framed a document that more than fulfilled all the requirements for admission to statehood, convention delegates hesitated to tempt the fierce partisanship that governed Congress in 1884. They wanted nothing controversial in the state's constitution, nothing that would justify either political party's denial of Montana's admission to the Union.

The conservative document drawn up by the delegates limited executive power and restricted legislative prerogative. The delegates' caution went for naught, however, for the delicate balance of power between the two major parties ordained Montana's future as a state. A Republican-controlled Senate blocked admission of potentially Democratic states, and the Democratic majority in the House stymied Republican candidates for statehood. This situation prevailed until 1888, when the Republicans won a majority in both houses. In early 1889, the "lame duck" Congress enacted the Omnibus Bill, which welcomed statehood petitions from eligible territories, including Montana.[12] Once again a Constitutional Convention convened in Helena; this time, delegates debated equal suffrage at some length.

The 1889 Constitutional Convention primarily aimed at securing the interests of groups who had prospered under the provisions of the old territorial constitution and who saw no reason to make fundamental changes. Drawing on the 1884 constitution as a model, the delegates fashioned a government that limited executive and legislative authority and maintained the *status quo*. The suffrage question, particularly woman suffrage, arose in the debates over who would be eligible to initiate governmental change. When the delegates discussed political privilege questions, they approached them pragmatically, with the same obdurate functionalism that they had applied to economic issues. They understood that the ballot could be a powerful tool.[13]

In this milieu, some delegates raised the question of equal suffrage, and suffrage advocate Henry Blackwell addressed the convention. Clara and Perry McAdow, Montana suffrage activists, had persuaded Blackwell to stop in Helena during his western tour. Clara McAdow had been successful in real estate in Billings, and she operated the Spotted Horse Mine near Maiden in central Montana. Married and a businesswoman, Clara represented one element of Montana women. She knew that alone she stood little chance of influencing convention delegates, but an articulate advocate such as Henry Blackwell could represent her views before the entire convention. Clara's initiative gave Blackwell and the cause of woman suffrage a golden opportunity. Experienced suffragists knew that approval during a constitutional convention, with its simple majority rule, was more likely than trying a surely more arduous amendment process. Blackwell rightly supposed that Montana's conservative delegates would block outright passage of equal suffrage, so he argued for the next best strategy—keeping the issue alive and trying to convert the delegates to a policy of legislative discretion in the matter.[14]

Suffrage appeared destined for defeat during the first round when a committee debated the issue on July 25, 1889. Legislators of the early 1880s had been willing to contemplate and experiment with suffrage and had thrown school governance open to women, but the over-arching conservatism of convention delegates quickly altered that policy. The suffrage committee recommended that women retain their school voting and board membership privileges, but it divested them of their tax ballot and eligibility for county school superintendency. It also rejected the legislature's discretionary power to enfranchise. The convention as a whole redressed some of the committee's subtractions reinstating the tax ballot and superintendency eligibility, but at the same time it voted down giving women the franchise in municipal and state school superintendency elections. Except for Clara McAdow moving discreetly behind the scenes, women neither spoke in behalf of suffrage nor appeared to take any interest in the proceedings. Clearly, the convention desired to maintain the *status quo* on women's issues, but the real question was one of legislative discretion.[15]

Delegate Walter Bickford exposed the ideological divisions in the convention when he proposed that the legislature be empowered to confer suffrage on women. Not particularly in favor of suffrage himself, Bickford made his proposal in the interests of good government and appealed to progressive delegates who had fewer economic interests to preserve and an idea of government that included flexibility for future exigencies. Bickford, Hiram Knowles, and Joseph K. Toole put their faith in the judgment of the legislature, but others disagreed. While Knowles rightly pointed out that women were entering into all areas of life and that public affairs were a logical end to their endeavors, former territorial delegate Martin Maginnis balked at any legislative modification on woman suffrage. In oratory fraught with oblique references to the "cult of true womanhood" and the doctrine of separate spheres, he contended that government was founded on the principle of force and that women, by their natural limitations, would not support the state's actions during times of conflict. The liberal element, a minority in the convention, lost on Bickford's proposal to the proponents of the Maginnis philosophy, 29 ayes to 34 nays.[16]

Woman suffrage would be achieved only by an amendment to the constitution, a laborious procedure that would require a two-thirds majority approval in both houses and submission to the electorate. Alignments in the Constitutional Convention foreshadowed the future politics of woman suffrage in Montana. Support for suffrage came from delegates living in Montana's nascent, eastern agricultural frontier, while opposition to the measure came from delegates acting for older, western mining communities.[17]

As a new state, Montana immediately disgraced itself. In 1890, the first legislature neglected the state's affairs as partisan quarrels over disputed election results and the selection of U.S. senators consumed the session. In the end, Montana blithely sent four senators to Washington, two Republicans and two Democrats. More bickering over Senate seats in 1893, a political fight over the permanent location of the state capital, and personal enmity among Montana politicians led to spectacular political corruption. The Panic of 1893 and the subsequent depression rocked Montana and aided the Populist party. As Montana's silver miners felt the effects of demonetization of silver and as the state's economy declined, the Populists' star rose. In the aftermath of political corruption and economic adversity, Montana inclined toward reform. The Republicans ousted the Democrats in the 1894 legislative election, while the Populists garnered thirteen seats in the lower chamber and three in the Senate. Two years earlier, Populists had demonstrated their support for women's rights by running Ella Knowles for Attorney General.[18]

The 1895 legislative session promised much for Montana's women. Early in the session, John Huseby, a Populist from Lewis and Clark County, introduced House Bill 46, a proposed constitutional amendment that would give women the ballot on the same basis as men. The bill left committee in modified form—it barred women from law enforcement positions and prohibited them from jury service—and the House passed it with a little over the required two-thirds majority and sent it on to the

Senate. Populist Senator T. W. Brosnan of Cascade County produced several petitions in support of the Senate bill and spoke in its favor. The amendment proposal drew mixed responses throughout the state. The *Butte Miner* observed that the solons were taking the discussions seriously and should consult women. The senators may or may not have polled their disenfranchised constituents, but when the time came they soundly defeated the bill 14 to 4 in a non-roll call vote. After the measure's defeat, several Montana newspapers reproved the senators' action and the *Helena Independent* faulted Governor J. E. Rickards for failing to support the measure. As had earlier observers, the *Independent* also noted that women themselves seemed unsupportive of the suffrage cause. The editor urged women to ready themselves for "a long pull, and a strong pull, and a pull all together. . . ."[19]

The near success of the suffrage bill had impressed the National American Woman Suffrage Association (NAWSA) enough that it sent Emma Smith DeVoe on an organizing tour through Montana. NAWSA originally had intended to send Emma DeVoe to aid the Idaho woman suffrage campaign, but the national organization now saw an additional opportunity in Montana. DeVoe began her tour in Miles City on May 15, 1895, and organized fourteen suffrage clubs in cities and towns along the route of the Northern Pacific Railroad. In June, she founded the Helena chapter of the suffrage association with eighteen members.[20]

The membership of the Helena club and Helena's delegates to the state suffrage convention in September 1895 reflected the changing demography of Helena's female population and disclosed much about women's failure to fulfill the *Revolution*'s rosy expectations of a vital women's rights organization under the aegis of Emma Ashley.[21] A combination of pioneer women and late-arriving reform-minded women, the members shared several characteristics; the women had been politically active and involved in community affairs. Ida F. Rosecrans was the sister-in-law of Joseph K. Toole, lawmaker and future governor.[22] Laura Howey had been active in the WCTU, in school board politics, in poor relief work, and in the state historical society as librarian.[23] Mrs. H. V. Wheeler and Isabel Kirkendall had participated in the Women's Helena for the Capital Club campaign.[24] The Kellogg women's position on women's rights extended to women's reproductive freedom; both were related to Dr. Edwin S. Kellogg, one of Helena's two abortionists. Many also were connected to the male political world. Perhaps the most illustrative of this were the Sanders women: Sarepta Sanders, Harriet Peck Fenn Sanders, Mrs. James Upson Sanders, and Martha Edgerton Plassman. All were linked with Wilbur F. Sanders, one-time U.S. senator, and Sidney D. Edgerton, Montana's first territorial governor.

Sarepta Sanders, Wilbur F. Sanders's sister, shared an eccentric family background with her brother. Both Wilbur and Sarepta found little to admire in their father, an incompetent businessman and religious zealot who, in punishing his children, would set them to reading the Bible. Instead of increasing their religiosity, the forced Bible study had the opposite effect. Wilbur became agnostic, and Sarepta embraced Unitarianism. Alienated from their father, the children turned to their mother. Wilbur's niece wrote of the father's and son's relationship: "They had little in common, and for many years,—perhaps all his life, Wilbur cherished a bitter feeling against this parent, while loving his mother, and having a feeling of positive adoration for Grandmother Edgerton, these two women being an intellectual inspiration for him." Of Sarepta's relationship with her mother, her niece simply wrote: "She fairly worshipped her mother."[25]

Both Sarepta and Wilbur Sanders idolized an unusual woman with an even more unusual name: Freedom Sanders. In the words of her niece, she was

> a remarkable woman. I well remember a visit of hers in our Akron home, when she would lie on the couch in our library, blissfully smoking—not a cigarette, but a meerschaum your father [Wilbur F. Sanders] gave her—and read by the hour, not detective stories or romantic tales, but the speeches of dead and gone statesmen, contained in the Annals of Congress.[26]

In addition to her intellectual predilections, Freedom Sanders also possessed strength of character. Although Wilbur's father held the study of law in contempt, Freedom Sanders argued one entire night that Wilbur be allowed to read law. Sarepta took one of the few courses open to an intellectual woman in her time: she became a teacher. For Harriet Peck Fenn, who married Wilbur F. Sanders, this was a congenial group; she found kindred spirits in both her husband and sister-in-law. Harriet herself moved easily and wisely in political circles; according to Elizabeth Chester Fisk, Harriet helped her husband into the U.S. Senate by being "discreet and politic" in her ways.[27]

Helena's suffragists also had in common a solid, middle-class standing in the community, underpinned by property ownership and money held in their own names.[28] Many of them had spent their young adulthood in Helena and had been active in the town's cultural and benevolent societies from their inception.[29] Augmenting their numbers with women who had arrived in Helena from 1880 to 1883, they had provided the leadership for the community's reform and charitable groups. Through kinship and social ties, they formed a small, cohesive group that had been successful in community work and reform efforts. More significantly, they were part of Helena's growing group of older women. With an average age of nearly fifty, these women no longer faced the responsibilities of child care and the domestic demands of a large household. Their time had become their own.[30]

Still, the suffragists were a small group. Sarepta Sanders summed up the situation:

> We lack workers who are able to make it [suffrage] go . . . those appointed to do the work accept . . . and then stay away. Helena is a society town—the women who are capable are the women who are too busy (they think) to assume a new work—the society woman would not be in sympathy with us, or if she were, would have nothing to add to the interest of the Club.[31]

Sarepta rightly looked to Helena's middle class for support for suffrage, but perhaps too ungenerously she appraised women's ability to follow through on their commitments. Observers perceived a general apathy and inactivity among Montana's women, but the majority of Helena's women were between twenty-one and forty years old and preoccupied with children and household. Nonetheless, one national organizer was so frustrated by the situation that she wrote: "The women of Montana must be an inferior race of beings to take so little interest in their own concerns. . . . I assure you I am very glad that I am a western woman, but not a Montana woman. Nothing would tempt me to live in such a state. . . ."[32]

In June 1896, women in Helena organized a second suffrage organization, the Helena Business Women's Suffrage Club. Significantly different from the town's other club, the new organization's members were younger, an average of forty years old, and unmarried—the married members had no children. The group represented the middle stratum of society and professional accomplishment.[33] Mrs. H. C. Sterling's mother, for example, was Dr. Emma S. Stevenson, a physician. Elinor Walsh's husband, lawyer T. J. Walsh, would distinguish himself as a progressive senator in Washington. Mary C. Wheeler's mother, a Helena pioneer, was a member of the matrons' suffrage organization.[34] The most obvious difference between the two suffrage groups was the businesswomen's commitment to their callings. The businesswomen's club included Dr. Maria F. Dean, a physician; Ella Knowles Haskell, Montana's first female lawyer; Mary C. Wheeler, an artist and teacher; Nina Young, a nurse-administrator; Roena Medini, an actress, singer, and instructor; and Adelaide Staves, an elocutionist and teacher. These women had grown up on the frontier or had chosen to spend their young womanhood there.

Mary C. Wheeler graduated in the first class of Helena High School in 1879. She went on to study art at the Boston Conservatory and later to Paris, where she studied painting under some of the Impressionist masters, including Mary Cassatt. Returning to Helena in the 1880s, Mary became a high school art teacher and eventually head of the department. Originally from Cedar Rapids, Iowa, Adelaide Staves came to Dillon, Montana, after teaching a few years in Iowa. In Dillon, she entertained the town's citizens with recitations and ran for county superintendent of schools. After her defeat at the polls, she returned to Iowa's Cornell College where she received a college degree. By 1896, Adelaide had returned to Montana as an instructor at Montana Wesleyan University in Helena. Adelaide had great expectations. Having saved enough money from her declamations and teaching, she read law with Ella Knowles Haskell from 1899 to 1900.[35]

Besides their devotion to their work and their political interest in suffrage, members of the businesswomen's suffrage group showed flashes of personal independence. Madame Roena Medini, who was deputy clerk of court and a part-time piano instructor, was married to Henry Casedy but she elected to keep her maiden name. Madame Medini was an accomplished singer and author who wrote two books of epic love poems in the style of Tennyson. Ella W. Foote also penned a handsome book of lyrics in various poetic forms. Likewise, Anna Barbour wrote two novels of romance, one of which was set in the world of frontier finance. For Maria Dean, Mary Wheeler, and Nina Young, their association went beyond their club membership; the three women lived together in Maria Dean's house on Benton Avenue until Dean's death in 1919. Other young women in Helena made similar living arrangements. In their work and lifestyles, the businesswomen's club represented the cutting edge of the change in women's lives. By the end of the century, more women would be unmarried and more would be living outside the nuclear family.[36]

The alliance of these two age cohorts and their separate organizations re-invigorated the suffrage activity in Montana. Helena's two suffrage groups remained cordial throughout the summer of 1896, and in August they decided to join forces. In November, the state organization, composed of the local clubs, held its second meeting in Butte. As outgoing president Harriet Sanders delivered the major addresses, laying out the basic tenets of the Montana suffrage movement. Drawing her text from Plato, Abraham Lincoln, and John Adams, she rationalized woman suffrage principally on the basis of natural rights and historical precedent. As she articulated these abstractions, she touched on a new element, one congruent with the ideological turn toward arguing from women's moral superiority taken by the national suffrage organization:

> . . . the state is but an aggregation of individuals and homes, and that whatever elements secure peace, purity, justice, love and harmony in the home will secure the same conditions in the government or state.[37]

Harriet Sanders said it clearly and directly: the ballot made women better mothers, better mothers created better homes and more enlightened offspring, and better homes and educated children improved the nation.

Harriet Sanders also referred to her audience's special experience, the women's kinship in the frontier life:

> It has been the fortune of some of us to be pioneers in Montana in many ways. We have seen the foundtion of the State laid,

> a civilization slowly formed from the rude elements of life. . . . we have marked the change in the social order. Among those none have seemed to us more worthy of our thought and effort, that this [suffrage] which is gradually occupying the minds of the women of Montana.[38]

She also alluded to the diffidence of Montana's women. "We have to confess," she said, "that but for the indifference and thoughtlessness of some of our own sex, we should before this have been granted this right." She urged that suffrage support not only be cultivated among the state's men but also among its women.[39] When the convention elected its new officers, the Helena coalition garnered most of the offices and contributed the new state president, Ella Knowles Haskell.

Haskell, who was no political ingenue, set about organizing an efficient suffrage lobby. Because they had the advantage of living in the state capital, the Helena women shouldered the major part of the burden with the help of suffrage representatives from each county. Haskell had no illusions about the challenge ahead for the lobby. The group's goal was to wrench the issue from the legislature and place it before the electorate. The strategy was "to make a systematic attack upon the strongholds of those who have been so unwary as to betray the fact that they are opposed to it" and to apply constant pressure to refractory legislators.[40]

The fourth Montana legislature met in January 1897, and suffrage became an issue early in the session. Petitions containing about twenty-five hundred signatures in support of suffrage arrived the day before the House committee was to discuss House Bill 37, a proposed constitutional amendment for suffrage introduced by Democrat R. B. Hill of Missoula County. On January 18, 1897, the committee sent the bill to the House, and on February 9 the House entertained debate on the question. Hill made the principal address in support of the bill. Reminiscent of speeches made before the constitutional convention, Hill's appeal shunned suffrage ideology and concentrated on the equity of allowing the state's voters to make the final decision. After a vote to suspend the rules, Ella Knowles Haskell was permitted to speak before the assembly. In her short speech, she reiterated Hill's basic premise and promised innumerable petitions if fairness did not prevail.[41]

Opponents to the suffrage bill argued in a different direction. Instead of speaking to the issue of equitable civil procedure, they hammered at the failings of woman suffrage ideology. In lengthy oratory, they treated their listeners to philosophical treacle and the unalloyed doctrine of separate spheres. Representative George L. Ramsay of Gallatin County regaled his audience with separate spheres dogma from the Bible and history by citing illustrations of women's misuse of power. Departing from the courtesy displayed by his predecessors, Ramsay suggested that suffragists were unbecoming models of womanhood. Dennis Shovelin of Deer Lodge County took up this theme, implying that suffrage work unsexed women and estranged them from their familial duties. Other suffrage opponents mocked women's petitions. Ella Knowles Haskell, who also received floor privileges, pled the cause of political justice and chastised those who sneered at women's petitions. The next day, the suffrage bill went down to defeat, 41 to 27, five votes short of the necessary two-thirds majority. A small minority in the House had prevented suffrage from going before the electorate.[42]

The debate and vote in the 1897 session revealed a subtle shift in the sources of support for suffrage and indicated, perhaps, a reason for its defeat. Support now came from the urban areas of western Montana, the strongholds of Populism, Socialism, and unionism that were friendly to women's rights.[43] But it was clear that something more than partisanship, ideology, or geography accounted for the bill's demise. Increasingly, the legislature was composed of frontier parvenus, men who had experienced Montana's settlement in its mature urban development and who had little knowledge of what women had contributed and accomplished.[44] Women who were veterans of the mining camp frontier were confronting men who did not share women's perception of their sex's capabilities or achievements.

In November 1897, heartened by their strong showing, the Montana suffragists convened in Helena for their third annual convention and began to prepare for the next session of the legislature. The convention's speakers still stood on natural rights as the best rationale for suffrage but leaned toward women's special moral capabilities as a particular incentive for giving the ballot to women. The delegates even felt pluckish enough to invite Populist Governor Robert B. Smith to give account of himself before the convention. Smith had omitted mention of woman suffrage in his inaugural speech, even though suffrage was part of the Populist platform. Understandably, convention delegates wanted to know where Smith stood. What they received was a fine show of tepid support.[45]

The Reverend Carleton F. Brown, a Unitarian minister and husband of one of Helena's leading suffragists, sounded a frankly radical note at the convention when he attacked male chivalry. Brown saw male etiquette as simple patronization that obscured the unequal social relations between the sexes:

> They [women] will see that it is false chivalry which implies condescension of superiors to inferiors. Women will cast aside angrily compliment and flattery and ask for simple equality. The soul of womanhood will dare to think, speak, and act independently.[46]

The delegates adopted a more moderate position than Brown's, one that frankly attributed special virtues to women. Montana women had firmly compromised their natural rights argument and had given themselves over to a modified version of separate spheres. The convention elected its state officers primarily from Helena and Butte, its suffrage bastions, but new faces from cities far east of the Continental Divide also made their appearances.[47] Roena Medini, a member of the Helena businesswomen's group, was elected to the presidency, but she resigned halfway through the year and Dr. Mary Atwater took up the organization's leadership.

Medini's resignation and the 1897 suffrage convention signaled a major realignment in the movement's leadership and membership. The earlier suffrage standard-bearers were growing older and could no longer meet the demands of lobbying. Harriet Sanders, for example, was too ill to attend the convention in 1897 and sent her speech to be read *in absentia*.[48] As one cohort aged, the younger cohort weakened. In the wake of Montana's general economic decline, middle-class businessmen and professionals were leaving the state, taking their politically active wives with them. Near the turn of the century, both dominant groups of Montana's suffrage movement were in disarray, but there were signs of order. More women with the honorific title of "Miss" joined the suffrage rank-and-file. Many of the new members were professionals or working women, and those who were married were young. Suffrage advocacy was passing from one generation to another, from one kind of woman to another, and from one region of the state to another.

The period of transition affected women's efforts in the next legislative sessions. When the legislature convened in 1899, the election of a U.S. senator once again overshadowed all else. W. A. Clark, a Butte copper magnate, finally attained the honor he had so long coveted, but at the cost of bribery and political corruption. Clark went to Washington, D.C., but the U.S. Senate refused to seat him, citing bribery and election irregularities as reasons. The legislature, controlled by an uneasy alliance of Populists and Democrats and distracted by the Clark affair, evinced no interest in major political reforms.[49] In this atmosphere, women mounted their third effort to secure suffrage.

As might be expected, the 1899 bid for suffrage failed. Introduced by J. R. Toole of Deer Lodge County, the bill attached property and legal qualifications to women's eligibility as voters. Women had to own $100 worth of property and be free of any felony convictions to be eligible for the franchise. Neither supporters nor opponents showed much enthusiasm for this mongrel bill, and it went down to quick and easy defeat—ten favoring the measure and forty-nine opposing it. Disorganization among suffrage adherents also contributed to the bill's demise. Helena suffrage club members disagreed about affiliation with the national group; a pervasive general apathy prevailed in the few meetings held in preparation for the session; and they made no concrete plans for the upcoming session. In contrast to the activity of 1895-1897, the future of suffrage looked bleak in 1900.[50]

The Helena Business Women's Suffrage Club reorganized as the Helena Equal Suffrage Club in late 1899, but woman suffrage continued to languish in Montana. In 1901, Adelaide Staves shepherded a half-hearted bill through committee only to see it lost in the shuffle as the House passed control to a steering committee in the interests of expedience. In 1902, NAWSA again took an interest in Montana and sent Carrie Chapman Catt, Gail McLaughlin, and Laura Gregg to drum up support for suffrage, to rejuvenate defunct clubs, and to organize new ones. They called a mass meeting in Butte, which was significant in confirming earlier trends that had been developing within Montana's suffrage movement.[51]

By 1900, Helena had lost one-quarter of its population and was in decline. In contrast, Butte was growing concomitantly with the increased production of its copper mines. With a population nearly double that of Helena, Butte showed promise of continued growth and health. Because of its unionism, Butte remained the center of Populist and Socialist sentiment, and women's clubs, another seedbed of suffrage, abounded. Butte's opportunities attracted men and also women, such as Sarepta Sanders and Ella Knowles Haskell.[52] The transferral of suffrage leadership away from Helena denoted the general diffusion of suffrage support throughout the state.

The suffrage assembly in 1902 marked the abandonment of natural rights as the chief argument for suffrage and the surrender to the argument of women's special moral virtue. In one way or another, assembly speakers appealed to nativist sympathies in their audience by pointing out that woman suffrage would offset the political advantage of undependable, ignorant, immigrant men, would improve the quality of politics, and would preserve American values. One suffrage writer carried this argument to the extreme and attributed to women the potential for political salvation. "Now, it is woman, only woman," she wrote, who "can rescue poor, indiscreet, and misguided man and lift him to the height above the seething, rotten conditions into which he has got himself."[53] What had begun as a straightforward philosophical position had been reduced to political efficacy. Montana's women fell back on the Victorian concept of woman possessed of special virtue, heightened it to moral superiority, and applied it to the public realm.

Commingled with these conservative rationales was a new, although muted, development. In her work among the unions, Gail McLaughlin had been remarkably successful in securing endorsements for the suffrage cause. During the 1902 meeting, the theme of the working woman made its first appearance, reflecting the increased number of women in the work force. Women needed the ballot to make their presence felt in the workplace and in the legislature.[54]

Despite the legislature's nascent progressivism and Governor Joseph K. Toole's avowed support, the suffrage bill in 1903 went down to defeat in both chambers—38 to 27 in the House and 16 to 10 in the Senate. Although many suffrage supporters had testified and attended the debates, a small minority continued to block the amendment's passage. Despite the legislators' numerous objections to the simultaneous submission of suffrage with other amendments, the measure narrowly failed and finally died on reconsideration.[55]

In 1905, a suffrage bill was again introduced in the House, and once again, in the face of widespread interest and support, the bill failed. Petitions backing the measure revealed the sources of suffrage support: Helena's pioneer women were among the first signers. Mrs. Jacob Switzer, Margaret Pyle, Mrs. John Horsky, Mrs. M. E. Tracy, and others added their names to the ranks of young women. The young signers had either been born in Montana or in the West or they had spent their young womanhood there. On the average, they were thirty-five years old, all born around 1870. The petitioners, in short, represented the same groups as Elizabeth Chester Fisk and her daughter, Grace—the pioneer mothers and the frontier daughters.[56]

After the 1905 effort, woman suffrage lay dormant. Perhaps because of the general economic decline between 1907 and 1909, women did not disturb the solons with suffrage bills. If the legislature had been diverted by the infighting of the copper barons in earlier sessions, copper corporate interests absorbed them after the turn of the century. Yet, even as Amalgamated Copper schemed to gain control of the Butte hill, developments of a different kind were occurring in eastern Montana.[57]

Most of Montana's population in its first half-century resided in the western part of the state. But improved dry-land farming techniques and promotion by the railroads invited settlement on Montana's arid eastern plains. Amendation of the original homestead act materially assisted this settlement. Formerly, settlers' claims had been limited to 160 acres, parcels too small for dry-land agricultural techniques. The Enlarged Homestead Act of 1909 offered 340 acres to those who could "prove up." Many families migrated west to take up farms, lured by a Milwaukee Railroad poster in which gold dollars sprang from a freshly turned plow furrow. The result was a dramatic increase in Montana's eastern, rural population and an accompanying shift in the state's economy toward agriculture. These new arrivals were hardly raw immigrants; they were young veterans of successive, earlier migrations, and they possessed some capital. Unlike the earlier predominantly male emigrants to the mining frontier, these new settlers arrived in family groups; like their predecessors in western Montana, they replicated the age profile of the mining frontier and recreated a new frontier environment. This new frontier would affect the progress of women's rights in Montana.[58]

In 1911, agitation for woman suffrage in Montana renewed. Kindled by the passage of suffrage in Washington state in 1910, the issue was revived in Montana by Jeannette Rankin, a veteran of the Washington campaign. In Rankin, Montana's suffrage cause found a new champion. In February 1911, a few months after the Washington victory, Rankin addressed the Montana House, sharing the platform with Dr. Maria M. Dean, Dr. Mary Atwater, and Mary Alderson, seasoned members of previous legislative campaigns. Few of the suffrage movement's senior members remained. Ella Knowles Haskell had died a few days before on January 28, 1911, and Harriet P. Sanders had died on September 23, 1909. Laura Howey, active in both the WCTU and the suffrage movement, would die in September 1911.[59] The suffrage cause had passed successfully to the next age cohort.

Born in 1880, Rankin spent her childhood and young womanhood in Missoula, Montana. Coming from a family of some means, she attended the University of Montana, graduating in 1902. Her college course had hardly inspired her, and like many young women of her class at the turn of the century she found herself without direction. After several years of experimentation, which included advanced study at the New York School of Philanthropy, a flurry of social work in Missoula, and a brief sojourn at the University of Washington, she found her vocation in politics.[60]

In Rankin were gathered all those qualities that set Montana's new women apart and some qualities that contributed to her political effectiveness. The frontier population had always been affected by the force of personality, and Rankin possessed a winning combination of physical attractiveness and persuasive reason. She managed to keep her femininity and assertiveness in careful balance. When she opened her address before the legislature in 1911 with the statement that she had been born in Montana, the assembly applauded loudly. She also belonged to a large group of women who were unmarried, frontier-bred, and working. Rankin's support would not only come from her own age group but also from the petition-signers of 1905, an older group with similar experiences. Despite Rankin's efforts, woman suffrage was defeated in 1911, with the House voting down the bill by 33 for and 30 against. Nevertheless, the women were encouraged; the legislative debate and the vote indicated a renaissance in the woman suffrage movement. The vote also demonstrated a geographical shift in suffrage support, which was now anchored in the predominantly rural, eastern counties. Montana's older, urban, mining communities had grown less supportive of women's admission to citizenship.[61]

Buoyed by their success on such short notice, suffragists looked forward to having better luck in the next session. They were aided by the new mood of progressivism that was overtaking the state. At the urging of Rankin and her band of loyal followers, both major parties made suffrage part of their platforms. In 1912, voters swept Democrats into office, mandated approval of all four progressive ballot initiatives, and warned the legislature that the electorate would tolerate no political shenanigans. Democratic politicos were expected to make good their campaign promises. They did. Woman suffrage glided easily through the legislature: 26 ayes and 2 noes in the Senate and 74 for and 2 against in the House. The voters would have their first opportunity to accept or reject the amendment in 1914.[62]

In February 1914, Rankin officially opened the headquarters of the Montana Equal Suffrage Association in Butte. She had learned several political stratagems in doing her suffrage work in other states: keep suffrage a single issue, keep the ballot wording non-specific, and organize the state at the precinct level. Rankin followed these precepts throughout the campaign. In concrete terms, it meant that suffrage had to disassociate itself from temperance. For some, like Mary Alderson, this strategy was a cruel blow; temperance groups had kept the suffrage lamps burning, however dimly. Nonetheless, the WCTU kept its counsel and worked its own campaign for both suffrage and prohibition. Both groups were politically canny enough to keep the rift quiet.[63]

Montana suffrage campaigners walked the thin ideological line between playing to the voters' fear of un-American encroachments on their lives and courting the non-American element, especially the heavily immigrant labor groups in Butte and Anaconda. On the one hand, suffragists pointed out how woman suffrage would counter the growing political clout of foreign-born men; on the other hand, suffrage partisans promised the immigrant electorate that woman suffrage would augment its power. Whatever their audience, suffragists framed their case accordingly. The old arguments of women's moral superiority and the special need for women in public affairs, however, still held sway and were effective.[64] Suffragists won a narrow victory at the polls—41,302 for and 37,558 against. Lewis and Clark County, the early stronghold of woman suffrage in Montana, could only muster 47 per cent of its vote in support of suffrage. The agricultural counties of eastern Montana and the mixed-economy counties of the far northeastern corner of the state provided the necessary majority to the amendment, balancing the losses incurred in older, urban mining counties.[65] Eastern Montana residents had a constellation of reasons for increasing the electorate, not the least of which was the prospect of redrawing the boundaries of existing counties to create new ones. Establishing a new county seat would not only move governmental offices closer to a scattered, rural population and prove attractive to businesses allied with agriculture but the proximity of a county seat would also bring public health and welfare services nearer to women. For both eastern Montana men and women, passage of woman suffrage promised material gains. More striking than the geographical support for woman suffrage, however, was its timing. From start to finish—from 1895 to 1914—the suffrage movement had taken nearly twenty years to triumph, the span of a generation.

The fortunes of woman suffrage in Montana were tied to the vicissitudes of the state's politics. Populism and Progressivism aided the suffrage cause, and the internal wrangling over national appointments hindered enactment of popular reforms, suffrage among them. At these times, legislators not only neglected consideration of reform but also left normal state business unattended. Nonetheless, these political movements were not the decisive factor in the winning of suffrage, nor was partisanship responsible for woman suffrage's successive defeats. The most that can be said is that a small minority of the legislature, whose membership changed from battle to battle, successfully blocked submission of the suffrage question to the electorate and that, in the final years, suffrage garnered its support from the eastern part of the state. Political reform movements of political parties, therefore, cannot entirely account for the course of woman suffrage. More important than external forces were the participants in the suffrage movement—the women themselves.

The idea of women's rights was not new in 1864, when the discovery party stumbled into Last Chance Gulch, and it was certainly an old issue by 1890. But women as suffrage activists did not make their appearance in Helena until 1895. Certainly, Helena harbored women's rights supporters. There were women like Emma Ashley who arrived in Helena with experience in the suffrage campaign and those like the Sanders women who inclined toward feminism. Yet, nothing happened for thirty years. The reasons for women's early indifference to suffrage lay in the peculiar demography of Helena's female population, in the fluctuating responsibilities inherent in the cycles of their lives, and in their attention to local reform issues.

At the outset, there were few women in Helena, most of whom were married and raising children. Most of those, unencumbered by familial responsibilities, engaged in what they came to do—make money. The rigors of urban, frontier life, moreover, soon overwhelmed women who had sympathy for the suffrage cause. Frontier society also made local reform and organization a more immediate concern than national, more abstract issues. Women's familial and local civic responsibilities occupied them until the early 1890s, affecting women's lives much as they had during the 1870s.

By 1895, Helena had aged and so had its women. The first suffrage group, composed of women whose mean age was fifty and whose preoccupation with children and household had ended, took up the cause when they were free to do so. Born between 1840 and 1850, this cohort marked the succession of Helena's first generation of grandmothers. This group of women, which included Harriet P. Sanders and Elizabeth Fisk, was reinforced by a second group, who were members of the Helena Business Women's Suffrage Club. Born between 1850 and 1860, this younger cohort facilitated the transfer of suffrage leadership to the second suffrage wave and sustained it between 1899 and 1911. This group of mostly professional, single women or independent, married women, represented frontier women who had not taken the long detour into the home and women for whom the frontier held out the promise of increased opportunity. Moreover, as the rhetoric of the woman suffrage movement changed from natural rights to an appeal to recognition of women as "civilizers," the male electorate had ample evidence at close quarters to sustain women's claim. In a world of metropolitan towns and urban villages, women had promoted culture in Montana's mining communities and entrepôt centers, had helped meet the needs of the less fortunate residents, and had attempted to uplift the moral life of the communities by establishing schools, churches, and benevolent organizations.

Born between 1870 and 1880, the next cohort marked the generation point. This company included Grace Fisk and the majority of the frontier daughters and the young signers of the petition in 1905. Unlike the cohort before them, these women were married and had small children; but like the preceding group, they possessed some work experience and an interest in broader social issues. After the fashion of their mothers, the Sanders' generation, they remained at home, and their chief expression of support for suffrage came through their petition signatures. The cohort born between 1880 and 1890, which included Jeannette Rankin, provided the leaders and foot soldiers of the suffrage movement; they took up the suffrage standard and moved onward.

By 1914, the Sanders'generation had all but passed away. Grace Fisk's generation was entering into its post-child-rearing years, and the Rankin cohort was composed of numbers of young women, both married and unmarried, who had been born on the mining frontier and who included work outside the home as part of their life experience. For the first time, as generation joined with generation, women with a shared frontier experience were present in numbers enough to claim the political badge of equal citizenship.

CHAPTER SIX

No Step Backward

IN 1879, THE FIRST GRADUATING CLASS of Helena High School—Ann Warfield, Mary C. Wheeler, and Ida Wilson—chose for their class motto, "No step backward." The reasons for their choice went unrecorded, but some glimmering of their thinking and the extent to which they had adopted the values of their frontier society appeared in their commencement addresses. Influenced by Ralph Waldo Emerson, Ann Warfield took as her theme "self-reliance" and applied its principles to women. Ann was aware that women learned self-reliance through experience and that a lack of self-reliance contributed to women's dependence. Mary C. Wheeler, feminist, suffragist, and future student of Mary Cassatt, spoke on a favorite nineteenth century topic: progress. Like many Helena boosters, Mary had been captivated by the idea of infinitely forward social movement and betterment; she embellished this commonplace idea by adding the improvement of women's status. Ida Wilson, another proto-feminist, in a stock piece of valedictory oratory, "Twenty Years Hence," predicted female lawyers, the arrival of the railroad, and the stabilization of the community. Not far off the mark, Ida predicted that Montana would furnish the first female president of the United States.[1]

Interwoven with adolescent optimism and naiveté were themes common to other women's lives. Ann Warfield's piece echoed the theme of self-reliance in Elizabeth Chester Fisk's letters, and Ida Wilson imagined Ella Knowles's admission to the bar and Jeannette Rankin's political victory. Mary Wheeler spoke of women's involvement in public and community service, another theme that ran through the lives of the pioneer mothers and frontier daughters. Common to the three graduates was a vision of womanhood that combined elements of traditional nineteenth century "true womanhood" and values more commonly associated with masculine society—independence, work, and participation in public life. As they alluded to their own growth in Helena, they implied that their environment had provided experiences and opportunities that had altered their perspective on nineteenth century womanhood; the frontier had shaped a new vision of what was necessary and possible for women.

From the vantage point of 1900, a review of Helena's first thirty-five years delineates the relationship between the mining frontier and its women and lends credence to the speakers' perceptions. The effect of the frontier on women was neither startling nor abrupt; it did not occur during an overland journey or a riverboat trip up the Missouri. Instead, it varied from one class of women to another over decades and generations. The frontier was an enduring, not an ephemeral, condition. In Helena's case, the failure of the city to incorporate, its relative isolation, and the persistence of its peculiar demography testify to the durability of frontier conditions and suggest an environment redolent with the possibilities for change.

From the outset, the possibilities for change in women's status inhered in the town's demography. In 1870, the family was a minority institution, representing 44 per cent of the population; by 1880, when families constituted 61 per cent of the population, a sizable minority of the general population lived outside the purview and control of the family and its captains, women. The concentration of women between twenty-one and forty years old, the prime childbearing years, assured that Helena women would spend their time devoted to household maintenance and child care. The lack of domestic servants intensified women's confinement to the home and their domestic responsibilities; prospective domestics found more lucrative opportunities or chances to create homes of their own. Finally, Helena was unequivocally a man's world, and the institutions fostered in Helena were geared to men's social and economic activities, leaving little space for women's traditional nineteenth century endeavors. For middling women who primarily experienced the frontier through the family, the frontier embodied values antithetical to those defined by their girlhood homes. Instead of the town hall or home or church, the saloon was the locus of most social interaction for men, the majority of the population, until the turn of the century.

Helena's isolation also affected women's lives, throwing women back on themselves and their own resources. Their husbands' long absences guaranteed that women would have sole charge not only of their households but also of their husbands' business affairs and, in some cases, enterprises. Out of this experience, Helena women developed a sense of their own capabilities and self-worth. These circumstances also encouraged an ideology that competed with the "cult of true womanhood," the cornerstones of which were selflessness, dependency, and self-sacrifice.

The frontier, moreover, eroded the "cult of true womanhood" by undermining the traditional centers of female influence and strength: churches and informal female networks. In making accommodations to frontier society, churches had promoted dancing, raffles, and fetes—activities inimical to serious-minded church-goers—and had fallen prey to internal bickering. The transiency of the frontier population constantly reformed women's social groups, truncated women's friendships, and finally sent women reeling back into the only stable institution in an unsettled world, their homes. Often left to manage by themselves, bereft of domestic help and the society and assistance of other women, middling women endured unmitigated domesticity. As a result, they nurtured a vague criticism of their roles as wives and mothers.

Also between 1880 and 1890, the children of the middle-class matured, and middle-class mothers perceived that the homes they had fashioned as havens from an immoral world were not as impregnable as they had imagined. Outside women's homes, the frontier threatened to corrupt their children and to disrupt orderly social reproduction. Social institutions—schools and churches—that normally helped bear the family's burden of inculcating the young with a common set of values were weak, unorganized structures that accommodated themselves to a new society. Consequently, families became the last line of defense in a hostile, tolerant, worldly society. Under siege, the family's role was exaggerated and women's sense of their own importance as household guardians increased proportionally. Realizing that safeguarding the home was insufficient to protect their children, middling women bent their energies toward reforming the society around them. In this, they were aided by the renaissance of the "cult of true womanhood" in a new form.

Coincident with Helena women's attention to the socialization of their children was the transformation of the community's population with the advent of the railroad. Among other things, Helena's newcomers brought a renewed dedication to the "cult of true womanhood." A sizable group of Helena women, pioneer and *arriviste* alike, now at an age that freed them from unrelieved supervision of children and encouraged by sufficient numbers, sought to reinstate the "cult of true womanhood" both in public affairs and in private life. Some women were content with the outward trappings of "true womanhood" and settled on etiquette, fashion, and smartness to demonstrate genteel womanhood; other women, under the umbrella of local organizations and national reform movements such as the WCTU, emphasized community reform. But in reinstating "true womanhood" the latter group refurbished it to their own taste. Women retained prescriptions from the old ideology that were useful and were sources of power: women's moral superiority, an inclination toward collectivity, household superintendency, and socialization of their offspring. To this streamlined version of the "cult of true womanhood" women grafted individuality, self-reliance, and economic and personal independence.

These changes brought an important result: an effective reordering of the social relationships between the sexes. That reordering was best exemplified by the alterations in domestic law. By 1895, the state civil code regarding divorce favored women's marital expectations by outlining men's obligations in several important clauses. The changes stacked the marital deck for women. Women's long detour into the home, their resurrection of the "cult of true womanhood," and the resulting public activism had also brought them to a critical chronological and political pass. During the same years, they contemplated significant social reform for themselves and their daughters by initiating the drive for the ballot, an ultimately successful effort carried to fruition by succeeding generations.

Despite the best efforts of Helena's middling women, the frontier maintained its hold on the community and conditioned the lives of its daughters. Helena's second generation did not have to shift from one perspective to another; Helena's society was the only one they had known, and it was markedly different from the one their mothers had experienced as girls. The second generation grew up in a world suffused with masculine values and models. As children, these girls were accustomed to receiving men's attentions and praise, and in their adolescence they were surrounded by examples of male independence and individualism. As a result, Helena's daughters assimilated, to some degree, the values of the dominant group in their society.

Besides these male models, Helena's daughters were also provided with examples of women who belied the cultural female images that arrived in monthly issues of *Ladies Home Journal* and *Godey's Lady's Book*. Their mothers managed in their fathers' absences, and working women were sprinkled throughout the strata of Helena's work force. Helena's daughters and granddaughters developed, as one of the 1879 Helena High School graduates called it, self-reliance, and this all-encompassing term marked their adulthood. More of the pioneers' daughters elected to remain single and more evidenced a commitment to work outside the home. Those who followed in their mothers' footsteps by marrying and bearing children took pains before marriage to establish a separate identity, no matter how tenuous. More telling, the daughters showed impatience with the prescribed gender roles by divorcing more often than their mothers and their counterparts in other regions. Where their mothers had endured, the next generation refused. In sum, the orderly socialization of young women on the frontier suffered a dislocation, resulting in the creation of a generation of women who differed from their mothers in several respects and who shared, to a much lesser extent, an orientation to a revised "true womanhood."

While the majority of women on the frontier operated within the family structure, a significant minority did not. The largest group among Helena's working women were the town's fancy ladies, who in one sense dramatized frontier economic opportunity. During the city's early years, they were able to capitalize on the frontier's peculiar demography and become entrepreneurs. By the same token, the end of Helena's boom period signaled their demise. Despite their physical and social separation from the town's respectable women, Helena's soiled doves served a variety of functions and affected the lives of their virtuous counterparts. First, Helena's prostitutes helped control the single-male population by providing social and sexual entertainments. Second, in doing so, they effectively marked off the boundaries of women's social space. Because "bad" women were confined to a particular neighborhood, the rest of the public sphere was thrown open to other women. And third, the Wood Street regulars provided Helena's better sort with ever-present examples of the antithesis of the nineteenth century concept of women as morally superior beings and with a reminder that the vices of the community appealed to illicit male pleasures. In tacit recognition of this darker side of female nature, women like Elizabeth Fisk concentrated on safeguarding their sons from temptations of the flesh and allied vices. In turning their attention so fully to their sons, these mothers overlooked factors that might influence their daughters to think differently about their roles. Away from the full force of their mothers' moral scrutiny, daughters like Grace Fisk escaped full indoctrination in "true womanhood" and, as a result, fashioned a new womanhood for themselves.

The twentieth century does not remember the frontier's other working women so well as it remembers its sporting women, but these less flamboyant workers played their part. Helena's service economy increased the demand for women's domestic skills. Once women had a toehold in the marketplace, they remained there, parlaying their service skills into other channels. Helena's respectable working women made the combination of women and work an acceptable phenomenon and laid the foundations for women's work, marking not merely a stage in the female life cycle but the entire life of a woman.

Helena's wives were not left out of the economic scramble. As many women's historians have demonstrated, women's realization of economic opportunity has not been wholly limited to wage earning nor is it as obvious as a census label. While historians have painstakingly described and cataloged informal, elementary economic transactions, they have not explored the more sophisticated means to profit: manipulation of capital, patterns of investment, or property ownership. Women's experience in Helena suggests that the urban frontier provided economic opportunities for middle-class, married women and that women took advantage of these opportunities in a manner not normally included in women's work. While city lots and mortgages may have lacked the stereotypical association with landownership, they provided the potential for considerable profit and power. Helena women who did not leave their homes brought the marketplace into their parlors, manipulating real estate investments and helping the next generations to acquire their homes. In a national environment that was generally inimical to women's employment, women were able to enter the work force, applying their domestic skills and profiting accordingly. Similarly, women's conception of themselves pushed the courts to new interpretations of the law. As generation joined with generation, women were also able to realize their political aspirations.

Despite women's legal, economic, and political achievements, it is also clear that Frederick Jackson Turner's detractors are correct in their arguments that the frontier intensified the negative aspects of nineteenth century domesticity and the inequity of the social relationships between the sexes. Certainly Elizabeth Fisk's letters home lend credence to this conclusion. They also substantiate the Stasists' claims for the general continuity of nineteenth century ideology from coast to coast, from settlement to frontier, at least for the duration of the overland journey. But Elizabeth's correspondence and the lives of her peers also illustrate outcomes other than women's spiritual and physical debilitation and the geographical persistence of "true womanhood." Just as Turner and his early partisans asserted, the frontier opened wider avenues and provided greater political and economic opportunities for Helena's women, and the preponderance of evidence from Helena weighs in favor of the Turnerians' contentions. By shifting the focus of Turner's interpretation toward women and testing the validity of his thesis in terms of women's experience, the Turner thesis takes on new explanatory vitality—in part.

While the scenario set forth here in a sense embraces Turner's arguments for an extension of personal and public democracy, it ignores utterly his points about national character, frontier types, an order of settlement, and the vanishing frontier, except as the frontier prostitutes' control of their enterprise coincided with Turner's end of the frontier. The most helpful components of Turner's frontier still remain: "its focus on the history of how human beings have interacted with the American landscape; its ability to relate local and regional history to the wider history of the nation; its interdisciplinary focus; and, not least, its commitment to putting ordinary people at the center of the story."[2] The chronicle of Helena's women augments this masterful summation of the Turner thesis by adding not only the human response to the landscape but also humans' responses to one another. In other words, the study of Helena's women suggests the ways in which men and women, daughters and mothers spoke to one another out of their experience with a landscape. To speak about relations with a landscape was (and is) simply not enough; the human geography made a difference, at least in the nineteenth and early twentieth centuries.

Yet, one final piece of evidence from the twentieth century argues for this neo-Turnerian revision. One historian, re-examining a Roper poll taken in 1943, shows that western women between the ages of twenty and thirty-five were better educated, evinced greater excitement and optimism about their futures, demonstrated a greater openness to change, and advocated equal moral standards for men and women more than their eastern, midwestern, and southern counterparts. "On the personal morality scale" (that is, questions aimed primarily at gauging the sexual expectations of both men and women), the researcher concluded, "*there was a western regional effect* on top of, or apart from, education alone."[3] Hence, although education was the best predictor of post-war attitudes, those questions most closely associated with equity between men and women showed a definite regional bias. As far as thinking about the relationships between men and women was concerned, westerners were the wave of the future. A subset analysis comparing Mountain states women to their Pacific states counterparts, moreover, revealed an interesting attitudinal emphasis. Besides being better educated and anti-union, the Mountain states women believed that a large number of both men and women were unfaithful to their wedding vows, alluding perhaps to the frequency of adultery in Helena's divorce proceedings.[4]

The world of Rosie the Riveter might seem far removed from both today's society and nineteenth century Helena, but the link connecting the two is neither tenuous nor strained. The women of the Roper poll were the granddaughters or great-granddaughters of the Elizabeth Fisks of the frontier. Their answers reflect themes common to the generations of pioneer mothers and daughters and mark *leitmotifs* in the Helena High School commencement addresses made more than a half-century before.

In the valedictories of 1879, the young graduates did not imagine the alternative routes, sidesteps, and detours that would consume women's energies before women would prove Ida Wilson's foretelling. The young women, filled with the freshness of educational accomplishment and great expectations, did not conceive of the time that would elapse, the generations to be dedicated to changing women's status in Montana. Not merely commencement rhetoric, the class of 1879 wrote out of their lives on the frontier and described the essence of that experience as opportunity, individual self-fulfillment, optimistic expectation, and advancement for themselves as women. Unwittingly, they summed up women's experience on the mining frontier and heralded attitudes espoused by their twentieth century western sisters. As they made their farewell, the woman graduates anticipated the result of women's frontier experience and greeted their womanhood, promising "no step backward." They and the generations of western women who followed them made good on their words.

Appendices

1. Research Methodology
2. Statistical Tables
3. Property Owned by Helena Prostitutes, 1870-1890

APPENDIX ONE

Research Methodology

THE QUANTITATIVE INFORMATION in the appendices is based on statistics derived from an analysis of the total population of Helena, Montana, taken from the *U.S. Census* for 1870, 1880, and 1900. Considerations of sampling techniques, therefore, do not apply.

At the initial stage, ten variables were coded

Household	Numeric
Family	Numeric
Name	Alphabetic
Race/Sex	Alphabetic
Age	Numeric
Household Relationship	Alphabetic
Marital Status	Alphabetic
Occupation	Alphabetic
Geographical Origin	Alphabetic

For the 1870 census, an additional variable, Wealth, was coded, as that enumeration made the value of property and personal wealth a category. The 1870 census did not include Marital Status; hence, marital status and other household relationships were inferred. If a man and woman had similar surnames and were relatively the same age, they were coded as "married" and as "husband" or "wife." Children listed in the same household were given the appropriate label. In some instances, it was possible to discern other relationships. Similarity in male surnames and ages suggested they were brothers, and elder men and women in a household intimated that they were grandparents. From the inclusion of maiden names, it was often possible to isolate a sister. These relationships were coded under the term "relative." Those with no discernible relationship to any family member were coded as boarders. Failure to come to terms with these household members would have resulted in the gross underestimation of extended family groupings and an overestimation of boarders.

In the 1880 and the 1900 censuses, an additional variable, Presence or Absence of Spouse, was added. There were a number of male and female household heads listed as married whose spouses were not in evidence. In view of information gleaned from a cursory examination of the manuscript sources, it seemed appropriate to determine the number of spouses who were left to manage by themselves. The 1900 census included the category of Household Ownership and Rental, which was included in the variable list for that data set. The second stage of data analysis produced three additional variables: Household Type, Number of Servants, and Number of Boarders.

Helena's residents arranged themselves in households in a variety of ways: these arrangements were compressed into nine broad classifications under Household Type. A *nuclear family* was composed of a husband and wife with or without children or a household head of either sex with children. An *extended family* comprised a nuclear family with any additional relative. A *two-family household* was defined as any combination of the nuclear and extended types occupying the same dwelling. These three categories composed a larger class of "familial" households. A *wholly male household* was composed of two or more men; similarly, a *wholly female household* contained only women. *Solitary female* and *solitary male* groups were simply men or women living alone. A *sexually mixed household* was defined as men and women living together who had no discernible marital or familial relationship. Finally, there was a small category of *institutional households*, which included jails, hospitals, and boarding schools. These six groupings constituted a larger class of "non-familial" households.

Occupational tables were adapted from those divisions laid out by Stephen Thernstrom in *The Other Bostonians: Poverty and Progress in the American Metropolis, 1880-1970* (Cambridge, Massachusetts: Harvard University Press, 1923). This facilitated comparison with another nineteenth century city and provided the initial framework for an occupational structure. Some occupations were unique to Helena, and the appropriate categories were expanded to accommodate such oddities as bullwhacker and whip braider. Two problems immediately became apparent: how to separate the petty shopkeepers from the major proprietors and how to classify correctly a large number of the city's population who were listed simply as "miner." The first problem was solved by linking those who advertised in the city directories and those for whom wealth could be definitely established via bank records. Advertisers and those with documented wealth (over $5,000 in property or $2,000 in cash) were assigned to the major-proprietor category; the others fell into the petty-proprietor group.

The second problem was more difficult. The census taker seldom differentiated skill levels among miners. For lack of a better expedient, the general level of mining development in the Helena area determined a wholesale definition. Because most mining in 1870 was still at the placer level—which required little more than simple machinery, strong bodies, and a watchful eye—miners in 1870, unless the census specified otherwise, were lumped into the category of semiskilled labor. The presence of a large number of Chinese miners in Helena during this period also supports this decision, because the Chinese normally worked the tailings with the simple tools of surface mining. By 1880, however, the nature of mining had changed. Surface ore deposits had been depleted, and it became necessary to employ more complex methods to extract silver ore and replacement gold deposits. Quartz mining techniques and deep-shaft operations replaced simpler methods and necessitated a variety of skills. In this light, unless otherwise indicated, miners listed in the 1880 and 1900 censuses were grouped with skilled workers.

WHITE-COLLAR OCCUPATIONS

High White-Collar

Professionals: architect, chemist, clergyman, editor, engineer (except for locomotive and stationary), lawyer, pharmacist (apothecary), physician, social worker, teacher, veterinarian.

Major Proprietors, Managers, and Officials: banker, capitalist, broker, builder/contractor, government official (state and county), hotel keeper, merchant (with sufficient property).

Low White-Collar

Clerks and Salespeople: accountant, bookkeeper, advertising agent, agent, auctioneer, bank teller, debt collector, canvasser, cashier, clerk, insurance agent, mail carrier, messenger, salesman, stenographer, typist, telegrapher.

Semi-Professionals: actor, artist, ballplayer, draftsman, mortician, entertainer, reporter/newspaperman, librarian, musician, photographer, surveyor, writer, gambler.

Petty Proprietors, Managers, and Officials: foreman/forewoman, huckster/peddler, minor government official (city), small shopkeeper, railroad conductor, boardinghouse keeper.

BLUE-COLLAR OCCUPATIONS

Skilled: baker, blacksmith, boilermaker, bookbinder, bricklayer, brickmason, carpenter, cabinetmaker, compositor, printer, confectioner, engineer (locomotive or stationary), fireman (railroad), furrier, glover, jeweler, machinist, steamboatman, mechanic, molder, painter, paperhanger, patternmaker, plasterer, plumber, gas fitter, shoe/bootmaker, precious metalsmith, stonemason, stonecutter, tailor, tinsmith, upholsterer, stagedriver, bullwhacker, mule skinner, chainmaker, seamstress/dressmaker, milliner, saddlemaker, gunsmith, beekeeper, stencil cutter, whip braider, wheelwright, lather, harnessmaker, miner (1880 and 1900).

Semi-Skilled and Service Workers: barber, bartender, cab/hack driver, other transportation workers, cook, cooper, bellboy, elevator operator, janitor, butcher, policeman, sailor, soldier (except officers), railroad workers (below fireman), watchman, teamster, waiter/waitress, prostitute (except demimonde proprietors), miner (1870), miscellaneous worker connected with skilled occupations, whitewasher, ironer.

Unskilled Laborer and Menial Service Workers: coachman, gardener, livery stable/corral worker, laborer, servant, woodcutter and miscellaneous wood workers, porter, scrubwoman, washer.

In all cases, the community was left to define itself; that is, the adult population was marked off by its age at nuptiality and entry into the work force. Few Helena residents married before the age of eighteen, and only a handful were gainfully employed before that age. Thus, occupational statistics are based on the adult population, those who were eighteen years old or older.

Locating prostitutes in Helena proved to be the most complex research problem. The 1870 census listed no fancy ladies; the 1880 census counted only Chinese prostitutes; and the 1900 census differentiated between the lower-class, working girls on Clore Street and the higher-class brothel workers of Wood Street, labeling the former as "sporting women" and the latter not at all. Initially, my search began with several scattered bits of information. Oral history preserved the names of Josephine "Chicago Joe" Hensley and Lillian Ashton, a turn-of-the-century madam who ran a whorehouse known as "The Castle," as well as the general location of Helena's red-light district on Wood and Clore streets. Coroner's records listed a suicide at "Lillie McGraw's *maison de joie*" on Wood and Joliet streets.

The 1870 census recorded an abundance of female households whose occupants had no evident means of support but held personal wealth or property. Although the census routinely overlooked marginal people, it is highly probable that a number of Helena's "soiled doves" were counted and that a distinguishing feature might be their living arrangements. To that end, a subset of women who lived in exclusively female groups, lone women, and inhabitants of sexually mixed households was drawn from the 1870 census. Obviously inappropriate candidates were eliminated by age or information from archival sources. In addition to their shared living arrangements, these women had another common trait: they held property.

The trail led to the grantee/grantor books and the original plat map. All of these women's property holdings were located in a two-block area of Wood Street, the known location of Helena's tenderloin. The next step was an examination of criminal records, a common source for prostitution research. Helena was apparently highly tolerant of the skin trade, so the records were inconclusive; but they did provide evidence of interesting associations and relationships as the same names reappeared as litigants and witnesses in cases involving assault, public drunkenness, and disorderly conduct, crimes associated with prostitution. In a few instances, some women were identified as "soiled doves." Civil cases, divorce records, mortgages, and probate files ultimately provided the sources for positive identifications, as suspects admitted their connection with the skin trade trade in the course of their testimony. Women occupying a house with a known madam were also placed among the fancy ladies. In other instances, adultery cases specified the house, the manager, or the correspondent involved, further identifying prostitutes and places of business. Comparison of known prostitutes' mortgages with other women's revealed a single, outstanding difference: fancy ladies regularly listed a number of spittoons in their chattel inventories. This item was utterly absent from respectable women's inventories. Conveyance of property from one woman to another provided additional corroborating evidence. Potential whorehouse purchasers would likely be women interested in operating such an establishment. Through positive identifications and an abundance of circumstantial evidence garnered from myriad sources, it was possible to achieve a high level of certainty regarding Helena's demimonde population.

An example illustrates the array of evidence utilized and its accuracy. Louise Courselle was initially a promising demimonde candidate, but no piece of evidence definitely identified her as a Wood Street dove. She had the necessary associations with known fancy ladies; her chattel mortgages contained the ubiquitous spittoons; and she appeared in court in both criminal and civil actions that associated her with tenderloin personnel and activity. Louise's last property conveyance, however, was notarized in 1876 in Bozeman, where the census enumerator listed her as a prostitute in 1880.

Having once established the addresses of houses of prostitution on Wood Street for the earlier period, it was a relatively simple matter to match house numbers with those in the 1900 census, the first to record addresses. Lillie Ashton and her household at 105 Joliet could readily be identified as something other than an all-female boardinghouse, and the inmates of Allie Carleton's house, Lillie McGraw's former bawdy house, could be assigned their rightful occupations. In the same fashion, the new residents of Chicago Joe's old holdings could be ferreted out. These designations were, in turn, shored up with additional information from county records.

Similarly, the cohort analysis of mothers and daughters posed some problems in identification. The goal was to collect a numerically significant group of *represen-*

tative women who might have had similar frontier careers and experiences by virtue of the fact that they lived in the same community for a particular time. Hence, the pioneer mother contingent was based on the statistical mean description of a woman in Helena in 1870. This restrictive description was broadened to include all married women between twenty and thirty years old. Because there were 489 adult women in the community, this description comprised over 200 women or nearly 50 per cent of the population. These names were linked with those in the 1880 census to identify persisters, those who stayed on in Helena during the lean years. Of the initial 200 or so women, 56 remained. Because the 1890 census was destroyed by fire, the problem at this juncture became one of "at risk." Each candidate was traced through city directories, newspaper accounts, obituary files, and mug books to determine who died or left the community between 1880 and 1890. This is an important consideration in ascertaining who was eligible to participate in reform activities, because female reform did not become a factor until the mid 1880s. Reform activism was defined as involvement in one or more of the following: membership in the WCTU, inclusion on the female voter list of 1888, participation in the Poor Committee, membership in the Home for Working Women project, or engagement in the Helena for Capital Club.

Plainly, this method of constructing a composite biography has its problems. It excludes women with some claim to the pioneer cohort, who arrived shortly after 1870 and before 1883, the critical point at which the railroad radically changed Helena's population. It also rejects women who may have left Helena but who stayed on the mining frontier in Montana. The second instance especially applies to some women who removed to Butte when that community became an attractive investment opportunity for their financially minded husbands.

Construction of the composite biography of the daughters of the frontier proceeded by tabulating all female children born to the pioneer mothers, tracing them through marriage records to obtain their married names, and tracking them through the 1900 and 1910 censuses. In this fashion, it was possible to determine the status of approximately two-thirds of the frontier daughters in 1900. Their lives were then reconstructed from obituaries and oral histories.

Information for the divorce table was garnered from divorce records for the period between 1865 and 1900 and is based on 95 per cent of the divorce cases indexed in the county court; consequently, missing data are not a problem. Petitioners for divorce normally listed a constellation of grounds to support their suit. The reason occurring first was taken to be the principal reason for the action and defined the categories. The only exception occurred in considering cases that claimed both desertion and extreme cruelty. Establishing grounds then became more complicated. If the court granted a divorce without considering the year's absence rule, it seemed reasonable to assume that the magistrates were emphasizing cruelty as grounds rather than desertion. In this case, the suit was assigned to the cruelty classification. Even so, this judgment call was necessary in an insignificant number of cases and does not alter the percentages.

APPENDIX TWO

Statistical Tables

TABLE 1
Population of Helena and Lewis and Clark County, 1870-1900

	1870	1888	1890	1900
Helena	3,106	3,624	13,834	10,770
Lewis and Clark County	5,040	6,521	19,145	16,544

TABLE 2
Racial Composition, Marital Status, and Geographical Origin of Helena Residents, 1870, 1880, and 1900 (in percentages)

	1870[a]	1880[b]	1900[c]
Racial Composition			
White	77	89	96
Chinese	21	8	2
Black	2	2	2
Native American	—	1	—
Marital Status			
Married	22	45	57
Single	77	50	35
Divorced	—	.5	1
Widowed	—	4.5	7
Geographical Origin			
China	20.7	7.7	1.7
Europe	23	23.3	24.6
Midwest	16	13.2	22.3
Northeast	18.9	22.4	10.3
South	12.8	13.1	8.05
West	8.6	20.4	33.1

[a]For racial composition and marital status, *N* = 2,554; for geographical origin, *N* = 3,104.

[b]For racial composition and marital status, *N* = 2,536; for geographical origin, *N* = 3,624. Nine per cent of the population listed themselves as married but did not have a spouse in evidence.

[c]For racial composition and marital status, *N* = 7,095; for geographical origin, *N* = 10,665. Three and one-half per cent of the population listed themselves as married but did not have a spouse in evidence.

TABLE 3

Analysis of Miners, Lewis and Clark County, 1870, 1880, 1890

	1870[a]	1880[b]	1900[c]
Geographical Origin			
China	57%	33%	2%
Immigrant	18	34	47
Midwest	7	6	21
Northeast	12	17	17
South	6	9	11
West	—	1	2
Age			
Mean Age	32	41	46

[a]*N* = 719

[b]*N* = 252

[c]*N* = 225

TABLE 4

Age Structure and Sex Ratio of Helena Residents, 1870, 1880, 1900

	1870[b]	1880[c]	1900[d]
Age Structure[a]			
0-10	13%	19%	22%
11-20	10	13	16
21-30	38	25	18
31-40	28	22	21
41-50	9	14	13
51-60	2	5	7
over 60	1	2	3
Sex Ratio[e]			
0-10	127	103	101
11-20	139	117	*132*[f]
21-30	388	115	*123*
31-40	595	263	122
41-50	460	425	151
51-60	415	429	167
over 60	300	234	170

[a]In percentages

[b]*N* = 3,106

[c]*N* = 3,624

[d]*N* = 10,645

[e]Males per 100 females

[f]Italicized numbers indicate a reversal in the sex ratio: females per 100 males.

TABLE 5

Household Type and Population of Residents in Households for Lewis and Clark County, 1870, 1880, and 1900 (in percentages)

	1870[a]	1880[b]	1900[c]
Household Type			
Familial households	34.3	62.0	82.6
Nuclear family	30.7	39.8	69.0
Extended family	2.4	9.5	12.9
Two-family	1.2	2.7	.7
Non-familial households	65.7	38.0	17.4
Wholly male	39.0	20.7	1.9
Wholly female	2.8	.3	.7
Solitary male	17.6	9.9	10.1
Solitary female	4.0	2.7	4.2
Sexually mixed	2.1	4.0	.2
Institutional	.2	.4	.3
Population in Households			
Familial households	44.6	71.0	92.5
Nuclear family	33.3	53.3	74.3
Extended family	3.7	12.7	17.3
Two-family	2.6	5.0	.9
Non-familial households	55.4	29.0	7.5
Wholly male	43.5	21.4	1.1
Wholly female	2.1	.1	.4
Solitary male	5.2	2.2	2.6
Solitary female	1.2	.6	1.0
Sexually mixed	2.8	3.0	.3
Institutional	.6	1.8	2.1

[a]For household type, *N* = 906; for population in households, *N* = 3,106. Mean household size equals 3.4 persons; mean nuclear family size equals 4.2 persons.

[b]For household type, *N* = 791; for population in households, *N* = 3,624. Mean household size equals 4.5 persons; mean nuclear family size equals 4.8 persons.

[c]For household type, *N* = 2,506; for population in households, *N* = 10,752. Mean household size equals 4.3 persons; mean nuclear family size equals 4.6 persons.

TABLE 6

Occupational Distribution of Male and Female Labor, Lewis and Clark County, 1870, 1880, and 1900 (in percentages)

Class	1870[a]	1880[b]	1900[c]
Male			
High white collar	24	29	39
Professionals	3	4	6
Other	21	25	33
Blue collar	75	70	61
Skilled	8	22	21
Miners	37	14	7
Semi-skilled and service	16	19	17
Unskilled and menial service	15	15	15

TABLE 6 (continued)

Women			
High white collar	11	28	38
Professionals	3	13	13
Other	8	15	25
Blue collar	89	72	62
Skilled	6	13	17
Semi-skilled and service	79	56	38
Unskilled and menial service	4	3	7

[a]For men, N = 2,002; for women, N = 100.

[b]For men, N = 1,803; for women, N = 163.

[c]For men, N = 3,591; for women, N = 877.

TABLE 7

A Comparison of the Occupational Distribution of the Male Labor Force in Helena and Boston, 1900 (in percentages)

Class	Helena	Boston
High white collar	39	38
Professionals	6	6
Other	33	32
Blue collar	61	62
Skilled	28	32
Semi-skilled and service	17	18
Unskilled and menial service	16	12

TABLE 8

Distribution of Wealth in Lewis and Clark County, 1870 (in percentages)

	Men[a]	Women[b]
$100-2,000	67	74
$2,001-4,000	16	12
$4,001-6,000	10	15
over $6,000	6	—

[a]N = 551, or 27 per cent of the adult male population. The mean wealth figure for the total adult male population was $576.

[b]N = 34, or 7 per cent of the adult female population. The mean wealth figure for the total adult female population was $116.

TABLE 9

Percentage of Residents Owning or Renting Homes, Lewis and Clark County, 1900[a]

Owns free house	29
Owns mortgaged house	6
Rents house	65

[a]N = 2,542

TABLE 10

Women's Occupations, Lewis and Clark County, 1870, 1880, 1900

Occupation	1870	1880	1900
Actress	1	1	—
Artist	—	—	2
Baker	—	—	1
Boardinghouse keeper	4	7	47
Book agent	—	—	1
Book binder	—	—	3
Bookkeeper	—	—	9
Candy-maker			1
Canvasser	—	—	1
Capitalist	—	—	12
Cashier			4
Chambermaid	—	1	15
Clerk	—	1	21
Commercial broker	—	1	—
Complexionist	—	—	1
Confectionary store	—	—	1
Cook	4	3	37
Costumer	—	—	1
Dentist	—	—	1
Dressmaker	3	9	103
Editor	—	—	2
Factory worker	—	—	2
Farmer	—	—	2
Florist	—	—	2
Forewoman	—	—	1
Fortune teller	—	—	1
Gambler	2	—	—
General agent	—	—	1
Governess	—	—	2
Grocer	—	1	1
Hairdresser	—	1	4
Hide dealer	—	—	1
Hotel keeper	—	—	2
Hotel worker	—	1	—
Housekeeper	—	4	41
House rents	—	—	1
Laborer	—	1	9
Lawyer	—	—	1
Librarian	—	1	6
Librarian State	—	—	1
Mail carrier	—	—	1
Medium	—	—	1
Merchant	—	—	2
Merchant candy	—	—	2
Midwife	—	1	2
Milliner	1	3	16
Missionary	—	—	1
Nurse	—	9	29
Nurse-administrator	—	1	—
Nurse, children's	—	—	2

TABLE 10 (continued)

Occupation	1870	1880	1900
Officer	—	—	7
Officer, Salvation Army	—	—	2
Patent Medicine Vendor	—	—	1
Photographer	—	1	2
Physician	—	—	4
Preceptress	—	—	1
Prostitute	38	50	56
Rancher	—	—	1
Real estate owner	—	1	1
Saleswoman	—	—	13
Saloon keeper	1	—	1
School principal	—	1	—
School superintendent	—	—	1
Schoolteacher	3	19	86
Scrubwoman	—	—	14
Seamstress	2	8	12
Servant	19	32	145
Sister, religious	—	—	6
Sister Superior	—	—	1
Soap wrapper	—	—	1
Stenographer	—	—	40
Stock grower	—	—	1
Superintendent, reformatory	—	—	1
Superintendent, ass't reformatory	—	—	1
Tailor	—	—	2
Telegraph editor	—	—	1
Telephone clerk	—	—	1
Telephone operator	—	—	4
Traveling Agent	—	1	—
Typist	—	—	3
Waitress	8	—	33
Washerwoman	4	1	35
Keeping house	338	446	1,639
No occupation	36	126	747

Note: The female work force is defined as all women who were eighteen years old or older. The total number of adult women in 1870 was 489; 20 per cent of them were employed outside the home, 73 per cent were "keeping house," and 7 per cent listed no occupation. In addition, five women younger than eighteen years old worked as servants. The total number of adult women in 1880 was 735; 22 per cent of them were employed outside the home, 61 per cent were "keeping house," and 17 per cent listed no occupation. Twenty-six women younger than eighteen years old worked as servants. The total number of adult women in 1900 was 3,264; 27 per cent of them were employed outside the home, 50 per cent were "keeping house," and 23 per cent listed no occupation.

TABLE 11

Comparison of White Prostitutes, Helena, 1870, 1880, 1900

Geographic Origin	1870 Prostitutes	1870 General Population	1870 Population Stratified
Immigrant	27%	29%	34%
Midwest	31	20	24
Northeast	15	24	24
South	23	16	16
West	4 *N*=26	11 *N*=2,462	2 *N*=318
Geographic Origin	**1880 Prostitutes**	**1880 General Population**	**1880 Population Stratified**
Immigrant	24%	25%	29%
Midwest	30	14	23
Northeast	28	24	23
South	14	14	20
West	4 *N*=30	22 *N*=3,344	4 *N*=469
Geographic Origin	**1900 Prostitutes**	**1900 General Population**	**1900 Population Stratified**
Immigrant	45%	25%	31%
Midwest	28	22	32
Northeast	4	10	9
South	15	8	9
West	8 *N*=53	33 *N*=10,484	19 *N*=1,821

TABLE 11 (continued)

Household Type	1870		1880		1900	
Nuclear Family (NF)	4%		16%		2%	
Exclusively Female (SF)	38		10		51	
Sexually Mixed (SX)	4		50		9	
Single Female (1F)	54	*N*=26	23	*N*=30	38	*N*=53

Wealth	1870	1880	1886	1900
Prostitutes Reporting or Having Wealth	45% *N*=32	30% *N*=-30	22% *N*=42	0% N=53
Property Ownership	1870	1880	1886	1900
Prostitutes Owning Property	45%	13%	12%	0%
Combined Financial Resources	1870	1880	1886	1900
Prostitutes Reporting Wealth or Property or Both	57%	36%	22%	0%

[1]Statistics for household type and geographic origin were based on those women for whom demographic data were available. Figures for property ownership and financial resources were based on the total prostitute population. In order to determine how well the prostitute population's geographic origins reflected those of other women, an additional figure was computed on the basis of women in the general population who fell between the ages of eighteen and thirty-five, the age concentration of the prostitute population. This effectively removed the regional bias of the general population figure which contained a large number of young children born in Montana. The total percentage at points does not equal 100 per cent because of rounding.

TABLE 12

White Prostitutes in Helena, 1870

Name	Race	Age	Household	Origin	Wealth	Bank Acct.	Property
Fannie Spencer	W	23	1F	IL	$ 500		
Eliza Wearing	W	33	SF	CAN			
Eliza Thompson	W	28	SF	ENG	$5500		X
Henrietta Zipp (Bischoff)	W	28	SF	LA	$5500		X
Kate Strong	W	42	SF	FRA	$5000		
Lizzie Frazer	W	22	SF	IN			
Belle Backus	W	35	SF	MI			
Delores Jarra	W	28	NF	CHINA			X
Delilah Finger	W	25	1F	KY	$ 200		
Louise Courselle	W	37	1F	FRA	$ 100		X
Florence Bentley	W	27	1F	OH			
Julie Bunker	W	31	1F	OH	$6000		X
Mollie Grahm	W	33	SF	ME	$1000	X	X
Jennie Wilson	W	23	SF	KY			
Charlotte Rich	W	26	SF	ME			
Sarah Herbert	W	23	SF	MO			
Carrie Bedell	W	29	SF	MO			
Ami Hope	W	29	1F	OH			
Carrie Whitman	W	28	1F	OH			
Caroline Whitney	W	25	1F	CT			X
Catherine Harrison						X	X
Isabella Grosse (Lance)							X
Nellie Perkins	W	21	1F	CA	$1500		X
Louisa Philip	W	33	1F	VA	$1100		X
Celia Goldman	W	35	SX	BAV	$ 600		X
Hannah Kates							X
Anna Belsford							X
Kate Silvers							X
Julie Levi							X
Kate Smith	W	27	SF	MD	$3000		
Jennie Foster	W	24	SF	MI			
Mary Parker	W	23	SF	IRE			

TABLE 13

White Prostitutes in Helena, 1880

Name	Race	Age	Household	Origin	Wealth	Bank Acct.	Property
Josephine Hensley	W	35	NF	IRE	X		X
Nellie Reynolds	W	24	NF	NY			
Elizabeth Lynch	W	22	NF	NY			
Annie Williams	W	22	NF	NY		X	
Rosa Diamond	W	22	SX	IW		X	
Fannie Spencer	W	30	SX	IL			X
Elizabeth Kimbal	W	25	SX	CA			
Nancy Waters	W	47	SX	MD			
Catherin Ross	W	32	1F	PA			
Annie M. Fisher	W	29	1F	ENG			X
Mary Young	W	21	1F	IL			
Blanche Emerson	W	29	SX	NY		X	
Anna Southhard	W	23	SX	IN			
Celia Davis	W	35	1F	AL			
Bertha Porter	W	29	1F	IN		X	
Maud Stevenson	W	22	SF	ENG			
Jessie White	W	22	SF	OH			
Grace Thurston	W	22	SF	IL			
Caroline Schneider	W	17	SX	PRU			
Margaret Ligget	W	24	SX	PRU			

Diana Will	W	18	SX	PRU			
Lizzie Keller	W	19	SX	NY		X	
Dora Reece	W	30	SX	NY		X	
Dora Ose	W	22	SX	IL			
Jennie Blair	W	27	SX	AK			
Mary Gon	W	39	SX	LA			
Mary Lavenash	W	36	NF	WI			
Mattie Sheppard	W	31	SX	CAN			
Belle Crafton	W	22	1F	LA		X	
Lillie McGraw	W	43	1F	MO	X		X

TABLE 14
Chinese Prostitutes, Helena, 1880

Name	Race	Age	Household	Origin
Ah Fung	C	38	SX-Loafer	C
Chung Fow	C	33	1F	C
Sing Toy	C	29	1F	C
Ah Faw	C	22	1F	C
Ang Gang	C	21	SX-Loafer	C
Ah Ho	C	18	1F	C
Du Toy	C	21	SX-Loafer	C
Pae Toy	C	26	SX-Loafer	C
Ah Lai	C	32	SX-Servant	C
Ah Gue	C	24	SX-Loafer	C
Toy Gun	C	19	SX-Baker	C
Han Wong	C	37	SX-Baker	C
Ah Hong	C	28	SX-Restaurant Owner	C
Ah Look	C	19	SX-Restaurant Owner	C
Liu Gue	C	21	SX-Loafer	C
Gives Ung	C	22	SX-Loafer	C
Ying Gon	C	32	SX-Loafer	C
An My	C	32	SX-Loafer	C
Woon May	C	16	SX-Acrobat	C
How Wong	C	41	1F	C
Heung Gue	C	36	1F	C
Gue Lung	C	38	SX-Loafer	C
Hong Gim	C	39	SX-Loafer	C
Ye Hab	C	30	SX-Cook	C

TABLE 15
Prostitutes in Helena, 1900

Name	Race	Age	Household	Origin	House Ownership Status
Ah Fou	C	44	1F	C	R
Phoebe Hafer	W	31	Jail	WI	R
Ak Hou	C	48	1F	C	R
Kitty McEvoy	B	35	1F	NC	R
Ding Young	C	30	1F	C	R
Choy Now	C	45	1F	C	R
Mamie Pratt	W	17	NF	IW	R
Satan Tore	J	24	SF	JAP	R
Hannah Okio	J	22	SF	JAP	R
Lizzie Tracey	W	36	1F	WI	R
Annie Ferris	W	22	SX	SCO	R
Dora Cain	W	20	SX	IW	R
May Lehman	W	22	SX	NO	R
Addie DeBuck	W	23	1F	FRA	R
Carrie Kinney	W	26	1F	MT	R
Lillian Ashton	W	37	SF	OH	R
Mae Stanton	W	21	SF	CA	R
Gertrude Morton	W	28	SF	LA	R
May Davidson	W	23	SF	SWE	R
Belle Hundington	W	26	SF	NY	R

TABLE 15 (continued)

Name	Race	Age	Household	Origin	House Ownership Status
Carmen Livingston	W	21	SF	MN	R
Kate Hutten	W	31	1F	IRE	R
Kitty Lewis	W	22	1F	KY	R
Allie Carleton	W	27	SF	MA	R
Margaret Livingston	W	19	SF	IL	R
Lillian Holmes	W	18	SF	ND	R
Violet Melbourne	W	20	SF	TN	R
Elsie Hammond	W	23	SF	IL	R
Dollie Knowles	W	35	1F	IL	R
Ella Ritchie	W	34	1F	CUB	R
Minnie Johnson	W	24	1F	RUS	R
Alvina Herlin	W	20	1F	DEN	R
Sarah Johnson	W	31	1F	MN	R
Millie Ford	W	25	1F	GER	R
Lottie O'Neil	W	30	SF	MO	R
Minnie Emmett	W	32	SF	TN	R
Blanche Mirar	W	22	2F	FRA	R
Margaret Marchy	W	37	2F	FRA	R
Ella Miller	W	19	2F	GER	R
Sophie Miller	W	25	2F	GER	R
May Stewart	W	40	SF	OH	R
Frankie Miller	W		SF		R
Millie White	W		SF		R
Stella Arnold	W	31	SX	OH	R
Callie McAllister	W	32	SX	NB	R
M. Frank	W	34	1F	GER	R
Ella Walters	W	26	1F	BEL	R
Gabriel Roberts	W	39	1F	FRA	R
Alda Hull	W	25	1F	MI	R
Eura Phillips	W	27	1F	IL	R
Russia Dease	W	24	1F	SWE	R
Gladys Conley	W	29	1F	KY	R
Isabella Miller	W	38	1F	AUS	R
Louise Fleuret	W	42	1F	FRA	R
Rose Dunay	W	34	SF	FRA	R
Lucien Glaudine	W	35	SF	FRA	R
Sophie LeCanat	W	33	SF	FRA	R
Jennie Remond	W	24	SF	FRA	R
Adeline DeBois	W	32	1F	FRA	R

TABLE 16

Women in the Work Force, Helena, 1870-1910 (in percentages)

1870	1880	1890	1900	1910
3	5	14	20	30

Note: Statistics are derived from an analysis of the working population in Helena in the *U.S. Census* for 1870, 1880, and 1900 and from a linear trend analysis to supply the missing data points for 1890 and 1910. Although there are not enough data points in this model to make any conclusive statements about the significance of women's increasing participation in the labor force, a preliminary analysis of the 1910 census suggests that the figure for that year is not far off the mark. At this point, the table is meant to be suggestive only.

TABLE 17

Ratio of Marriages to Divorces in Lewis and Clark and Los Angeles Counties, 1867-1900

	California	Montana
1867-1870	25.6:1	2.6:1
1871-1875	7.3:1	4.4:1
1876-1880	9.0:1	6.2:1
1881-1885	9.0:1	6.4:1
1886-1890	7.0:1	7.3:1
1891-1895	4.9:1	5.6:1
1896-1900	4.2:1	5.0:1

Source: Carroll D. Wright, *A Report on Marriage and Divorce in the United States, 1867 to 1886* (Washington, D.C.: Government Printing Office, 1891), 344-345, 228-229.

Note: Additional data from Lewis and Clark County for 1865-1866 pertaining to divorce and marriage does not appreciably change the ratio for the early period. For 1865-1870, the figures would be 2.7:1. It should be noted that figures forwarded to the Department of Labor by the county offices were grossly overestimated for any particular year. Nonetheless, the ratios based on data gleaned from local records approximate the ratios garnered from Wright and indicate the same trends.

TABLE 18

Frequency of Grounds for Divorce in Lewis and Clark County, 1865-1900 (in percentages)

	Desertion	Cruelty	Drink	Adultery	Other
1865-1870	59	15	—	26	—
1871-1875	68	10	12	7	2
1876-1880	69	13	3	13	2
1881-1885	53	21	13	6	6
1886-1890	48	31	8	9	4
1891-1895	44	31	5	14	5
1896-1900	48	27	7	11	11

Note: N = 668. The numbers of divorces for the five-year periods are 1865-1870 = 47; 1871-1875 = 42; 1876-1880 = 40; 1881-1885 = 47; 1886-1890 = 143; 1891-1895 = 181; 1896-1900 = 168. Other grounds for divorce included bigamy, conviction of a felony, venereal disease, and non-support without abandonment before 1895.

TABLE 19

Comparison of Grounds for Divorce in Lewis and Clark and Los Angeles Counties, 1880-1889 (in percentages)

	Los Angeles	Lewis and Clark
Desertion	39	49
Cruelty	35	26
Adultery	9	9
Neglect	10	—
Intemperance	6	11
Felony Conviction	1	1
Bigamy	1	1
Fraud	—	—
Other	—	3

Source: Statistics for Los Angeles are derived from Elaine May, *Great Expectations: Marriage and Divorce in Post-Victorian America* (Chicago: University of Chicago Press, 1980), 175.

TABLE 20

Duration of Marriage in Years Before Divorce by Specific Cause for Montana, California, and the United States, 1867-1886

Cause	Montana	California	United States
Adultery	*N*=	*N*=	N=
To husband	(53) 6.75	(626) 8.09	(38,184) 7.84
To wife	(18) 6.83	(536) 9.35	(29,502) 9.51
Cruelty			
To husband	(10) 13.33	(269) 9.73	(6,122) 9.75
To wife	(169) 8.34	(2,166) 9.16	(45,473) 9.25
Desertion[a]			
To husband	(117) 9.92	(1,541) 10.73	(51,485) 9.80
To wife	(248) 8.83	(1,979) 10.55	(75,191) 9.14
Drunkeness/ Habitual Intemperance			
To husband	(6) 7.67	165) 10.41	(1,434) 10.92
To wife	(28) 8.07	(252) 11.07	(12,432) 10.97
All Causes			
To husband	(207) 9.22	(2,999) 9.84	(112,540) 8.97
To wife	(615) 8.69	(9,119) 9.83	(216,176) 9.27

Source: Statistics abstracted from Wright, *A Report on Marriage and Divorce to the United States*, 701, 613-614, 182.

[a]Since the courts made no practical distinction between abandonment and desertion in Montana, the numbers from the separate causes of abandonment and desertion have been combined to facilitate comparison.

TABLE 21
Pioneer Mothers, Helena, 1880

	Property	Employment/ Sole Tradership	Community Activism	Marital History
Bridget Allen				D-1886
Nellie Beach	X			
Mary Bartos	X			W-1886
Ann Beveridge	X			
Helena Birkenfeld				
Elizabeth Blake		washer		D<1880
Anna Brainerd				
Catherine Cannon	X		X	
Margaret Carr	X	boardinghouse		
Norma Chadwick	X		X	W<1890
Loretta Crounse	X			d. 1881
Ann Cuthbert	X			
Vestina Davis	X			
Rebecca Davis	X	washer		W<1880
Caroline Dutro	X			
Mary Eckert	X	photographer		D-1873
Mary Edwards	X			
Eliza Farrell	X			
Elizabeth Fisk	X		X	
Elizabeth Flowerree				d. 1882
Emma Frank	X			
Mary Hamilton			X	
Mary Holter				
Sarah Herrick		dressmaker		
Mary Hoback	X			
Molly Kemp	X			d. 1889
Jeanette Kinna	X		X	
Isabella Kirkendall	X		X	
Mary Kleinschmidt	X		X	
Mary Lavenash	X	rancher		D-1873 D-1880
Caroline Lehman	X		X	
Emily Lockey	X			
Jeannette Loeb	X		X	
Mary McEvily	X			
Louisa McGinnis	X		X	
Sophie McHugh	X		X	W<1880
Catharine Ming	X	broker	X	W-1889
Elizabeth O'Connell			X	d. 1889
Jennie Paynter				
Hannah Pope				
Matilda Reinig			X	
Catherine Richardson	X	broker	X	
Hannah Rumsey	X		X	
Ester Sands				W-1887
Mattie Sheppard	X	prostitute		
Fannie Spencer	X	prostitute		d. 1881
Eliza Sweeney	X		X	W-1887
Ruby Walker				
Laura Wells	X	milliner		W-1890
Maria Wentworth				
Annie Williams				
Anna Woolfolk	X			
America Wright				
Emma Zimmerman				d. 1894

TABLE 22

Frontier Daughters, Helena, 1900

	Employment	Community Activism	Marital Status
Mary Beveridge	kh		M-1907(36)
Florence Fisk	reporter		M-1904(22)
Grace Bryan	editor	X	M-1890(21)
			D-1898
			M-1919?
Bertha Frank	none		?
Anna Frank	none		?
Clara Holter	kh	X	M-1888(18)
			W-1900
			M-1925
			D-1925
Nettie Kirkendall	county clerk	X	single
Clara Kirkendall	kh/enumerator		M-1898(21)
			D-1904
			M-1934
Bessie Kirkendall	milliner		single
Mary Lockey	headmistress	X	single
Rose Bartos	dressmaker		single
Emily Bartos	dressmaker		single
Marie Kleinschmidt	kh	X	M-1906(31)
Elizabeth McEvily	stenographer		M-1902(28)
Alice Pope	teacher	X	single
Catherine Pope	none		M-1909(21)
Harriet Pope	kh		M-1899(28)
Mary Pope	kh		M-1898(23)
Lottie Rumsey	none	X	M-1913(45)
			D-1913
			M-1929
Elise Sweeney	none		M-1902(26)
Anne Reinig	none	X	M-1907(33)
Jessie Eckert	none		M-1888(18)
			D< 1900
Eudora Flowerree	kh		M-1889(19)
			D-1896
Elizabeth Flowerree	kh		M-1889(18)
Helen Lehman	kh/business	X	M-1895(24)
Norma Kinna	kh		M-1889(20)
Polly Davis	seamstress		M-1885(20)
Alice Dutro	kh		M-1890s?
Flora Dutro	kh		M-1890s?
Mary McHugh	principal	X	single
Susan McHugh	kh		M-1890s?
Celia McHugh	kh		M-1895(24)
Mary Williams	kh		M-1893(24)
Rose Farrell	kh		M-1889(23)
Clara Cuthbert	kh		M-1895(22)

Note: No record can be found for the following frontier daughters: Mary Crounse, Helena Wright, Rourna Wright, Harriet Blake, Nellie Cuthbert, Fanny Carr, Alice Crounse, Cora Crounse, Mary L. Davis, Victoria Farrell, Mary Farrell, Margaret Farrell, Josephine Hoback, Nettie Kinna, Catherine Paynter, Theresa Sands, Yetta Sands, Annie Sands, Ada Woolfolk, Susan Woolfolk, Katie Lavenash, Rachel Coleau, Hattie Brainerd, Gertrude Herrick, Josephine Edwards, Mary McEvily, Anna Flowerree. There are scattered bits and pieces for several of the women. Mary Crounse, Helen Wright, Rourna Wright, and Anna Flowerree married, but where they went after their marriages is unknown. And, clearly, some of the women left Helena for other communities. The Sands apparently went to Salt Lake City; the Crounse and Woolfolk families departed for Illinois; and the Hobacks migrated to Butte. The table, therefore, represents 55 per cent of the daughters, and the biographical narratives in Chapter 3 represent 10 per cent of the total number of daughters, a sufficient number upon which to base generalizations.

APPENDIX THREE

Property Owned by Helena Prostitutes, 1870-1890

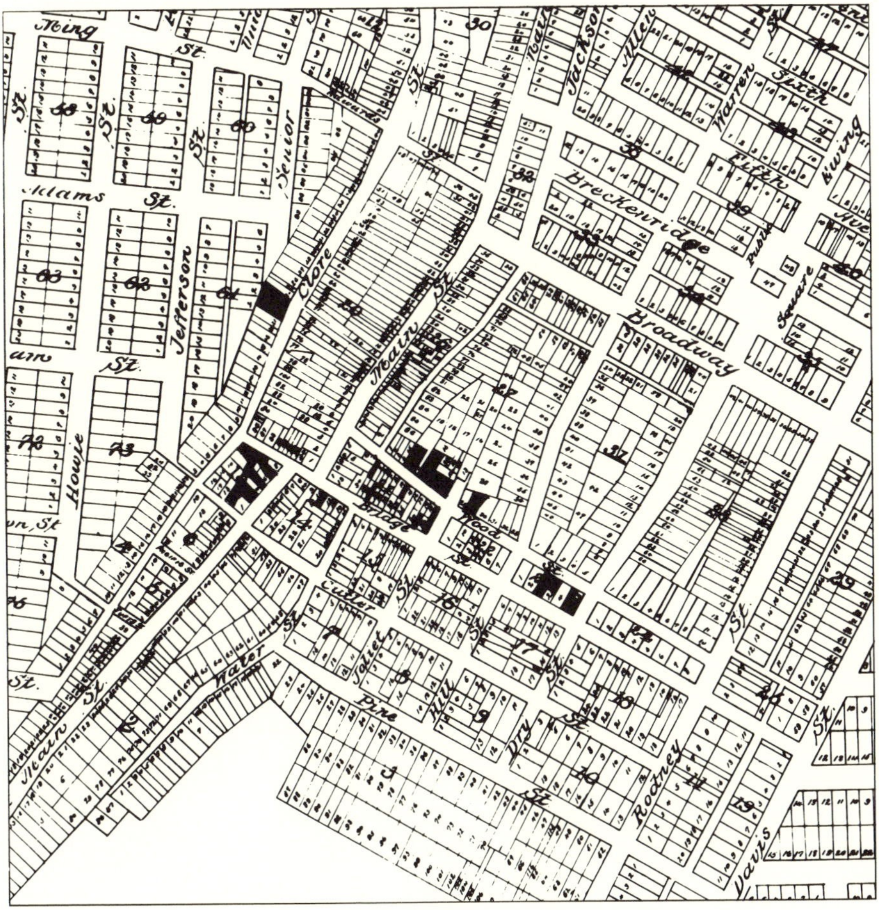

MAP 1
Property Owned by Helena Prostitutes, 1870

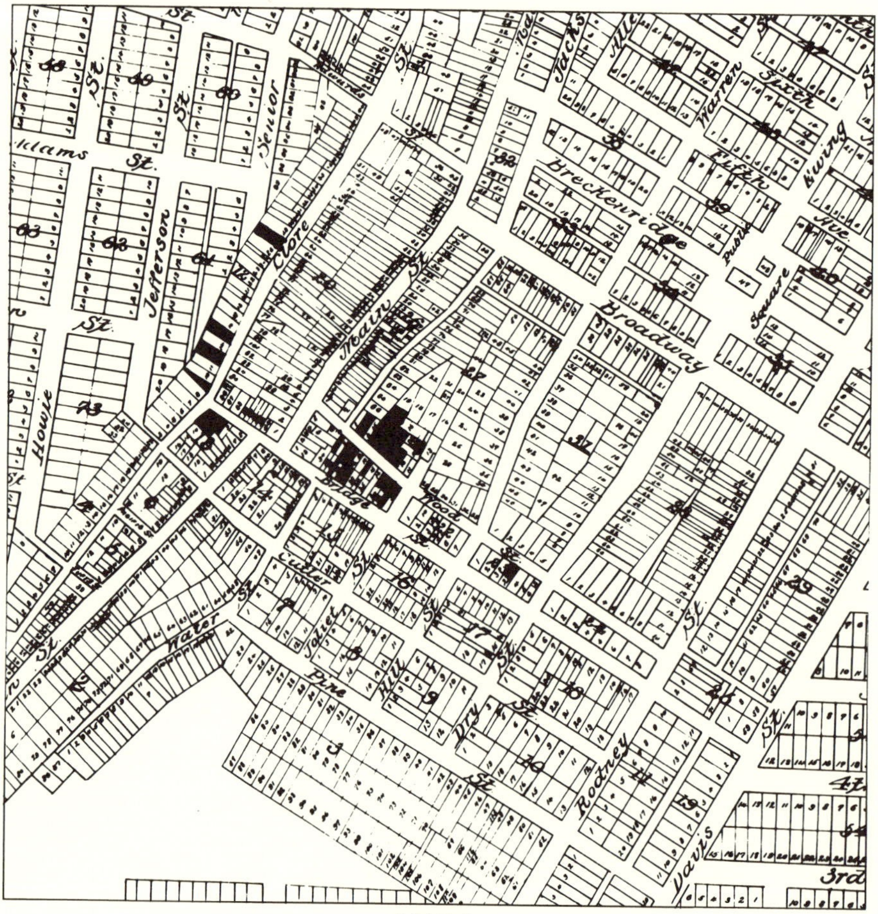

MAP 2

Property Owned by Helena Prostitutes, 1880

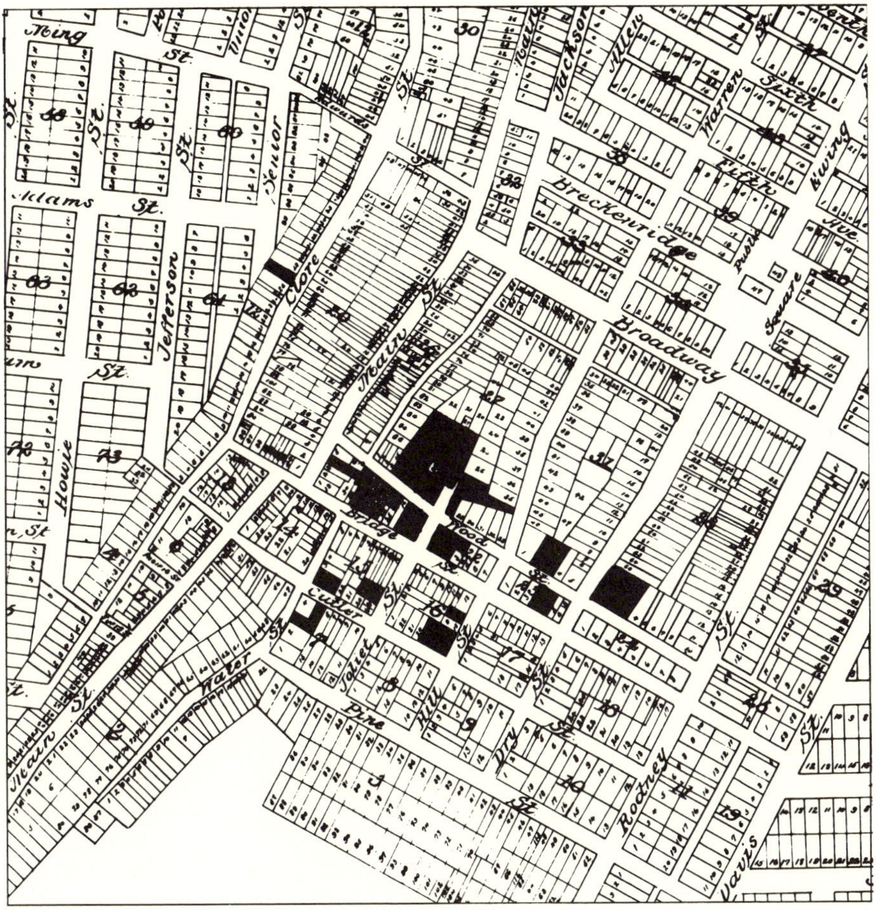

MAP 3

Property Owned by Helena Prostitutes, 1890

Notes

Author's Note: Special surveys or lists cited are statistical cross-tabulations in the author's possession. Unless otherwise specified, all county records are from Lewis and Clark County and are located in or through the following offices:

Office of the Clerk and Recorder
- Deed Books
- Helena Townsite Records
- Plat Books
- Mortgage Books
- Miscellaneous Records
- Register of Deaths

Office of the Clerk of the Court
- Civil Cases, Old Series
- Civil Cases, New Series
- Criminal Cases, Old Series
- Criminal Cases, New Series
- Coroner's Inquisitions
- Marriage Records
- Record of Civil Actions, vol. 1-4
- Record of Criminal Actions, vol. 1-2 (Inverse and Direct)
- Wills
- Probates

Office of the Treasurer
- Tax Assessment Records

Office of City Engineering
- McIntyre Survey Maps

INTRODUCTION

1. Ray A. Billington, *America's Frontier Heritage* (New York: Holt, Rinehart and Winston, 1966), 25; Sandra L. Myres, *Westering Women and the Frontier Experience, 1800-1915* (Albuquerque: University of New Mexico Press, 1982). Like Billington and Myres, I am using frontier both as a process and as a place. In this case, the frontier as a place is more narrowly defined as the Rocky Mountain mining frontier, and the process is obviously modified to accommodate women.

2. Frederick Jackson Turner, "The Significance of the Frontier in American History," in *The Turner Thesis, Concerning the Role of the Frontier in American History*, ed. George Rogers Taylor (Lexington, Massachusetts: D. C. Heath, 1972), 28.

3. Carolyn Stefanco-Schill, "Women on the American Frontier: An Historiographical Essay" (paper delivered at the Social Science-History Conference, Nashville, Tennessee, October 30, 1981).

4. Ibid. For examples of work done in the Turnerian tradition, see Dee Brown, *The Gentle Tamers: Women of the Old Wild West* (New York: Putnam, 1958); William W. Fowler, *Woman on the American Frontier* (Ann Arbor: Plutarch Books, 1971); Agnes Morley Cleaveland, *No Life for a Lady* (Boston: Houghton Mifflin Company, 1941).

5. Stefanco-Schill, "Women on the American Frontier." For examples of works treated by the Reactionists, see Ole Rolvaag, *Giants in the Earth: A Saga of the Prairie* (New York: Harper Brothers, 1927); Agnes Smedley, *Daughter of Earth* (Westbury: The Feminist Press, 1973); Mari Sandoz, *Old Jules* (Boston: Little, Brown and Company, 1935); Nannie T. Alderson, *A Bride Goes West* (New York: Farrar & Rinehart, 1942); Everett Dick, *The Sod House Frontier, 1854-1890: A Social History of the Northern Plains from the Creation of Kansas and Nebraska to the Admission of the Dakotas* (Lincoln, Nebraska: Johnsen Publishing Company, 1954).

6. Stefanco-Schill, "Women on the American Frontier." For examples of the Stasist school, see John Mack Faragher, *Women and Men on the Overland Trail* (New Haven, Connecticut: Yale University Press, 1979); Johnny Faragher and Christine Stansell, "Women and Their Families on the Overland Trail, 1842-67," *Feminist Studies* 1:2/3 (1975): 150-166; Julie Roy Jeffrey, *Frontier Women: The Trans-Mississippi West, 1840-1880* (New York: Hill and Wang, 1979).

7. Jeffrey, *Frontier Women*, 80. In 1870 and 1880, 21 and 23 per cent of the nation's population was classified as urban. In Montana, two-thirds of the populace lived in cities or towns. Department of the Interior, Census Office, *Statistics of the Population of the United States at the Tenth Census* (Washington, D.C.: Government Printing Office, 1883), xxix, 250; idem, *Compendium of the Ninth Census* (Washington, D.C.: Government Printing Office, 1872), 252.

8. See Jeffrey, *Frontier Women*, chapters 4 and 5; Glenda Riley, *Frontierswomen, the Iowa Experience* (Ames: Iowa State University Press, 1981); Lillian Schlissel, *Women's Diaries of the Westward Journey* (New York: Schocken Books, 1982); Myres, *Westering Women*. The Myres work does not conform entirely to this classification; in her final chapter, she suggests that the frontier possibly had an effect on women, especially through the generations.

9. Women's networks and their function during the nineteenth century have been discussed by several historians, including Jeffrey, *Frontier Women*, Chapter 4; Nancy Cott, *The Bonds of Womanhood: "Woman's Sphere" in New England, 1780-1835* (New Haven, Connecticut: Yale University Press, 1978); Carroll Smith-Rosenberg, "The Female World of Love and Ritual: Relations Between Women in Nineteenth-Century America," *Signs*, no. 1 (Autumn 1975): 1-30. A number of articles and books have explored the complexities of the "cult of true womanhood"; of these the discussion that draws all the interpretations together is Mary P. Ryan, *Cradle of the Middle Class: The Family in Oneida County, New York, 1790-1865* (New York: Cambridge University Press, 1981), 191-198, 146-155, 179-185.

CHAPTER ONE: From Urban Village to Metropolitan Town

1. William C. Campbell, *From the Quarries of Last Chance Gulch*, 2 vols. (vol 1: Helena: The Montana Record Publishing Company, 1951; vol. 2: Helena: Bell-Arm Corporation, 1964), 1:4-12. In microcosm, the discovery party and the fate of its members typified the nature of mining camp populations as heterogeneous, mobile, and partially successful. Southerner D. J. Miller returned to Alabama and John Cowan went back to Georgia, where he opened a sawmill. Reginald Stanley, a Britisher, returned to his homeland and entered the colliery and foundry business with his profits from Last Chance Gulch. Iowan John Crabb died penniless.

2. Ibid., 12.

3. Duane A. Smith, *Rocky Mountain Mining Camps: The Urban Frontier* (Bloomington: Indiana University Press, 1967); Roger Lotchin, *San Francisco, 1846-1856: From Hamlet to City* (New York: Oxford University Press, 1974), 5.

4. Michael A. Leeson, ed., *History of Montana, 1739-1885* (Chicago: Warner, Beers and Company, 1885), 701; Campbell, *From the Quarries of Last Chance Gulch*, 1:8, 12; J. D. McIntyre Survey: Plats of Helena Townsite, 1884. When the original townsite was resurveyed in 1883, few major changes were made except for renumbering several blocks and lots. See Appendix 3, Map 1 for an indication of the city plan and block and lot measurements.

5. Rodman Wilson Paul, *Mining Frontiers of the Far West, 1848-1880* (New York: Holt, Rinehart and Winston, 1963), 144. In 1870, the census enumerator counted all unoccupied dwellings. Using these empty dwellings and the mean size of the household in 1870, it is possible to arrive at a more accurate estimate of Helena's population during its boom period: 295 (empty dwellings) x 3.4 (mean household size) = 1,003 (residents). This does not take into account the number of residents who occupied impermanent structures, such as tents, or those who lived outside the city but were near enough to be visible. This figure is considerably lower than previous estimates but accords with the general decline of 25 per cent experienced by the state as a whole. See *U.S. Census, 1870: Territory of Montana*, Montana Historical Society Library, Helena [MHSL].

6. See Appendix 2, tables 4 and 5, and Chapter 2.

7. *U.S. Census, 1870.* I am indebted to John Chaffee, State University of New York at Binghamton, for his assistance in analyzing Helena's Asian population. From the naming patterns in the census, it is apparent that Helena's Chinese emigrated from two or three villages in Canton Province and were generally related to one another. The prejudice against the Chinese was evident in the census enumerator's inclination to lump them under the general description of "Chinaman" or "Chinawoman." By 1880, the enumerator made his rounds with an interpreter, and the census information concerning the Chinese is more accurate. The large Chinese population in 1870 is also indicative of the general decline in Helena's mining activity. Chinese on the mining frontier worked the tailings, and their presence signaled the end of profitable placer operations.

8. Chinese men outnumbered Chinese women by ten to one, and there was not one child present in the population. Because marital status was not a category in the 1870 census, it is especially difficult to discern marital relationships among the Chinese, where often there are no names recorded or where the names may or may not have conformed to Chinese tradition wherein women incorporated their maiden names into their married names. Nonetheless, it is evident that Helena's Chinese lived in households markedly different from those in their native country. This was especially true of Helena's Asian women who lived in exclusively female households, an arrangement that was virtually unknown in China. This raises questions about these women's motivations for emigration and the means by which they managed to arrive in the hinterland. Unfortunately, no records survive that would shed light on these issues. Of all Helena's groups, the Chinese left the fewest traces.

9. What is known of Helena's population agrees with modern accounts of Chinese in the United States and explains, in part, the absence of familial households among the Chinese. See Maxine Hong Kingston, *China Men* (New York: Alfred A. Knopf, 1980).

10. See Appendix 2, Table 2.

11. From the birthplaces of successive children in the same family, it is evident that families moved with some regularity over long distances. James and Eliza Rodda, for example, both from England, migrated to Iowa, where their twin daughters, Addie and Norma, and another daughter, Iota Mae, were born. Their next migration took them to Helena, where their last child, Helena, was born.

12. For an example of one resident's itinerant existence, see Patricia L. Dean, "The Jewish Community of Helena, Montana, 1866-1900" (Honors Thesis, Carroll College, Helena, Montana, 1977), 19.

13. Smith, *Rocky Mountain Mining Camps*, Chapter 5.

14. Analysis is based on special aggregate occupational listing from the *U.S. Census, 1870.*

15. Elizabeth Chester Fisk [ECF] to Frances Chester, November 1, 1869, Fisk Family Papers, Montana Historical Society Archives, Helena [MHSA]. All correspondence cited from Elizabeth Chester Fisk is in the Fisk Family Papers.

16. Michael P. Malone and Richard B. Roeder, *Montana: A History of Two Centuries* (Seattle: University of Washington Press, 1976), 140-143; Paul, *Mining Frontiers of the Far West*, 145-148.

17. ECF to Frances Chester, January 2, 1870.

18. Leeson, *History of Montana*, 712-718.

19. Campbell, *From the Quarries of Last Chance Gulch*, 1:55-56.

20. Malone and Roeder, *Montana*, 84-85.

21. ECF to Azubah Clarke Chester [ACC], April 4, 1875.

22. *Helena Weekly Herald*, January 16, 1868.

23. ECF to ACC, November 22, 1874; *Helena Daily Herald*, November 9, 1874. For a full discussion of the charter controversy, see Joan Bishop, "A Season of Trial: Helena's Entrepreneurs Nurture a City," *Montana the Magazine of Western History* 28 (Summer 1978): 62-71.

24. *Helena Daily Herald*, March 27, 1877.

25. ECF to ACC, February 6, 1877.

26. Leeson, *History of Montana*, 704, 707.

27. Ibid., 708.

28. This analysis is based on Helena Board of Trade membership in 1878 and 1887 and linkages between those numbers and *U.S. Census, 1870* and *U.S. Census, 1880: Territory of Montana*, MHSL. Decision making at stages of the human life cycle has been the subject of a number of recent studies. As Lillian Schlissel points out, young men's overland experience marked a rite of passage to adulthood; see Schlissel, *Women's Diaries of the Westward Journey*, 106. As has been suggested by other researchers, perhaps adults feel a particular need to put down roots around the age of forty.

29. Bishop, "A Season of Trial," 69.

30. Montana and Nevada Territories Vol. 1, pp. 288, 245, 214, 240, 298, R. G. Dun & Co. Collection, Baker Library, Harvard University Graduate School of Business Administration [R. G. Dun & Co. reports]; Delores J. Morrow, "Jewish Merchants and the Commercial Emporium of Montana," in *Montana and the West*, ed. Rex C. Myers and Harry W. Fritz (Boulder, Colorado: Pruett Publishing Company, 1984), 17-36. R. G. Dun & Company was the forerunner of Dun and Bradstreet.

31. R. G. Dun & Co. reports, 298, 288.

32. Ibid., 217.

33. Ibid., 245, 288.

34. Ibid., 298.

35. Ibid., 268.

36. Ibid., 284.

37. Ibid., 240.

38. Ibid., 290.

39. Leeson, *History of Montana*, 703.

40. See Appendix 2, tables 4 and 5.

41. In order to arrive at the best estimate for the proportion of the population that boarded, figures are derived from household relationship frequency distribution and frequency distribution of the presence or absence of a husband or wife when the census respondent is listed as married. These statistics should be taken with caution and viewed as conservative. Because the census was taken during the summer, the population was affected in two ways: first, the number of boarders decreased as men went to work in nearby areas or took business trips to the East; second, husbands or wives took advantage of the summer to travel. See Appendix 2, Table 5.

42. See Appendix 2, Table 6.

43. Analysis is based on special aggregate occupational listing from the *U.S. Census, 1880*.

44. See Appendix 2, Table 6.

45. (Helena) *Montana Radiator*, January 27, February 3, 1866.

46. This analysis is based on a special survey of servant population in 1870 and 1880.

47. ECF to ACC, January 6, 1871. A number of Elizabeth Fisk's servants departed to work in the public sphere, and others were lured away by the promise of marriage. Elizabeth did not entirely solve the problem until twelve-year-old Mary Knipper came into the household as a servant. When Mary's father was killed in the International Hotel fire and her family dispersed, the Fisks became Mary's legal guardians. Elizabeth acquired a built-in servant until Mary became so much a part of the family that Elizabeth thought it no longer ethical to consider her as hired help.

48. In 1870, seven children were engaged as servants in Helena. Several were in their teens, but the remainder were under twelve years old. The same phenomenon occurred in 1880, when twenty-seven children were working as servants.

49. See Chapter 4 for a discussion of the effects of the paucity of servants on middle-class women. Statistics are derived from a special survey of servant population in 1870 and 1880.

50. ECF to ACC, May 20, June 15, 1873.

51. Ibid.

52. ECF to ACC, July 27, October 22, 1873.

53. See Appendix 2, Table 6.

54. See Appendix 2, Table 10.

55. Clyde Griffen and Sally Griffen, *Natives and Newcomers: The Ordering of Opportunity in Mid-Nineteenth-Century Poughkeepsie* (Cambridge, Massachusetts: Harvard University Press, 1977), 229-233. The Griffens define their work force as being from age fourteen, whereas

Helena's demographic profile shows that the age demarcation was greater than or equal to eighteen. Even so, the percentages are roughly comparable. In Poughkeepsie, women comprised 20 per cent of the labor force in 1870 and 24 per cent in 1880; this calculation included a large number of workers under the age of eighteen. While Helena neither had the industries nor a large female population, women still entered the work force in significant numbers.

56. See Appendix 2, tables 10 and 16.

57. Statistics are derived from a comparison of total population listings of *U.S. Census, 1870* and *U.S. Census, 1880*. Figuring the rate of persistence in a community is always risky, and Helena is no exception. Because of the marriage of Helena women during the period, this figure underestimates the number who stayed on, although not by very much, considering the small number of single women. In addition, this figure does not include women who continued their frontier careers in neighboring communities. Butte was beginning its phenomenal growth, and it is clear that several women moved there. The point is that the rate of persistence was significantly less than that found in Hamilton. See Michael Katz, *The People of Hamilton, Canada West: Family and Class in a Mid-Nineteenth-Century City* (Cambridge, Massachusetts: Harvard University Press, 1975), 122.

58. *Helena Daily Herald*, June 12, 1883.

59. *Helena Daily Herald*, April 18, 1887.

60. *Helena City Directory, 1886-7* (Helena: Geo E. Boos, 1886). From the addresses of some of the women listed, it is evident that the compiler included prostitutes in the directory. By 1886, the addresses were known bordellos; the women also appear in criminal court records and newspaper accounts for the same period.

61. Jean Baucus, *Gold in the Gulch* (Helena: Bar Wineglass Publications, 1981), 50; *Helena Daily Herald*, August 28, 1882.

62. Rex Myers, "Trolleys of the Treasure State," *Montana the Magazine of Western History* 22 (Spring 1972): 34-47.

63. Alexander Botkin, *The Charter and Ordinances of the City of Helena with the Rules of Order for the Government of the City Council, 1887* (Helena: Journal Publishing, 1887), 130-135. See also Chapter 5. Generally, ordinances governing citizens' social and moral behavior were clustered in the brief period between 1884 and 1887. Earlier ordinances were aimed at the general organization and governance of the community.

64. *Helena Daily Herald*, July 17, 1885.

65. Jean Baucus, *Helena Her Historic Homes*, vol. 1 (Helena: J-G Publications, 1976); Jean Baucus, interview with author, August 13, 1980.

66. Jean Baucus, *Helena Her Historic Homes*, vol. 2 (Helena: Bar Wineglass Publications, 1979); Baucus, *Gold in the Gulch*.

67. *Helena Board of Trade Report for 1887* (Helena: Helena Board of Trade, 1888), 5-6.

68. *Helena Daily Herald*, January 11, 1883; Helena Board of Trade, Vertical File, MHSL; Leeson, *History of Montana*, 702; Ellis L. Waldron and Paul B. Wilson, *Atlas of Montana Elections, 1889-1976* (Missoula: University of Montana Publications in History, 1978); Ellis L. Waldron, *Montana Legislators, 1864-1979* (Missoula: Bureau of Government Research, University of Montana, 1980).

69. *Helena Daily Herald*, January 3, 1888.

70. *Helena Daily Herald*, March 13, 1888.

71. Rex C. Myers, "The Montana Club: Symbol of Elegance," *Montana the Magazine of Western History* 26 (Autumn 1976): 30-51.

72. See chapters 3 and 4.

73. Comparison of residents' addresses in the *Historical Sketch and Essay on the Resources of Montana; Including a Business Directory of the Metropolis* (Helena: Herald Book and Job Printing, 1868) and the *Helena City Directory, 1886-7* demonstrates that various occupational groups were mixed in both their places of residence and places of business during the early period. An analysis of the *U.S. Census, 1900: State of Montana*, MHSL, suggests that the new residential groupings became permanent features in the city's geography.

74. Campbell, *From the Quarries of Last Chance Gulch*, 1:123, 2:22-26.

75. A cursory analysis of East Helena's population suggests a greater percentage of foreign-born workers connected with the smelter. See Appendix 2, Table 6.

76. *Helena Board of Trade Report for 1887*, 22.

77. *Helena Daily Herald*, September 6, 1890.

78. *Helena Daily Herald*, May 7, March 11, 1890; *Helena City Directory, 1889* (Helena: A. W. Ide, 1889); *Helena City Directory, 1890* (Helena: R. L. Polk & Company, 1890); Campbell, *From the Quarries of Last Chance Gulch*, 2:21; Waldron, *Montana Legislators*.

79. *Helena Herald*, April 4, April 21, April 22, April 24, May 12, May 29, June 12, July 11, July 21, September 1, 1891, April 16, 1892.

80. Miscellaneous Records, vol. 13, 148-154; *Helena Herald*, July 27, 1893; First National Bank of Helena Records, MHSA; Merchants National Bank Records, MHSA; *Helena Herald*, August 1, 1893.

81. *Helena Herald*, August 7, August 9, August 18, August 25, 1893; *Record of Civil Actions*, vol. 1.

82. *Helena Herald*, February 27, 1894.

83. *Helena Herald*, August 15, 1893. Chicken pilfering was also a popular way of augmenting the larder; see *Helena Herald*, September 5, 1893.

84. *Helena Herald*, July 12, 1893.

85. *Helena Herald*, August 28. 1893.

86. *Helena Evening Herald*, September 4, 1896, February 13, 1897.

87. First National Bank of Helena Records; Merchants National Bank Records. Nineteenth century banking was a personal affair, and bank officers were accustomed to using the bank's resources to finance their own projects. Banking during the period was often an extension of an entrepreneur's success in another area. In short, internal personal loans were common and accepted practice. Unfortunately, the Panic of 1893 coincided with bank officers' large loans to themselves. There were, however, limits to which this personal loan policy could be carried. In the case of the Merchants National Bank, Eugene Wilson detected gross mismanagement and malfeasance on the brothers Hershfields' part and supported a suit against them. Judge Hiram Knowles dismissed the suit for lack of evidence in 1900. The collapse of the bank spelled the end of the Hershfields' career in Helena. Louis returned to New York City, presumably on his ill-gotten gains, and Aaron, having disgraced himself on numerous occasions, was left in the West to manage as best he could.

88. Rollin Lynde Hartt to his mother, November 2, 1896, Rollin Lynde Hartt Letters, SC 155, MHSA.

89. *Helena Evening Herald*, October 23, 1899.

90. See Appendix 2, tables 1 and 5. The percentage of the population boarding in 1870 was 4.5 per cent; in 1880, 12.1 per cent; and in 1900, 11 per cent.

91. See Appendix 2, tables 2 and 4. Data are derived from an analysis of the total female population between the ages of twenty-one and thirty contained in the *U.S. Census, 1880* and *U.S. Census, 1900: State of Montana*, MHSL. Figures include women listed as single, divorced, or widowed. See Appendix 2, Table 4.

92. See Appendix 2, Table 4.

93. *Helena Daily Herald*, December 12, 1889; *Helena Herald*, January 26, 1891; *U.S. Census, 1900*.

94. *Helena Herald*, June 4, June 5, 1895; *Helena Daily Herald*, December 4, 1884; *Helena Evening Herald*, April 8, 1895.

95. Richard B. Roeder, "Crossing the Gender Line: Ella L. Knowles, Montana's First Woman Lawyer," *Montana the Magazine of Western History* 32 (Summer 1982): 64-75.

96. See Appendix 2, Table 7.

CHAPTER TWO: Capitalists with Rooms

1. *Report of the Secretary of the Helena Board of Trade for the Year 1878* (Helena: Fisk Brothers, 1879), 27; see Appendix 2, Table 10.

2. Deed Book A, p. 280; Deed Book C, pp. 135, 166; Deed Book F, pp. 194, 388, 438; Deed Book E, pp. 142, 491-492; Deed Book G, p. 99; Deed Book H, p. 108; Deed Book I, p. 98; Book A of the Helena Townsite, 90, 91, 99, 100. Property transactions between 1865 and 1870 are derived from the grantor and grantee books and represent a reconstruction of information contained in Plat Book 1, which was destroyed in a boiler explosion in the early twentieth century. Analysis of property transactions is limited to the sixty-block area of the original townsite.

3. *Historical Sketch and Essay on the Resources of Montana*, 1868; *U.S. Census, 1870*. Comparison of the two sources suggests that the city directory asked for place of last residence rather than place of birth or origin.

4. Deed Book C, p. 200; Deed Book D, p. 324; Deed Book I, p. 98. Some property transfers from the early period include the wholesale transfer of household articles, making it possible to obtain some idea of a demimondaine's personal property. Among the items moved from prostitute to prostitute were gold scales, suggesting that the fancy ladies were in the mainstream of the mining economy.

5. Statistics are derived from an analysis of 116 property transactions of prostitutes between 1865 and 1870.

6. The figure 265 represents the number of transactions by women who bought and sold property solely in their own names. Prostitutes dealt primarily with male businessmen associated with the district (54 per cent), with other women (30 per cent), or with the probate judge (16 per cent).

7. Mortgage Book A, pp. 19, 123, 373; Mortgage Book C, pp. 17, 174; Mortgage Book B, pp. 173, 267; Mortgage Book D, pp. 135, 338, 363; Mortgage Book E, p. 79; Mortgage Book F, pp. 38, 120, 131, 143, 377, 379, 395, 422.

8. Statistics are derived from an analysis of twenty mortgages made to prostitutes; thirteen of the mortgages went unpaid, nine of them made by men to prostitutes. The greatest losses were incurred by Edward Zimmerman and Louise Courselle. Mortgage cancellation does not seem to have been a task that the county clerk was especially meticulous about. Often, a record of a mortgage went uncancelled, yet the same parties did business again.

9. Civil Case no. 1405, Old Series.

10. Civil Case no. 1342, Old Series. *Lavenberg v. Bischoff* and *Harrison v. Pounds* are only two of a number of civil suits involving demimonde residents. Mollie Teats, Dolores Jarra, Carrie Bedell, Eleanor Alphonsine Dumont, Fannie Bird, Louise Courselle, Nellie Perkins, Belle Crafton, and Josephine "Chicago Joe" Hensley all appeared in court as plaintiffs or defendants in civil litigation. Clearly, these women believed that they had recourse to the law in spite of their profession. As the nature of prostitution changed, however, Wood Street denizens, with the exception of the demimonde's leaders, made fewer attempts to settle their differences in the courts.

11. Plotted on the J. D. McIntyre Survey map of 1884. The McIntyre Survey, with a few changes, represents the plat of the town in 1865-1870. See Appendix 3, maps 1-3.

12. (Helena) *Montana Post-Fire Express,* May 3, 1869; Book A of the Helena Townsite, 63-105; (Helena) *Montana Post,* May 14, 1869; *U.S. Census, 1870*; Coroner's Inquisition no. 332; *Historical Sketch and Essay on the Resources of Montana,* 1868; Deed Book H, p. 314; Book A of the Helena Townsite, 365.

13. See Appendix 2, Table 10. The census enumerator in 1870 was reluctant to describe any woman as a prostitute, so the figure for white prostitutes is derived from other sources. Like any other census, Helena's was prey to underestimation, and marginal individuals were usually those most often passed over. Although the lines between legitimate but often shady occupations and prostitution were often blurred, it is clear from the sources that these occupations and the individuals involved were engaged in prostitution. The figure, therefore, is a conservative but accurate one for the population of prostitutes. The number of Chinese prostitutes is an estimate based on figures in the 1880 census. Helena's population remained fairly constant between 1870 and 1880, and it seems fair to assume that the Chinese prostitute population hovered in this neighborhood even though the total Chinese population decreased. Again, this figure errs on the side of conservatism. In the absence of more definite data, no attempt will be made to discuss Chinese prostitution during the early period.

14. See Appendix 2, Table 12.

15. Marion Goldman, "Sexual Commerce on the Comstock Lode," *Nevada Historical Society Quarterly* 21 (Summer 1978): 112-117.

16. See Appendix 2, Table 11.

17. Information is derived from an analysis of property transactions from 1865 to 1870 and is based on dates of property sales and purchases.

18. Josephine Airey "Chicago Joe" Hensley has been the subject of what little research has been done on prostitution in Helena. See Rex Myers, "An Inning for Sin: Chicago Joe and Her Hurdy Gurdy Girls," *Montana the Magazine of Western History* 27 (Spring 1977): 24-33; Herbert M. Peet, " 'Chicago Joe' Found Dictionary Better Defense Than Statutes in 'Hurdy Gurdy' House Trial," *Great Falls Tribune,* July 10, 1955. Chicago Joe was illiterate and could not write her name. Her name in various sources is spelled at least seven differ-

ent ways; I have chosen the one used with the most frequency. There can be no doubt that Mary Welch, Josephine Airey, and Josephine Hensley are one and the same person. Numerous notarized documents attest to the fact that Josephine Hensley was at one time known as Josephine Airey. The only times Chicago Joe reverted to her given name were at her two marriages.

19. Deed Book F, p. 194; Mortgage Book B, p. 173. The actual record of the deed is made to a Josephine Aeary; the grantee index lists that buyer as Josephine Neary. Close examination of the transaction reveals that Neary is a miscopy of Aery, one of the many variants of Josephine Airey's name. There is no record that this mortgage was ever cancelled.

20. Marriage Record of Lewis and Clark County, Book A, 1865-1907. Albert Hankins was an apparent intimate of the demimonde and had previously been associated with another fancy lady, Anna Belsford, whom he had fleeced of $2,000. Criminal Case no. 60, Office of Clerk of Court, Deer Lodge County Courthouse, Anaconda, Montana [DLCC].

21. Book A of the Helena Townsite, 13; Deed Book I, p. 399.

22. Myers, "An Inning for Sin," 27; *Helena Independent,* October 26, 1899. This seems a reasonable assumption, although there is no record of their presence in Nevada nor is there any record of a divorce between Albert Hankins and Josephine Airey.

23. R. G. Dun & Co. reports, pp. 240-240[20]; Deed Book L, p. 230; Mortgage Book F, pp. 337, 379; Mortgage Book G, p. 149.

24. Deed Book M, p. 438.

25. Mortgage Book F, p. 432; Mortgage Book G, p. 392; R. G. Dun & Co. reports, p. 240; Mortgage Book H, p. 70.

26. Mortgage Book H, p. 70; Leeson, *History of Montana,* 681.

27. Leeson, *History of Montana,* 717. Josephine Airey may have lost as much as $3,500 in the fire, although the tabulation is speculative because of variations in the spelling of her name and the colloquial designation of buildings. Leeson lists a "Mrs. Ayre's house" and "Jo's Mason house." One or both or neither could have been Airey's.

28. Leeson, *History of Montana,* 717; Deed Book N, p. 564; Frank W. Warner, *Montana Territory, History and Business Directory* (Helena: Fisk Brothers, 1879), 149. The Red Light Saloon appears with James T. Hensley listed as proprietor, but Josephine Airey Hensley owned the property and had been the owner since 1874. First mention of James Hensley occurs in a subpoena relating to the insanity hearing of Mary Kelly on May 2, 1874. Hensley joined with Josephine Airey, Dolores Jarra, and Lillie McGraw in petitioning the court for Mary Kelly's incarceration. Subsequently, Dr. William Bullard of Radersburg wrote an assessment of Mary Kelly's mental state in which he asserted that the Kelly woman was a victim of designing demimonde leadership that sought to defraud her of her property. Records of the Montana Territory, Executive Office, Record Series 40, MHSA. Insanity petitions seem to have been a device used in the demimonde to control its residents and illegally obtain property through guardianship. Early insanity cases were unnumbered.

29. Deed Book S, p. 246.

30. Miscellaneous Records, vol. 3, 423, 567, 583.

31. Deed Book U, pp. 37, 146, 266, 405; Deed Book S, pp. 330, 364, 637, 639; Deed Book T, p. 305.

32. See Appendix 2, tables 10, 13, 15. The census enumerator in 1880 was unwilling to designate white women as prostitutes but was less reluctant to count Chinese women as tenderloin workers. The statistics for white prostitutes are derived from and corroborated by other sources. The base population is a conservative but accurate estimate.

33. Goldman, "Sexual Commerce on the Comstock Lode," 111-114. See also Appendix 2, Table 11.

34. See Appendix 2, Table 11; *U.S. Census, 1880;* Sanborn Map and Publishing Company, Ltd., Helena, insurance map, 1883, MHSL.

35. In 1896, two of Helena's major banks failed magnificently. Through fortuitous circumstance, their records were preserved. See First National Bank of Helena Records, and Merchants National Bank Records, MHSA. Statistics derived from these sources are minimums. It is quite possible that prostitutes maintained accounts in one of several other Helena banks. Evidence from later mortgages suggests that the Thomas Cruse Savings Bank had

connections with prostitution. Individual account ledgers are among those items missing from the Thomas Cruse Papers, MHSA. Statistics are based on an analysis of seven bank accounts. First National Bank of Helena Records, vols. 21, 22; Merchants National Bank Records, vols. 32, 33.

36. *Helena Board of Trade Report for 1887*, 12, 14.

37. Chattel inventories and probate inventories include fur items, bar crystal, and furniture made of hardwoods and marble. Fannie Spencer's list of creditors provides evidence of prostitutes' expenditures. Probate no. 196, Old Series.

38. Statistics are based on an analysis of seven bank accounts. First National Bank of Helena Records, vols. 21, 22; Merchants National Bank Records, vols. 32, 33.

39. Deed Book V, pp. 9, 546; Deed Book Y, pp. 268, 305; Deed Book 2, pp. 205, 296, 632; Deed Book 2, p. 569.

40. The *Helena City Directory, 1883-4* (Helena: Geo E. Boos, 1884) indicates that the tenement housed a variety of working-class men.

41. Probate no. 2605, New Series; Deed Book O, 218; Deed Book W, 90; Deed Book Y, 377; Deed Book 1, 171; Sanborn insurance map, 1883; First National Bank of Helena Records, vols. 22, 23.

42. Probate no. 4571, New Series; First National Bank of Helena Records, vols. 20, 21, 22; Deed Book W, p. 149.

43. Deed Book 2, p. 149; First National Bank of Helena Records, vols. 20, 21; Probate no. 196, Old Series; Deed Book 2, p. 560.

44. Deed Book I, pp. 206, 208; Mortgage Book G, p. 144; Mortgage Book D, p. 93; Book A of the Helena Townsite, 95-97; Baptismal Records, St. Helena's Cathedral, Diocese of Helena Archives, Helena, Montana; Deed Book M, p. 406; Deed Book N, p. 538. The priest's notation on the daughters' baptismal certificates lists Dolores Jarra's relationship to the father as "concubina."

45. Apart from the record of the 1876 property conveyance, Dolores Jarra's last official appearance in Helena occurs in an unnumbered insanity petition that she filed with Lillie McGraw, Josephine Airey (later Josephine Hensley), and James T. Hensley against Mary Kelly; Mortgage Book E, p. 15, Office of the Clerk and Recorder, DLCC; Criminal Case no. 1213, Office of the Clerk of Court, DLCC; *Butte Miner*, April 4, 1878.

46. Marriage Record Book A (typescript in the volume), Office of the Clerk of Court, DLCC; Mortgage Book 1, 202, Office of the Clerk and Recorder, Silver Bow County Courthouse, Butte, Montana [SBCC]; Deed Book B2, 263, Office of the Clerk and Recorder, DLCC; Miscellaneous Records I, 202, Office of the Clerk and Recorder, SBCC; *U.S. Census, 1880*.

47. Probate no. 187, Old Series; Miscellaneous Records, vol. 3, 538-540, 561-562, 590-591, 604, 628. In September 1876, Dolores transferred the property in the Prickly Pear Valley to her minor daughters. See Deed Book Q, 237. On September 9, 1886, the *Helena Independent* reported Charles Stanchfield's arrest for causing a disturbance in a bawdy house on Clore Street. Apparently, Stanchfield did not entirely forsake his social interest in the demimonde after his marriage, and Dolores's caution was well-advised.

48. Deed Book E, p. 758, Office of the Clerk and Recorder, SBCC; Miscellaneous Records, vol. 5, 25-27; Miscellaneous Records, vol. 6, 423.

49. Undated newspaper clipping attached to the Magnolia Hotel Register (internal evidence suggests the year 1889), Magnolia Hotel Records, SC 1098, MHSA; Marriage License no. 1786; Deed Book 28, pp. 327, 329; Deed Book 33, p. 230; Deed Book 43, p. 570; Mortgage Book 12, p. 259; Mortgage Book 15, p. 25; *Helena City Directory* (Helena: R. L. Polk & Company, 1892-1894). The narrative of these sources suggests the following scenario: In 1891, the Stanchfields used the profit from the farm to finance an ice business managed by Charles Stanchfield in Helena. By 1894, in the aftermath of the panic, they were strapped for capital and mortgaged their property for $1,500. Successful in repaying their debt, the Stanchfields found themselves in need again. In 1895, they secured an additional mortgage for $5,000 from Corlea Cullen. Three years later, they had paid nothing, and Cullen had to take action. Although their mortgagee obviously did not want to be encumbered with the farm, she had no choice and foreclosed.

50. *Helena Independent*, June 11, 1886; Records, vol. 6, p. 24, Office of the Clerk and Recorder, Madison County Courthouse, Virginia City, Montana; Civil Case no. 454, Office of the Clerk of Court, SBCC; *U.S. Census, 1880*; Deed Book V, p. 423; Deed Book W, pp. 288-289; Criminal Case nos. 841, 843, 988, 989, 1035, 1068, 1033, 1101, 1214, 1216, 1159.

51. Civil Case no. 454, Office of the Clerk of Court, SBCC; Civil Case nos. 2860, 3553, Old Series.

52. Civil Case no. 3866, Old Series; Deed Book 19, p. 306; Miscellaneous Records, vol. 6, 606; Miscellaneous Records, vol. 7, 161. The final record of Sarah Dubay Stevenson appears in an unidentified jail record book kept for the purposes of recording board charges for prisoners for 1889. Sarah's name appears on the roster for an unknown offense. See Lewis and Clark County Sheriff Records, SC 1633, MHSA. There is also some indication that Sarah remarried and was deserted, again by James Gorman. See Civil Case no. 1302, New Series.

53. Civil Case no. 1302, New Series; Criminal Case nos. 998, 996, 1201, 1288, 1317, 1328, 1417, 1156, 1305, 1208, 1298, 1147, 1202, 1017, 1055, 946, 1003, 1002, 1097, 1039, 975, 1016, 916, 746, 772, 662, 548, 724, 715, 672, 336, 196, 337.

54. Sanborn insurance map, 1883.

55. *Report of the Secretary of the Helena Board of Trade, for the Year 1878*, 30-32.

56. This analysis is based on an examination of prostitutes' property transactions between 1865 and 1870, court cases between 1873 and 1883, and the *U.S. Census, 1870* and *U.S. Census, 1880*. An examination of divorce cases between 1865 and 1883 indicates that no prostitute was named as a correspondent in any divorce suit involving a legitimate member of the community. During the same period, however, fancy ladies were named in suits brought by residents of the demimonde. After 1883, several scattered suits suggest that the residents of the tenderloin had become bolder in their associations with married gentlemen and were responsible for undermining several marriages.

57. No death register exists for the period, but coroner's inquests into unattended or suspicious deaths are complete from 1875 forward, and no prostitute appears in these records. Similarly, newspaper accounts list no tenderloin suicides between 1865 and 1875.

58. Brown, *The Gentle Tamers*; Curt Gentry, *The Madams of San Francisco* (Sausalito, California: Comstock Editions, 1977); Goldman, "Sexual Commerce on the Comstock Lode," 99, 118.

59. Deed Book 4, pp. 160, 240; Deed Book 8, p. 303; Deed Book 12, p. 254; Deed Book 12, p. 358; *Helena City Directory, 1883-4*, 121; Deed Book 21, p. 424; Mortgage Book 12, pp. 250, 369. There is no record of Josephine Hensley's purchase of two properties: Lot 4 and the south half of Lot 16, Block 21. The former was property that contained the International Hotel. Nonetheless, Joe must have held clear title to these properties, as she was able to mortgage and sell them without hindrance. Earlier in 1879, Joe had made a loan to one of the wily Lavenbergs, who had defaulted on the agreement. See Mortgage Book J, p. 341.

60. Deed Book 3, p. 285; Deed Book 5, p. 426; Deed Book 6, p. 427; Deed Book 15, pp. 373, 375; Book C of the Helena Townsite, 99; Deed Book 21, p. 374; Deed Book 20, p. 375; Deed Book 4, p. 378.

61. Deed Book 6, pp. 393, 396; see Appendix 2, Table 11; Deed Book 16, p. 2; Deed Book 20, p. 199.

62. The figure for the number of prostitutes is derived from the *Helena City Directory, 1886-7*. Lot and block number were matched with the 1888 Sanborn insurance map for addresses. Newspaper accounts for the period substantiate the directory entries. See Paula Petrik, "Strange Bedfellows: Prostitution, Politicians, and Moral Reform in Helena, Montana, 1885-1889," *Montana the Magazine of Western History* 35 (Summer 1985): 2-13. First National Bank of Helena Records, vols. 23, 24, 25; Merchants National Bank Records, vols. 38, 39; see Appendix 2, Table 11. Women owned property on Clore Street but for various reasons never sustained their ownership for very long. The careers of Sarah Dubay Stevenson, Fannie Spencer Fordanski, and Dolores Jarra are typical of this pattern. See Paula Petrik, "Capitalists With Rooms Revisited: Prostitution in Helena, Montana, 1865-1900" (paper presented at the Women's West Conference, Sun Valley, Idaho, August 12, 1983).

63. Mortgage Book N, p. 210; Mortgage Book 3, p. 23; *Helena Board of Trade Report for 1887*, 10; *Helena Daily Record*, January 1, 1889; Sanborn insurance map, 1888.

64. *Helena Daily Record*, January 1, 1889; Myers, "An Inning for Sin," 31, 33.

65. *Helena Daily Independent*, October 26, 1899.

66. ECF to Frances Chester, January 22, 1871; ECF to ACC, March 30, 1873, September 7, 1890. Sexual matters were difficult topics for Elizabeth. In her letters, she barely alluded to her own pregnancies and euphemistically referred to the impending arrival of the "little

stranger." Perhaps like other nineteenth century women, Elizabeth had the unlimited capacity to ignore those subjects that she found distasteful. Vague hints in her letters indicate that Elizabeth was very much aware of Wood Street's skin trade, but she preferred to keep her counsel on the subject and to bend her efforts toward isolating her children from the district's influence.

67. *Helena Independent*, August 14, 1884.

68. *Helena Independent*, February 25, February 27, February 14, February 23, February 24, 1885.

69. *Helena Independent*, June 23, 1885.

70. Botkin, *The Charter and Ordinances of the City of Helena*, 126-127.

71. *Helena Daily Herald*, December 13, 1887; *Helena Independent*, June 12, 1886. Hendry correctly perceived a market for detailed local news. Whereas the *Herald* made little mention of police court doings, except to note the most sensational, and reported city council meetings in the most perfunctory manner, the *Independent* reveled in its minute descriptions of the most interesting offenders and meetings, accompanying them with appropriate commentary and recreating dialogue from the city council meetings. The *Herald* concentrated on national and state news, and its editorial columns were filled with the paper's interpretations of these events in addition to scathing attacks on its competing journal. The circumstance was probably a result of the political aspirations of *Herald* editor Robert E. Fisk, who spent much of his time angling unsuccessfully for political administrative appointments. Hence, historians must rely almost entirely on the *Independent* for a record of local events.

72. *Helena Independent*, September 9, 1885, April 3, April 5, 1886. The *Independent*'s sole reform interest before Joseph Hendry's tenure was the opium problem and the presence of the Chinese. It is interesting that Hendry began his reform journalism with the same topic, thereby maintaining the continuity established by the previous management.

73. *Helena Independent*, April 6, April 15, April 30, 1886.

74. *Helena Independent*, June 4, June 18, June 26, July 27, July 17, 1886. The monthly general report of the police magistrate to the city council for 1886-1887 included only a handful of prostitution arrests; neither journal mentioned notorious women, with the exception of the multiple arrests on July 17, 1886. The newspapers used this occasion, however, to provide a lesson in the fate of fallen women. One woman, the daughter of a New York bank president, was being assisted by "one of the best known of the younger residents of Helena" to escape her sad fate.

75. Criminal Case no. 1767, Old Series; *Helena Daily Herald*, August 23, 1886; *Helena City Directory, 1886-7*.

76. *Helena Independent*, August 31, 1886.

77. *Helena Independent*, August 31, 1886; *Helena Daily Herald*, August 31, 1886.

78. *Helena Independent*, January 30, February 2, February 16, February 26, 1887.

79. *Helena Independent*, March 3, June 14, June 21, 1887.

80. *Helena Independent*, April 5, April 6, 1887. It is interesting that John Worth's election from Helena's second ward marked only the second time that a Democrat had been successful from that area of the city. One might reasonably assume that Worth's occupation and his probable ties to tenderloin interests influenced his political win.

81. *U.S. Census, 1870*; *U.S. Census, 1880*; *Helena City Directory, 1883-4*; *Helena City Directory, 1886-7*; Leeson, *History of Montana*. The membership of the city council was composed of men who had settled in Helena before 1870, with the exception of Richard Howey, educator; Ernest Thieme, proprietor of the Grand Pacific Hotel; John H. Saul, proprietor of the Commercial Hotel; and Archer O. Simons, agent for the Singer Sewing Machine Company. William Lorey, a wallpaper dealer, arrived in 1874, and it seems fairly certain that Robert C. Wallace, a grocer, also came to Helena in the late 1870s.

82. Leeson, *History of Montana*, 1223-1224.

83. *Helena Independent*, April 14, June 4, June 19, 1887.

84. *Helena Independent*, June 25, 1887.

85. *Helena Independent*, October 7, October 9, 1887.

86. *Helena Independent*, October 14, 1887.

87. *Helena Daily Record*, January 1, 1889; *Helena Independent*, August 3, August 10, 1888; *Helena Daily Herald*, December 13, 1887; *Helena Independent*, April 20, 1889, December 13, December 16, 1890, January 24, 1891; *Helena Board of Trade Report for 1887*, 26. There is the

sense from later issues of the *Independent* that law enforcement officials found a way to circumvent Howey's resolution. By mid-1889, the *Independent* made a brief reference to a quarterly roundup of prostitutes and, in 1891, police arrested pimps instead of prostitutes on a regular basis.

88. Register of Deaths in Lewis and Clark County, pp. 1ff.

89. Coroner's Inquisition no. 278.

90. Ibid.

91. Coroner's Inquisition nos. 177, 176, 201, 242.

92. Record of Marriages, License no. 194.

93. *Helena City Directory, 1891* (Helena: R. L. Polk & Company, 1891); Abstract no. 2482, Helena Abstract and Title Company, Helena, Montana [HATCO].

94. Civil Case no. 4460, New Series.

95. Ibid.

96. Record of Marriages, License no. 2645; Abstract no. 2482, HATCO; Deed Book 43, p. 615; Civil Case no. 4646, New Series; Deed Book 44, p. 439.

97. Abstract no. 2482, HATCO; Will no. 349, New Series; Probate no. 349, New Series.

98. Probate no. 349, New Series; Will no. 349, New Series. All documents pertaining to the contestment trial are contained in the probate file. The Weinsheimer marriage had been a violent one from its outset. On September 25, 1899, Mollie filed a divorce action. The suit never came to court, but in her complaint Mollie claimed that "the defendant had threatened to kill plaintiff and to blow out her brains, and to split her head open with an ax." See Civil Case no. 4807, New Series.

99. Civil Case no. 4807, New Series.

100. *Helena Daily Herald*, February 10, 1870. Few, if any, newspaper accounts allude to a pimp/mistress relationship before the mid 1880s.

101. See William L. Lang, "The Nearly Forgotten Blacks of Last Chance Gulch, 1900-1912," *Pacific Northwest Quarterly* 70 (April 1979): 50-57; idem, "Tempest on Clore Street: Race and Politics in Helena, Montana, 1906," *Scratchgravel Hills* 3 (Summer 1980): 9-14. Lang points out that several notorious murder cases involving black fancy women and their men caused problems for the black community during the Progressive Era. Earlier newspaper references indicate that pimps became a feature of the district in the mid 1880s and often made their points with violence.

102. *Muller v. Buyck*, 12 Mont. (1893), 373, 360.

103. Ibid.

104. Ibid., 374-375; Mortgage Book N, p. 22. Because the mortgage is dated 1886, there is the sense that Sully Buyck had planned his fraud for some time and used his role as Anna's manager to gain Chicago Joe's confidence. Cautious about lending money, Joe had made no loans in the district since her experience with the Lavenbergs, and it seems reasonable to assume that she believed she was doing business with Anna and not with Buyck.

105. Civil Case no. 935.

106. *Muller v. Buyck*, 374, 372, 377, 379.

107. Tax Assessment List, 1890; Probate no. 187, New Series; *U.S. Census, 1900*; Sanborn insurance map, 1890.

108. Thomas Cruse appears in the list of boarders at the Cosmopolitan Hotel in the winters of 1871 through 1875.

109. Mortgage Book 10, pp. 284, 434; Deed Book 37, p. 396; Civil Case no. 3607.

110. Civil Case no. 3607.

111. Mortgage Book 5, p. 4; Mortgage Book 1, pp. 209, 382; Mortgage Book 8, p. 631.

112. Probate no. 187, New Series; Register of Deaths, p. 1ff.

113. Cancellation of the Switzer mortgages was made on July 18, 1899. Most of Joe's property transactions were signed "Josephine 'X' Hensley, her mark." In later years, Nellie Reynolds accompanied Joe and signed for her, saving Joe the embarrassment of her illiteracy. Register of Deaths, p. 1ff.

114. Civil Case no. 3706. Records of this case include the receivers' reports for 1897 through 1900. Ledger sheets show no attempt at improvement, merely maintenance. Finally, the receiver for the Cruse bank advised the firm to sell the property because the receiver was incurring heavy financial losses. Jacob Switzer evidently closed the Coliseum Theater; Josephine Hensley's obituary refers to the theater's closure several years before her death.

115. *U.S. Census, 1900; Helena City Directory* (Helena: R. L. Polk & Company, 1891-1903); *Helena Independent*, October 26, 1899; Probate no. 187, New Series; Abstract no. 2482, HATCO; Margaret Hibbard, interview with author, Helena, August 17, 1980.

116. See Appendix 2, tables 11, 12, 15. No accounts can be traced to prostitutes in the 1900 census from the Northwestern National Bank and the First National Bank of Helena, which have allowed me limited access to their early records. Register of Deaths, p. 1ff.

117. Goldman, "Sexual Commerce on the Comstock Lode," 99, 118; George M. Blackburn and Sherman L. Richards, "The Prostitutes and Gamblers of Virginia City, Nevada, 1870," *Pacific Historical Review* 48 (May 1979): 258; Nancy Cott, "Passionlessness: An Interpretation of Victorian Sexual Ideology, 1790-1850," *Signs* 4 (Winter 1978): 219-236; Kathryn Kish Sklar, *Catharine Beecher: A Study in American Domesticity* (New York: W. W. Norton, 1973).

118. Records of the Montana Attorney General, "Commercialized Prostitution Conditions in Helena, Montana and Environs, March 1953," Record Series 76, MHSA.

CHAPTER THREE: Mothers and Daughters of Eldorado

1. For example, see narratives of Elizabeth Chester Fisk, Fisk Family Papers, and Mary Pauline Holter, A. M. Holter Papers, MHSA. Because of Helena's proximity to Fort Benton and the Missouri River, the likely choice for Montana emigrants was riverboat travel. It is clear from the paucity of marriages recorded in Lewis and Clark County between 1865 and 1875 that men returned to the States to find wives after they had been successful on the frontier, a circumstance that contributed to the age difference between husbands and wives. For a typical example, see *Helena Independent*, December 5, 1900.

2. This analysis is based on an examination of "familial" households with boarders: extended family, nuclear family, and double-family arrangements. Women who worked outside the home and kept boarders were excluded, as were women who operated obviously commercial establishments, that is, boarding houses or hotels. These exclusions were made to gauge the extent of informal boarding in the population and, thereby, to better estimate women's economic involvement. The percentage of Helena women keeping boarders is greater than that in other cities outside the frontier but compares favorably with boarding rates in other mining frontier communities. Griffen and Griffen, *Natives and Newcomers*, 235-236; Ralph Mann, *After the Gold Rush: Society in Grass Valley and Nevada City, California, 1849-1870* (Chicago: Turnbull and Willoughby, 1985), 108-115.

3. *Second Annual Report of the Secretary of the Helena Board of Trade for the Year 1879* (Helena: Woolfolk, McQuaid and La Croix, 1880), 14.

4. This analysis is based on sole tradership declarations contained in Miscellaneous Records, vol. 1-6. Of the 119 sole tradership declarations, approximately one-quarter involved women who later divorced. Perhaps assertiveness within the marketplace induced the same trait in their marriages.

5. R. G. Dun & Co. reports, 231.

6. See Chapter 2. Successful female entrepreneurship occurred most often in the criminal economy.

7. R. G. Dun & Co. reports, 240; Miscellaneous Records, vol. 4, 450-451, vol. 5, 320, vol. 3, 79, 446, vol. 4, 265-266; Elizabeth Chester Fisk [ECF] to Azubah Clarke Chester [ACC], January 19, 1868, January 25, 1868. The Fisk Family Papers is an extraordinarily large collection. Elizabeth Chester Fisk's letters to her family number more than 550; I have drawn material from nearly 75 per cent of the correspondence addressed to her mother and her sister from 1867 to 1893. On a much smaller scale, I have made reference to other correspondence as it pertained to the narrative. Elizabeth Chester Fisk maintained an exceptionally open relationship with both her mother and sister. Even so, there is some indication of subtle differences in the quality of communication between Elizabeth and her mother and Elizabeth and her sister. Elizabeth felt free to confide her "blue feelings" and complaints to her mother. These letters she directed her mother to burn. Writing to her sister, Elizabeth was at liberty to mention "racier" topics.

8. For examples, see Miscellaneous Records, vol. 1, 78, vol. 3, 334, 339, 533, vol. 2, 207, 217, 258, 455, vol. 3, 131, 136-137, 149, 153, 163, 184, 190, 192, 202, 232, 270. The separate property transactions and sole tradership declarations were counted by hand and linked to the 1880 census. As such, the figure 10 per cent is liable to error, but on the conservative side.

9. Leeson, *History of Montana*, 681-686. Figures from 1870 and 1880 are derived from property transactions contained in Grantee Books I-IV and Grantor Books I-IV. Because this statistic is based on a reconstruction and is counted by hand, it is liable to error. The majority of those listed in Leeson's accounting are early prostitutes and madams: Fanny Bird, Louise Courselle, Eleanore Alphonsine Dumont, Belle Basque, and Josephine Airey.

10. Statistics are derived from an analysis of a sample—those whose last names begin with "B"—taken from Mortgage Record, Book I. Between 1865 and 1900, women financed 10 per cent of all mortgages; but between 1886 and 1893, the peak of their lending activity, they handled 25 per cent of the mortgages.

11. Clark Spence, *Territorial Politics and Government in Montana, 1864-89* (Urbana: University of Illinois, 1975), 201-202.

12. Campbell, *From the Quarries of Last Chance Gulch*, 1:185; *Helena Daily Herald*, April 7, 1888.

13. Elizabeth Chester Fisk, "The Associated Charities," n.d., minutes of the Poor Relief Committee, February 24, March 3, 1887, May 9, 1889, June 6, December 1, 1890, Helena Women's Relief Committee Records, SC 997, MHSA. In addition to providing personal charity and canvassing their friends for contributions, the women disbursed between $500 and $750 allocated to them on a quarterly basis. They also submitted detailed accounts to the council and were not above badgering the council when they believed its members were dragging their feet or were unappreciative of the women's activities.

14. The absence of any newspaper coverage of women's activities or women's columns testifies to the eclipse of "true womanhood" in Helena. Both Elizabeth Chester Fisk's correspondence and the testimony taken by chancery referees in divorce court during this period also reflect women's lack of attention to the ideology. Compared with the evidence found during the 1880s, this absence is striking. This is not to say that the "cult of true womanhood" was dead; it only lay dormant.

15. *Helena Independent*, July 19, November 13, December 12, February 27, 1887.

16. *Helena Independent*, March 5, 1886. See, for example, *Helena Independent*, August 12, 1886.

17. *Helena Independent*, April 6, April 8, April 22, March 11, March 28, April 1, 1888.

18. This statistic represents a mean and is based on a computer analysis of the female population in 1870.

19. See Appendix 1, Appendix 2, Table 21.

20. Ibid.; Mrs. Emma S. Cannon to Mrs. A. J. Davidson, October 27, 1894, Women's Helena for the Capital Club Records, MHSA.

21. See Appendix 2, Table 21.

22. For example, 3 per cent of the female population in 1880 listed themselves as married but with no spouse in evidence. In addition, the writings of Catharine Ming, Elizabeth Fisk, and Harriet P. Sanders document their husbands' frequent absences. These references are supported by the personal columns of both Helena newspapers that recorded the arrival and departure of Helena businessmen.

23. Civil Case no. 1987, Old Series; Miscellaneous Records, vol. 2, 449; Civil Case no. 2637, Old Series; Criminal Case no. 699, Old Series; *U.S. Census, 1880*; Deed Book U, p. 156; Deed Book Y, pp. 133, 233; Deed Book I, p. 374; Criminal Case no. 1473, Old Series.

24. Probate no. 196; unnumbered civil case, Box 3/4, Office of the Clerk of Court, Gallatin County, Bozeman, Montana. I am indebted to both Claudia Spencer Sadler and Rex W. Williams of Salt Lake City, Utah, for sharing with me portions of their family history.

25. Mortgage Book D, pp. 99, 361; Deed Book N, p. 477; Mortgage Book G, pp. 425-426; Mortgage Book H, p. 1; Deed Book U, p. 85; Probate no. 196. Papers contained in the probate include a copy of the auctioneer's inventory, the purchasers of the articles, and a public administrator's final report. Demimonde denizens were the estate's best customers.

26. John H. Ming to Catharine Ming, December 15, December 22, December 26, 1882, April 6, 1883, John H. Ming Papers, MHSA; Miscellaneous Records, vol. 4, 265-266.

27. John H. Ming Vertical File, MHSL; Civil Case nos. 4528, 4929, Old Series; Civil Case nos. 505, 1876, 2959, 2559, New Series; E. W. Toole and W. Wallace, Jr., to Catharine Ming, January 28, 1894, Ming Papers; *Helena Independent*, August 17, 1920.

28. *Helena City Directory*, 1867, 1883; *Helena Independent*, April 22, 1886; R. G. Dun & Co reports, 240[19].

29. *Helena Independent*, May 5, May 6, May 7, May 8, 1888; *Helena Daily Herald*, May 10, 1888. The *Independent*'s newshounds were especially assiduous in checking the veracity of Eckert's claim, ferreting out Wells Fargo waybills and scrutinizing Madison County newspapers. They asserted that Eckert could not have murdered John Denn because she was in Virginia City during the critical time. Law enforcement officials, however, guardedly admitted that Eckert knew more about the crime than she ever divulged. See Civil Case no. 1951, Old Series; Probate no. 349, New Series.

30. See Appendix 2, Table 21; *Helena Daily Herald*, December 23, 1875, July 7, 1884; *Helena Independent*, August 29, 1889; Civil Case no. 3633, Old Series; *Helena Independent*, July 8, 1887; Alexander M. Woolfolk to Martin Maginnis, January 12, 1885, Martin Maginnis Papers, MHSA.

31. It is clear from internal evidence that the list refers to tax assessments for 1889, but its exact date or source cannot be determined. *In situ*, the list is pasted into an old Magnolia Hotel register that seems to have been used as a scrapbook. See Magnolia Hotel records.

32. This statistic is derived from an analysis of individual tax assessments in a list in the Magnolia Hotel Register, Magnolia Hotel records. Corporate assessments were excluded.

33. *U.S. Census, 1900*. The female capitalists, in turn, were linked with the 1870 census and to other manuscript sources to determine the women's pioneer status.

34. See Appendix 2, Table 22. The occupations of the daughters' husbands also guaranteed that the pioneer daughters would experience little economic difficulty. Several of the daughters, moreover, became executors of their parents' estates and managed these holdings for the benefit of their siblings and interested relatives, continuing in the tradition of their business-minded mothers.

35. *Independent-Record*, December 15, 1951.

36. Marriage License no. 6315; Civil Case no. 8295, New Series; Jean Rumsey, Oak Park, Illinois, letter to author, n.d.; *Independent-Record*, April 28, 1947, December 15, 1951. I am grateful to Jean Rumsey for sharing excerpts from family diaries and letters pertinent to Lottie Rumsey's life.

37. *Independent-Record*, March 2, March 18, 1953.

38. *Fergus County Argus*, April 25, 1895; *Lewistown Democrat News*, April 22, 1930.

39. *Lewistown Democrat News*, April 22, 1930; *Fergus County Argus*, February 15, 1917.

40. Tom Stout, *Montana: Its Story and Biography*, 3 vols. (Chicago and New York: American History Society, 1921), 2:528. I am grateful to Ms. Perry McGilvray of the Castilleja School, Palo Alto, California, who shared with me additional information regarding Mary Lockey.

41. Hilda Potter, interview with author, Helena, Montana, December 12, 1983.

42. Joan Holter, telephone conversation with author, December 12, 1983, Helena; Barbara Kirkland, telephone conversation with author, December 13, 1983, Helena; Betty Lorbeer (Riverside, California), telephone conversation with author, December 12, 1983.

43. Ibid.

44. Quoted in Carl Degler, *At Odds: Women and Family in America from the Revolution to the Present* (New York: Oxford University Press, 1980), 152. I can find no comparative data for the nation as a whole; however, one historian indicates that women born between 1860 and 1880, the same birth years as the pioneer daughters, exhibited the highest rate of spinsterhood in the nation—10 to 11 per cent. Of the thirty-seven daughters who can be traced to 1900 with certainty, 19 per cent (seven) never married. The status of two frontier daughters who were single in 1900 is unknown after that period, although an examination of Lewis and Clark County records to 1910 reveals that no marriage licenses were issued to them.

45. Mary P. Ryan, *Womanhood in America from Colonial Times to the Present*, 2d ed. (New York: New Viewpoints, 1975), 119. See Appendix 2, Table 22 and Chapter 5. Marriage occurred late in life for a significant number of the frontier daughters, and many single women made careers for themselves after marriage prospects evaporated.

46. See Chapter 1.

47. *U.S. Census, 1880*. See also Appendix 1. Some argument could be made that the Fisks enjoyed a position among Helena's elite by virtue of Robert Fisk's part-ownership and editorship of the Republican newspaper, the *Helena Herald*. Another bit of evidence argues for Elizabeth's middle-class status: the absence of a servant in the Fisk household on a long-term basis. Whereas one in six U.S. households maintained domestic servants,

only one in ten Helena households could manage to retain help. Elizabeth had the services of Mary Knipper until Mary's marriage in 1886, but Mary became so much a part of the household that Elizabeth viewed her as simply another adolescent in the house, adding to Elizabeth's domestic responsibility. It seems best, therefore, to take Elizabeth at her word.

48. *Helena Independent*, April 22, 1927.

49. Guide to Fisk Family Papers, MHSA; ECF to Frances Chester, May 8, 1867; ECF to Chester family, May 17, 1867.

50. Faragher, *Women and Men on the Overland Trail*, chapters 3-5. Negotiating the overland route to the coast took the better part of a year, whereas the river route to Montana occupied only two months. Elizabeth's letters give no indication of the strains and stresses present among the overland immigrants, save toward the end of the journey when the passengers on the *Little Rock* succumbed to cabin fever. While Faragher rightly points out that nineteenth century gender roles survived the overland trip, he also isolates and highlights those inequities that irritated Elizabeth Fisk later in her life. Both the overland immigrants and the riverboat travelers were in transit; only an extended period of time on the frontier would transform the social relations between men and women.

51. ECF to Frances Chester, April 27, 1867; ECF to Chester family, May 26, 1867.

52. ECF to Frances Chester, June 1, 1867.

53. ECF to ACC, June 10, 1867; ECF to Frances Chester, April 27, May 8, May 13, May 24, June 1, 1867; ECF to Chester family, May 24, 1867.

54. ECF to Frances Chester, June 20, 1867.

55. ECF to ACC, July [?] 1867.

56. ECF to Frances Chester, July 31, 1867.

57. ECF to ACC, November 11, August 22, 1867.

58. ECF to ACC, August 22, August 7, October [?], November 6, 1867; ECF to Frances Chester, October 15, September 2, 1867. Elizabeth's complaints about the lack of a separate dwelling for her and her husband was a *leitmotif* in all of her letters and continued to be until the Robert Fisks obtained their own housing in June 1868. ECF to ACC, June 7, 1868.

59. ECF to ACC, November 6, 1867.

60. ECF to ACC, December 28, 1867; Harriet P. Sanders, Diaries, [1868], 1888, Wilbur Fisk Sanders Papers, MHSA. During that period and afterward, both the *Helena Daily Herald* and the *Helena Independent* reported the regular arrival and departure of various Helena entrepreneurs. While some of the men were taking short trips to nearby towns, many of the journeys, especially before the completion of the railroad, were to more distant places and took more time.

61. ECF to Frances Chester, January 25, 1868; ECF to ACC, January 19, 1868; ECF to Robert Emmett Fisk, January 8, 1868; ECF to Frances Chester, December 18, 1867; ECF to ACC, February 15, 1868. At Elizabeth's insistence, Robert engaged a Chinese servant to help Elizabeth meet the demands of his brother's household and her sister-in-law's illness. This marked the single instance when Elizabeth had adequate domestic help for any period of time.

62. ECF to Robert Emmett Fisk, January 12, February 1, 1868.

63. ECF to Frances Chester, January 25, 1868; ECF to ACC, February 29, 1868.

64. ECF to Frances Chester, January 25, 1868.

65. ECF to ACC, December 15, 1867, January 19, February 9, 1868.

66. ECF to Frances Chester, March 8, March 22, 1868; ECF to ACC, March 10, March 29, April 5, April 14, March 29, March 10, 1868.

67. ECF to ACC, April 14, 1868.

68. ECF to ACC, April 5, 1868.

69. ECF to ACC, April [?] 1868.

70. Ibid.

71. ECF to ACC, November 6, 1867.

72. Women's networks and their function in the nineteenth century have been discussed by several historians, including Jeffrey, *Frontier Women*, Chapter 4; Cott, *The Bonds of Womanhood*; Smith-Rosenberg, "The Female World of Love and Ritual."

73. ECF to ACC, May 17, May 24, 1868.

74. ECF to ACC, May 24, 1868.

75. ECF to Frances Chester, May 31, 1868.

76. ECF to ACC, December 15, 1867, June 21, 1868.

77. ECF to ACC, July 5, 1868.

78. ECF to ACC, June 21, July 13, 1868.

79. ECF to ACC, August 30, 1868.

80. ECF to ACC, September 21, September 27, October 25, 1868; ECF to Frances Chester, November 29, 1868.

81. ECF to ACC, January 15, 1869. The Fisks' decision to go back east seems to have been made on a moment's notice. Because Elizabeth's daughter was born at the end of May, by January Elizabeth was completely satisfied that she was pregnant.

82. ECF to ACC, November 14, 1869.

83. ECF to Frances Chester, November 1, 1869.

84. ECF to Frances Chester, February 13, 1870; ECF to ACC, November 2, December 18, 1870.

85. ECF to Frances Chester, November 21, 1869.

86. ECF to ACC, January 23, 1871, November 27, 1870; ECF to Frances Chester, October 2, 1870.

87. ECF to ACC, November 12, January 6, March 26, October 30, 1871; ECF to Frances Chester, March 23, 1871; ECF to ACC, November 12, 1871, January 29, 1874.

88. ECF to ACC, May 20, 1873, November 8, August 30, 1874, September 12, 1875, October 11, 1874, September 21, 1873, February 22, 1874.

89. ECF to ACC, October 28, 1877.

90. ECF to ACC, January 29, October 28, 1878, November 19, May 19, August 6, 1879.

91. ECF to ACC, March 24, 1879, July 27, 1880, March 7, July 12, 1881.

92. ECF to ACC, February 8, 1871, August 2, 1874, March 5, February 14, 1876.

93. ECF to ACC, March 31, 1881; *Helena Independent*, April 8, 1888.

94. ECF to ACC, March 28, 1882.

95. ECF to ACC, January 28, October 14, 1883.

96. ECF to ACC, April 29, May 18, 1885.

97. ECF to ACC, July 15, December 6, 1885; Diary of Harriet Sanders, April 7, 1888, Wilbur Fisk Sanders Papers, MHSA.

98. ECF to ACC, January 10, March 30, October 3, October 20, November 4, November 14, December 12, 1886.

99. ECF to ACC, November 14, December 12, 1886; ECF to Frances Chester, May 10, 1868; ECF to ACC, October 20, 1886, January 9, 1887.

100. Minutes of the Montana Woman's Christian Temperance Union [WCTU], 1886, Montana Woman's Christian Temperance Union Records, MHSA.

101. ECF to ACC, May 17, 1881.

102. ECF to ACC, January 24, 1886.

103. ECF to ACC, August 16, 1886.

104. ECF to ACC, June 4, June 13, 1886.

105. ECF to ACC, February 23, February 11, April 24, December 18, May 8, 1887; Minutes of the Montana WCTU Convention, 1887.

106. ECF to ACC, March 11, March 22, April 11, 1888, June 30, 1889; Minutes of the Montana WCTU Convention, 1888, 1889, 1890. Elizabeth's friend, Mrs. Richard Howey, also felt some alienation from the group. Long a crusader for temperance and other reforms, Mrs. Howey left the leadership of the WCTU in 1890.

107. ECF to ACC, September 26, September 30, November 11, October 21, 1888, August 11, 1889.

108. ECF to ACC, February 3, July 21, June 30, November 17, 1889, January 18, 1891. Elizabeth was dismayed to return from a trip and find that women in her reform groups had been unable to carry on in her absence.

109. ECF to ACC, January 18, 1891.

110. ECF to ACC, March 29, June 15, April 5, 1891.

111. ECF to ACC, January 15, 1888.

112. ECF to ACC, February 22, November 27, 1887, April 11, October 21, 1888.

113. ECF to ACC, June 1, August 24, September 7, 1890.

114. ECF to ACC, September 7, 1890.

115. ECF to ACC, September 23, 1890.

116. Ibid.

117. ECF to ACC, November 2, November 25, 1890.

118. ECF to ACC, March 9, March 15, May 15, September 9, 1891.

119. ECF to ACC, October 9, October 17, 1892.

120. ECF to ACC, January 24, March 7, March 14, April 25, 1892.

121. ECF to ACC, November 8, 1892.

122. ECF to ACC, February 15, March 5, 1893; Membership List, Women's Helena for the Capital Club Records, MHSA.

123. Malone and Roeder, *Montana*, 161-162; Miscellany, and Mrs. C. Cannon to Mrs. A. J. Davidson, October 27, 1894, Women's Helena for the Capital Club Records. Of the fifty-six ward canvassers, officers, and special committee members, thirty-six were women who had arrived in Helena before 1870 or shortly afterward. Ninety-five per cent of the club's membership were married and were between forty and forty-five years old.

124. *Helena City Directory*, 1896, 1897; Civil Case no. 4365, New Series.

125. See Chapter 4 for a discussion of divorce in Helena from 1883 to 1900.

126. Civil Case no. 4365, New Series.

127. Ibid.

128. Ibid.

129. *Helena City Directory*, 1898-1902; ECF to Robert Emmett Fisk, August 19, 1900; *Helena Semi-Weekly Herald*, December 27, 1902; *Helena Independent*, December 28, 1908, April 22, 1927.

130. Wallace Stegner, *Angle of Repose* (New York: Fawcett Crest, 1971), 90; ECF to ACC, December 18, 1892.

131. Jeffrey, *Frontier Women*, xv-xvi.

CHAPTER FOUR: Occasions of Unhappy Differences

1. Elizabeth Chester Fisk [ECF] to Azubah Clarke Chester [ACC], February 2, 1868, Fisk Family Papers, MHSA.

2. Because it seems fairly certain that the bulk of divorces in Lewis and Clark County involved Helena residents, "Lewis and Clark County" and "Helena" are used interchangeably in this discussion. Helena and Butte (in Silver Bow County) contributed the majority of Montana divorces, so to study divorce in these two communities is to obtain the fullest possible description of divorce in Montana. Butte's divorce profile stands in sharp contrast to Helena's. While courtroom events in Helena provided the basis for judicial and legislative reinterpretation of cruelty, cases in Butte suggest that the addition of "willful neglect" derived from this industrial mining community. See Paula Petrik, " 'If She Be Content:' The Development of Montana Divorce Law, 1865-1909" (manuscript in progress); Carroll D. Wright, *Marriage and Divorce in the United States, 1867 to 1886* (Washington, D.C.: Government Printing Office, 1891), 144-145; *Special Reports, Marriage and Divorce, 1867-1906*, Part 2 (Washington, D.C.: Government Printing Office, 1909).

3. *Helena Independent*, December 8, 1886; March 5, May 27, July 8, August 8, 1887.

4. Wright, *Marriage and Divorce*, 9-14, 154. Several recent studies contend that nineteenth century divorce cases indicate that an increasing number of women insisted on a recognition of their proper role in the home without undue subordination. The two points of contention in these arguments are whether or not this transformation worked to women's benefit and whether divorce was a phenomenon confined to the middle class or included couples from all classes. See William L. O'Neill, *Divorce in the Progressive Era* (New Haven, Connecticut: Yale University Press, 1967); Robert Griswold, *Family and Divorce in California, 1850-1890* (Albany: State University of New York Press, 1982); Elaine Tyler May, *Great Expectations: Marriage and Divorce in Post-Victorian America* (Chicago: University of Chicago Press, 1983); Degler, *At Odds*, 165-173.

5. Wright, *Marriage and Divorce*, 102. For the purposes of this investigation, states included in the Rocky Mountain mining frontier are Montana, Arizona, Colorado, Utah, Wyoming, Nevada, Idaho, New Mexico, and California. From 1863 until 1865, divorce suits were referred to the legislature; "private laws" enacted as part of the legislative calendar served to dissolve unhappy unions. By 1865, however, Montana lawmakers transferred jurisdiction over divorce contests to the district courts. Although territorial law distinguished between abandonment and desertion, desertion was subsumed under abandonment, and judges applied the criterion of abandonment to all cases involving a husband's disappearance. Whether women were deserted (when husbands left the territory with the avowed intention of never returning) or abandoned (when husbands departed without avowed intention), women were required to wait a year before they could obtain a divorce. This also

alludes to the difficulty the court encountered in ascertaining whether a spouse's disappearance was a bona fide desertion/abandonment or simply a spouse's necessary leave-taking to obtain employment.

6. Appendix 2, tables 6 and 17; Wright, *Marriage and Divorce*, 344.

7. See Appendix 2, Table 20.

8. Wright, *Marriage and Divorce*, 16.

9. See Appendix 2, Table 18; Civil Case nos. 39, 151, 330, 490, 370, Old Series.

10. Appendix 2, Table 18. See also Chapter 1.

11. Wright, *Marriage and Divorce*, 344; Civil Case nos. 1831, 1993, 1907, 2403, 1585, 2402, Old Series.

12. Civil Case nos. 2750, 3439, 4781, Old Series.

13. Civil Case nos. 3999, 3781, 4167, Old Series.

14. Ten per cent of the women testified that they had been forced to fall back on the charity of friends, neighbors, and family; less than 5 per cent filed a pauper's petition, claiming dire poverty and inability to pay the court costs necessary to prosecute their suits.

15. Civil Case nos. 2575, 2780, 1586, 1907, 2402, 2875, 3781, 4943, 3866, 2601. Of the 271 women who filed for divorce, 108 of them supported themselves by their own labor, although the nature of their work was not always evident. The cases cited do not represent the total number of divorcing women who worked; they are provided as an illustration of the kinds of employment available to women stranded on the frontier.

16. Civil Case nos. 2017, 2575, Old Series.

17. See Appendix 2, Table 18; Civil Case nos. 48, 51, 322, 223, Old Series.

18. Civil Case no. 573, Old Series.

19. Civil Case nos. 1, 56, Old Series.

20. Ibid.

21. Ibid.

22. Ibid.; Marriage Record, Book A. Although Montana provided for a jury trial in contested cases, few couples faced a jury. Only when members of the elite fought over property or daring middle-class wives argued over custody were couples vulnerable to a jury's verdict. Because the majority of cases involved desertion and because contested cases were expensive, the paucity of jury trials is not unlikely.

23. Civil Case nos. 1537, 1393, 2353. Old Series.

24. See Appendix 2, Table 18.

25. Civil Case nos. 3776, 4046, 4712, 2708, 2916, 2875, 84, 111, 4720, Old Series; Civil Case no. 489, New Series.

26. Because of the invariable appearance of complaints outlining three incidents of physical cruelty, I have termed the form the "three-beating rule." While persistence of the rule may indicate the persistence of a conservative definition of matrimonial cruelty, the rule may have been a kind of legal formula or ritual rhetoric to end marriages and, therefore, it may indicate little about attitudes regarding violence against women. The fact remains that apparently lawyers and magistrates encouraged and accepted the formulation of the complaint as the one most likely to secure a favorable hearing. Rhetoric, ritual, or formula, the form seemed important and serviceable to the court.

27. Civil Case nos. 126, 2501, 2571, 1706, 2490, Old Series.

28. Civil Case no. 2628, Old Series.

29. Ibid.

30. See Appendix 2, Table 18. Forty-nine divorce petitions alleging cruelty as the primary grounds were placed before the court between 1881 and 1890. Of these, twenty-one made no mention of physical violence.

31. *Montana Reports*, vol. 5 (Chicago: Callaghan and Company, 1885), 578.

32. Civil Case nos. 4021, 3763, 4164, Old Series.

33. Civil Case nos. 4943, 3537, 4306, Old Series.

34. Civil Case nos. 4215, 2829, 137, 5014, Old Series.

35. Civil Case no. 506, New Series; Civil Case nos. 3757, 4341, Old Series.

36. Appendix 2, Table 18.

37. Of the 271 women who filed for divorce between 1865 and 1885, fully 108 of them indicated they had supported themselves, although the nature of their work was not always evident. Women after 1890 increasingly alluded to the support of family members

during their divorces. No firm statistic is available, owing to the lack of verifiable information and the inconsistency of significant details in the later suits. Without engaging in undue speculation, family support would be a reasonable expectation during the 1890s when the second generation began marrying. The frequency of pauper declarations increased during the 1890s, suggesting that women divorcing in the later period were not as capable of obtaining employment as they had been earlier. One obvious factor contributing to this phenomenon was the poor economic climate in Helena after 1893.

38. Civil Case nos. 2580, 2300, 2823, 2204, 2345, 2072, 1439, 850, 764, 3939, 3227, New Series.

39. *Compiled Statutes of Montana Enacted at the Regular Session of the Fifteenth Legislative Assembly of Montana* (Helena: Journal Publishing Company, 1888), 920; *The Codes and Statutes of Montana in Force July 1st 1895* (Butte: Intermountain Publishing Company, 1895), 800-804.

40. U.S. Bureau of the Census, *Special Reports: Marriage and Divorce, 1867-1906*, 2 vols. (Washington, D.C.: Government Printing Office, 1908-1909), 1:99. The Bureau of Census reported that women asked for alimony in 13.2 per cent of the divorce cases in Montana and were granted alimony in 10.4 per cent of the cases. This accords with the rough estimates from Lewis and Clark County.

41. Ibid., 41; Griswold, *Family and Divorce in California*, Chapter 7. General indifference to children's well-being seems to have been relatively widespread in Helena. See Paula Petrik, "Who Killed Clara Rehberg? Violence Against Children on the Frontier" (unpublished paper).

42. See, for example, Civil Case nos. 3274, 2089, 3263, 3379, 4766, 4844, 4171, 4231, 3885, 4071, 3897, New Series.

43. Civil Case nos. 3413, 3370, 3263, 3241, 1802, 3879, New Series.

44. Civil Case no. 2196, New Series.

45. ECF to ACC, August 11, November 17, 1889, March 3, March 14, 1892; Civil Case nos. 3193, 2288, Old Series. See also Chapter 3. The phenomenon of dismissed divorce suits is difficult to gauge. Before 1887, women appear to have used the threat of divorce as insurance against the return of a spouse; after 1887, women appear to have used divorce as a means of regulating their husbands' drinking and obtaining minimal support.

46. Civil Case no. 1802, New Series.

47. Civil Case nos. 915, 1003, New Series.

48. Ibid.; *Montana Reports*, vol. 12 (San Francisco: Bancroft-Whitney Company, 1893), 122-149.

49. *Codes and Statutes of Montana*, 795.

50. *Montana Reports*, vol. 33 (San Francisco: Bancroft-Whitney Company, 1907), 408, 409, 410.

51. *House Journal of the Tenth Session of the Legislative Assembly of the State of Montana* (Helena: Montana Record Publishing Company, 1907), 182-183, 232, 332, 337, 387, 400, 498, 521, 581-582, 620-621, 646; *Senate Journal of the Tenth Session of the Legislative Assembly of the State of Montana* (Helena: Montana Record Publishing Company, 1907), 260, 262, 290, 309, 323-324, 332-333, 343, 351, 353, 391. District courts apparently ignored the legislature's guideline specifying a year's duration; judges happily sustained mental and physical cruelty on the basis of a single incident after 1907.

52. Griswold, *Family and Divorce in California*, 18-20.

53. For another analysis of the effect of new in-migration, see Jan Reiff, "Urbanization and Social Structure: Seattle, Washington, 1852-1910" (Ph.D. diss., University of Washington, Seattle, 1981).

54. Of the 668 divorce suits brought in Lewis and Clark County, 535 named women as plaintiffs.

55. Edward G. White, *The American Judicial Tradition: Profiles of Leading American Judges* (New York: Oxford University Press, 1976), 113.

CHAPTER FIVE: Generation Upon Generation

1. T. A. Larson, "Montana Women and the Battle for the Ballot," *Montana the Magazine of Western History* 23 (Winter 1973): 26. States with woman suffrage before 1920 were Wyoming (1869), Colorado (1893), Idaho (1896), Utah (1896), Washington (1910), California (1911), Arizona (1912), Kansas (1912), Montana (1914), and Nevada (1914). Alaska Territory legislated suffrage in 1913, and Illinois gave women the right to cast their ballots for

president in the same year. Utah and Washington had previous experience with equal suffrage, but it had been interrupted by various political changes.

2. Jeffrey, *Frontier Women*, 194. Jeffrey does not detail what in the western experience contributed to the region's suffrage successes.

3. Larson, "Montana Women," 26; Malone and Roeder, *Montana*, 81-82; ECF to Frances Chester, November 21, 1869, February 13, 1870.

4. ECF to ACC, November 19, 1879.

5. Helena's adult female population numbered 489 in 1870 and 735 in 1880; 353 of the adult women in 1870 were engaged in "keeping house," and 446 were so designated in 1880.

6. *Butte Miner*, August 2, August 3, 1883.

7. In her correspondence, Elizabeth Fisk makes numerous references to the social dangers that abounded in Helena. Her anxiety became a dominant theme as her children matured. Elliott West makes a convincing argument for the saloon as the social center of the frontier mining town in *The Saloon on the Rocky Mountain Mining Frontier* (Lincoln: University of Nebraska Press, 1979).

8. Minutes of the Woman's Christian Temperance Union Convention, 1887, Montana Woman's Christian Temperance Union Records, MHSA.

9. Ibid.

10. Minutes of the Woman's Christian Temperance Union Convention, 1889.

11. Records of the Montana Constitutional Convention, 1884, January 23, 1884, MHSA.

12. Malone and Roeder, *Montana*, 147-148; Doris Buck Ward, "The Winning of Woman Suffrage in Montana" (M.A. thesis, Montana State University, Bozeman, 1974), Chapter 1.

13. Ward, "The Winning of Suffrage in Montana," Chapter 1.

14. Henry Blackwell was the husband of Lucy Stone, a prominent suffragist. Their marriage reflected a commitment to feminist values and lifestyle. Blackwell was actively involved in the suffrage cause and did much public speaking in situations such as the one described here. "Woman-Suffrage," Vertical File, MHSL; Ward, "The Winning of Suffrage in Montana," 16-17.

15. *Proceedings and Debates of the Constitutional Convention, 1889* (Helena: State Publishing Company, 1921), 330, 404-408, 871, 915; Myres, *Westering Women*, Chapter 8. Myres makes the point that in many instances women were not present in any numbers in suffrage battles. Montana was no exception.

16. Ward, "The Winning of Suffrage in Montana," 19-24; *Proceedings and Debates*, 374, 459, 465-466.

17. Ward, "The Winning of Suffrage in Montana," 28.

18. Malone and Roeder, *Montana*, 150-151; Roeder, "Crossing the Gender Line."

19. Ward, "The Winning of Suffrage in Montana," 45; *Butte Miner*, February 22, February 25, 1895; *Helena Independent*, March 1, 1895.

20. *Helena Herald*, June 15, 1895; Larson, "Montana Women," 30. Members of the original club included Miss Sarepta Sanders, Mrs. M. S. Kellogg, Delia Kellogg, Mrs. Eliza Richards, Mrs. Margaret Pyle, Mrs. M. V. Wheeler, Miss C. L. Turnley, Mrs. M. L. Cunningham, Mrs. C. F. Ellis, Mrs. Wilbur Fisk Sanders, Mrs. J. U. Sanders, Mrs. F. L. Gaines, Mrs. Carrie Cox, Mrs. Hugh Kirkendall, Miss Ida P. Rosecrans, Mrs. Dotha Dolan, Mrs. Emma Remington, and Mrs. C. H. Avery.

21. See chapters 3 and 4.

22. ECF to ACC, November 9, 1891. Ida Rosecrans seems to have been involved in some kind of music education. Evidence suggests that she was the daughter of Ida Wilson, one of the first graduates of Helena High School.

23. *Helena Independent*, September 22, 1911.

24. Record Book, Women's Helena for the Capital Club Records, MHSA.

25. Harriet P. Sanders, "Diary of a Journey Across the Plains in 1863 and Reminiscences of Early Life in Montana," bound typescripts, 161-163, Wilbur Fisk Sanders Papers, MHSA.

26. Sanders, "Diary of a Journey," 162.

27. Sanders, "Diary of a Journey"; Diary of Harriet P. Sanders, 1888, Wilbur Fisk Sanders Papers, MHSA; ECF to ACC, January 18, 1890. From Harriet's diary entries it is evident that Sarepta and Harriet Sanders maintained a close relationship throughout their lives.

28. The analysis of suffrage club members is based on material drawn from the U.S. Census, city directories, and tax assessment lists. Biographical material is available for all but seven of the twenty-four women named as members of either the original suffrage group or as delegates to the first suffrage convention.

29. The associations of suffrage club membership are too entwined to disentangle sufficiently, but the same names reappear with regularity in cultural groups and on the rolls of reform and benevolent societies.

30. See Appendix 2, Table 9. This analysis is based on the fourteen members for whom verifiable age data are available.

31. Quoted in Larson, "Montana Women," 31.

32. See Appendix 2, Table 2; Larson, "Montana Women," 32.

33. This analysis is based on the ten members for whom verifiable age data are available.

34. Minutes of the Helena Business Women's Suffrage Club, June 14, 1898, Helena Business Women's Suffrage Club Minutes, SC 976, MHSA; *U.S. Census, 1900.*

35. Margaret Hibbard, interview with author, August 17, 1980, Helena; *Helena Independent,* February 14, 1934; Scrapbook, F. Adelaide Staves Reeder Papers, MHSA.

36. F. Roena Medini, *Edalaine: A Metrical Romance* (New York: Dillingham, c. 1891); Ella W. Foote, *Poems* (Oakland, California: George Arthur Kelley, c. 1898); Anna Barbour, *The Award of Justice: Or, Told in the Rockies: A Pen Picture of the West* (Chicago: Rand, McNally, and Company, 1901); Anna Barbour, *That Mainwaring Affair* (New York: American News Company, 1900); Margaret Hibbard interview; Appendix 2, Table 5. Single female and lone female households in 1900 nearly equaled the percentages of those households in 1870.

37. Minutes of the Helena Business Women's Suffrage Club, June 13, July 7, 1896.

38. Harriet P. Sanders, "Address of the President to the Second Annual Montana Equal Suffrage Association," November 17, 1896, 1, Wilbur Fisk Sanders Papers, W.A. Clark Library, University of California at Los Angeles.

39. Ibid., 5, 7.

40. Ibid., 7.

41. *Helena Independent,* January 10, 1897.

42. Ward, "The Winning of Suffrage in Montana," 55, 56, 58; *Butte Miner,* February 10, 1897; *Helena Independent,* February 10, 1897; *Helena Herald,* February 10, 1897.

43. Ward, "The Winning of Woman Suffrage in Montana," 58, 83.

44. Of the sixty-eight members of the House, arrival dates in Montana are available for thirty-six. Only eleven of these legislators had experienced Montana in its mining camp period before 1880. The rest of them had arrived in the post-railroad period. This analysis is derived from information contained in Waldron, *Montana Legislators, 1864-1979,* and Waldron and Wilson, *Atlas of Montana Elections, 1889-1976.*

45. *Helena Independent,* November 8, November 10, 1897.

46. *Helena Independent,* November 10, 1897.

47. Ward, "The Winning of Woman Suffrage in Montana," 68.

48. Ibid., 63.

49. Malone and Roeder, *Montana,* 164-167.

50. *Helena Independent,* January 24, January 26, February 14, 1899; Minutes of the Helena Business Women's Suffrage Club, June 14, June 21, 1898. There were only two meetings recorded for 1898.

51. Ward, "The Winning of Woman Suffrage in Montana," 78-79; *Butte Miner,* May 20, 1902.

52. See chapters 1 and 3; Malone and Roeder, *Montana,* 157-158, 162-163.

53. *Butte Miner,* September 19, 1902; *Great Falls Tribune,* October 26, 1902.

54. *Butte Miner,* May 20, May 30, 1902; *Helena Independent,* January 10, 1903.

55. Ward, "The Winning of Woman Suffrage in Montana," 93-94.

56. Ibid., 96-98. The data are derived from a random sample of 200 women taken from the original petition of 1905, Records of the Montana Ninth Legislative Assembly, Record Series 91, MHSA. This sample was then linked with the U.S. Census, which yielded information on age and birthplace.

57. Malone and Roeder, *Montana,* 170-171, 195-199.

58. Mary Wilma M. Hargreaves, *Dry Farming in the Northern Great Plains, 1900-1925* (Cambridge, Massachusetts: Harvard University Press, 1957); Malone and Roeder,

Montana, 178-189; Paul Petrik, Jr., interview with author, Sidney, Montana, May 25, 1981; Ward, "The Winning of Woman Suffrage in Montana," 103.

59. *Butte Miner*, January 28, 1911, September 23, 1909; *Helena Independent*, September 22, 1911.

60. Hannah Josephson, *Jeannette Rankin, First Lady in Congress: A Biography* (Indianapolis: Bobbs-Merrill Company, 1974), 19-25. There are a number of biographies of Jeannette Rankin; most agree on the chronology of her early years.

61. Ibid., 19-25, 28; Ward, "The Winning of Woman Suffrage in Montana," 109-111, 112.

62. Ward, "The Winning of Woman Suffrage in Montana," 119; Malone and Roeder, *Montana*, 202-204.

63. Josephson, *Jeannette Rankin*, 26, 40; Mary Long Alderson, "A Half Century of Progress for Montana Women," typescript, 16-17, Mary Long Alderson Papers, SC 122, MHSA.

64. Ward, "The Winning of Woman Suffrage in Montana," 124.

65. Waldron and Wilson, *Atlas of Montana Elections, 1889-1976*.

CHAPTER SIX: No Step Backward

1. *Helena Herald*, June 13, 1879.

2. William Cronon, "Revisiting the Vanishing Frontier: The Legacy of Frederick Jackson Turner," *Western Historical Quarterly* 18 (April 1987): 171; see also Patricia Nelson Limerick, *The Legacy of Conquest: The Unbroken Past of the American West* (New York: W. W. Norton, 1987).

3. D'Ann Campbell, "Was the West Different? Values and Attitudes of Young Women in 1943," *Pacific Historical Review* 47 (August 1978): 463.

4. Ibid., 453-463.

Selected Bibliography

UNPUBLISHED DOCUMENTS AND MANUSCRIPT COLLECTIONS

Office of the Clerk and Recorder, Lewis and Clark County
- Record of Deeds, 1865-1900
- Grantee Books, I-IV
- Grantor Books, I-IV
- Record of Mortgages, 1865-1900
- Miscellaneous Records, 1865-1900
- Original Plat Book, 1865
- Registry of Births and Deaths in Lewis and Clark County

Office of the Clerk of Court, Lewis and Clark County
- Index to Plaintiffs—Civil
- Index to Defendants—Civil
- Index to Defendants—Criminal
- Minute Books, Criminal Proceedings, 1865-1900
- Minute Books, Civil Proceedings, 1865-1900
- Judgment Books, Criminal Proceedings, 1865-1900
- Judgment Books, Civil Proceedings, 1865-1900
- Record of Marriages, Book I, 1865-1907
- Probate Index, Book I

Office of the Treasurer, Lewis and Clark County
- Tax Assessment List, 1888, 1889, 1890

Office of the Coroner, Lewis and Clark County
- Coroner's Inquisitions, 1875-1900

Montana Historical Society Archives, Helena, Montana
- Mary Long Alderson Papers
- Records of the Montana Attorney General, 1951, 1952, 1953, Record Series 76
- Thomas Cruse Papers
- First National Bank of Helena Records
- Fisk Family Papers
- Grand Army of the Republic, Women's Relief Corps Records
- Rollin Lynde Hartt Letters, SC 155
- Helena Businesswomen's Suffrage Club Records
- Helena Women's Relief Committee Records, SC 997
- A. M. Holter Papers
- Magnolia Hotel Records, SC 1098
- Merchants National Bank Records
- John H. Ming Papers
- Petition to the Montana State House for Woman Suffrage, 1905, Record Series 91
- Records of the Montana Constitutional Convention, 1884, 1889
- Records of the Montana Territory, Executive Office, Record Series 40
- Adelaide Staves Reeder Papers
- James Upson Sanders Papers
- Wilbur Fisk Sanders Papers

John Shober Papers
Montana Woman's Christian Temperance Union
Women's Helena for the Capital Club Records

Montana Historical Society Library, Helena, Montana
U.S. Census, 1870: Territory of Montana
U.S. Census, 1880: Territory of Montana
U.S. Census, 1900: State of Montana

W. A. Clark Library, University of California at Los Angeles
Wilbur F. Sanders Collection
Montana Suffrage Collection

Montana and Nevada Territories, Vol. 1. R. G. Dun & Co. Collection, Baker Library, Harvard University, Graduate School of Business Administration, Cambridge, Massachusetts.

Published Documents

State

Proceedings and Debates of the Constitutional Convention, 1889. Helena: State Publishing Company, 1921.

House Journals of the Legislative Assemblies of the State of Montana. 4th-13th sessions. Helena: Montana Record Publishing, 1895, 1897, 1899, 1901, 1903, 1905, 1907, 1909, 1911, 1913.

Senate Journals of the Legislative Assemblies of the State of Montana. 4th, 8th, and 13th sessions. Helena: Montana Record Publishing, 1895, 1903, 1907, 1913.

Report of Cases Determined in the Supreme Court of the State of Montana. San Francisco: Bancroft and Whitney, 1885, 1893, 1907.

Compiled Statutes of Montana Enacted at the Regular Session of the Fifteenth Legislative Assembly of Montana. Helena: Journal Publishing Company, 1888.

The Codes and Statutes of Montana in Force July 1st 1895. Butte: Intermountain Publishing Company, 1895.

Miscellaneous

An Act to Incorporate the City of Helena, Montana Territory and the Ordinances. Helena: Herald Publishing, 1882.

Alexander Botkin. *The Charter and Ordinances of the City of Helena, with the Rules of Order for the Government of the City Council, 1887*. Helena: Journal Publishing Company, 1887.

Helena Board of Trade Report for 1887. Helena: Helena Board of Trade, 1888.

Helena City Directory, 1883-4. Helena: Geo E. Boos, 1884.

Helena City Directory, 1886-7. Helena: Geo E. Boos, 1886.

Helena City Directory, 1888. Helena: Journal Publishing Company, 1888.

Helena City Directory, 1889. Helena: A. W. Ide, 1889.

Helena City Directory, 1890-1900. Helena: R. L. Polk & Company, 1890-1900.

Historical Sketch and Essay on the Resources of Montana; Including a Business Directory of the Metropolis. Helena: Herald Book and Job Printing, 1868.

J.D. McIntyre Survey: Plats of Helena Townsite, 1883, 1884.

Report of the Secretary of the Helena Board of Trade for the Year 1878. Helena: Fisk Brothers, 1879.

Second Annual Report of the Secretary of the Helena Board of Trade for the Year 1879. Helena: Woolfolk, McQuaid and Lacroix, 1880.

Sanborn Map and Publishing Company, insurance maps, Helena, 1883-1890.

INTERVIEWS

Jean Baucus, Helena, Montana, August 13, 1980
Margaret Hibbard, Helena, Montana, August 17, 1980
Paul Petrik, Jr., Sidney, Montana, May 25, 1981
Perry McGilvray, Palo Alto, California, December 12, 1983
Hilda Potter, Helena, Montana, December 12, 1983
Joan Holter, Helena, Montana, December 12, 1983
Barbara Kirkland, Helena, Montana, December 13, 1983
Betty Lorbeer, Riverside, California, December 12, 1983

BOOKS

Baucus, Jean. *Gold in the Gulch*. Helena: Bar Wineglass Publications, 1981.

______. *Helena Her Historic Homes*. Vol. 1. Helena: J-G Publications, 1976.

______. *Helena Her Historic Homes*. Vol. 2. Helena: Bar Wineglass Publications, 1979.

Blake, Nelson. *The Road to Reno: A History of Divorce in the United States*. New York: Macmillan, 1962.

Butler, Anne M. *Daughters of Joy, Sisters of Misery: Prostitutes in the American West*. Urbana: University of Illinois Press, 1985.

Campbell, William C. *From the Quarries of Last Chance Gulch*. Vol. 1. Helena: The Montana Record Publishing Company, 1951.

______. *From the Quarries of Last Chance Gulch*. Vol. 2. Helena: Bell-Arm Corporation, 1964.

Cott, Nancy. *The Bonds of Womanhood: "Woman's Sphere" in New England, 1780-1835*. New Haven, Connecticut: Yale University Press, 1977.

Degler, Carl. *At Odds: Women and Family in America from the Revolution to the Present*. New York: Oxford University Press, 1980.

Doyle, Don H. *The Social Order of a Frontier Community: Jacksonville, Illinois, 1825-1870*. Urbana: University of Illinois Press, 1978.

Dubois, Ellen Carol. *Feminism and Suffrage: The Emergence of an Independent Women's Movement in America, 1848-1869*. Ithaca: Cornell University, 1978.

Dykstra, Robert R. *The Cattle Towns*. New York: Alfred A. Knopf, 1968.

Faragher, John Mack. *Women and Men on the Overland Trail*. New Haven, Connecticut: Yale University Press, 1979.

Flexnor, Eleanor. *Century of Struggle: The Women's Rights Movement in the United States*. New York: Atheneum, 1970.

Goldman, Marion S. *Gold Diggers and Silver Miners: Prostitution and Social Life on the Comstock Lode*. Ann Arbor: University of Michigan, 1981.

Gordon, Michael, ed. *The American Family in Social-Historical Perspective*. 2nd ed. New York: St. Martin's Press, 1978.

Gray, James Henry. *Red Lights on the Prairies*. Toronto: Macmillan, 1971.

Griffen, Clyde and Sally Griffen. *Natives and Newcomers: The Ordering of Opportunity in Mid-Nineteenth-Century Poughkeepsie*. Cambridge, Massachusetts: Harvard University Press, 1977.

Grimes, Alan P. The Puritan Ethic and Woman Suffrage. New York: Oxford University Press, 1967.

Griswold, Robert. *Family and Divorce in California, 1850-1890.* Albany: State University of New York Press, 1982.

Hargreaves, Mary Wilma M. *Dry Farming in the Northern Great Plains, 1900-1925.* Cambridge: Harvard University Press, 1957.

Harper, Ida Husted, ed. *History of Woman Suffrage.* Vols. 5-6 (1900-1920). New York: National Woman Suffrage Association, 1922.

_____ and Susan B. Anthony, eds. *History of Woman Suffrage.* Vol. 4 (1883-1900). Rochester: Susan B. Anthony, 1902.

Jeffrey, Julie Roy. *Frontier Women: The Trans-Mississippi West, 1840-1880.* New York: Hill and Wang, 1979.

Josephson, Hannah. *Jeannette Rankin, A Biography.* New York: Bobbs-Merrill Company, 1974.

Katz, Michael. *The People of Hamilton, Canada West: Family and Class in a Mid-Nineteenth-Century City.* Cambridge, Massachusetts: Harvard University Press, 1975.

Kingston, Maxine Hong. *China Men.* New York: Alfred A. Knopf, 1980.

Kraditor, Aileen S. *The Ideas of the Woman Suffrage Movement.* Garden City: Doubleday and Company, 1971.

Leeson, Michael A., ed. *History of Montana, 1739-1885.* Chicago: Warner, Beers and Company, 1885.

Lotchin, Roger. *San Francisco, 1846-1856: From Hamlet to City.* New York: Oxford University Press, 1974.

Malone, Michael P. and Richard B. Roeder. *Montana: A History of Two Centuries.* Seattle: University of Washington Press, 1976.

Mann, Ralph. *After the Gold Rush: Society in Grass Valley and Nevada City, California, 1849-1870.* Palo Alto, California: Stanford University Press, 1982.

May, Elaine Tyler. *Great Expectations: Marriage and Divorce in Post-Victorian America.* Chicago: University of Chicago Press, 1980.

Moynihan, Ruth Barnes. *Rebel for Rights: Abigail Scott Duniway.* New Haven, Connecticut: Yale University Press, 1983.

Myres, Sandra L. *Westering Women and the Frontier Experience, 1800-1915.* Albuquerque: University of New Mexico Press, 1982.

O'Neill, William L. *Divorce in the Progressive Era.* New Haven, Connecticut: Yale University Press, 1967.

_____. *Everyone Was Brave: A History of Feminism in America.* Chicago: Quadrangle Books, 1971.

Paul, Rodman Wilson. *Mining Frontiers of the Far West, 1848-1880.* New York: Holt, Rinehart and Winston, 1963.

Perry, Eugene S. *Montana in the Geological Past.* Butte: Montana Bureau of Mines and Geology, 1962.

Riley, Glenda. *Frontierswomen: The Iowa Experience.* Ames: University of Iowa Press, 1981.

Rosen, Ruth. *The Lost Sisterhood: Prostitution in America, 1900-1918.* Baltimore: Johns Hopkins University Press, 1982.

Ryan, Mary P. *Cradle of the Middle Class: The Family in Oneida County, New York, 1790-1865.* New York: Cambridge University Press, 1981.

______. *Womanhood in America from Colonial Times to the Present.* 2nd ed. New York: New Viewpoints, 1975.

Schlissel, Lillian. *Women's Diaries of the Westward Journey.* New York: Schocken Books, 1982.

Sklar, Kathryn Kish. *Catharine Beecher: A Study in American Domesticity.* New York: W.W. Norton, 1973.

Smith, Duane A. *Rocky Mountain Mining Camps: The Urban Frontier.* Bloomington: Indiana University Press, 1967.

Spence, Clark. *Territorial Politics and Government in Montana, 1864-89.* Urbana: University of Illinois Press, 1975.

Stegner, Wallace. *Angle of Repose.* New York: Fawcett-Crest, 1971.

Taylor, George Rogers, ed. *The Turner Thesis: Concerning the Role of the Frontier in American History.* Lexington, Massachusetts: D.C. Heath, 1972.

Thernstrom, Stephen. *The Other Bostonians: Poverty and Progress in the American Metropolis, 1880-1970.* Cambridge: Harvard University Press, 1973.

U.S. Bureau of the Census. *Special Reports: Marriage and Divorce, 1867-1906.* 2 vols. Washington, D.C.: Government Printing Office, 1908-1909.

Waldron, Ellis L. *Montana Legislators, 1864-1979: Profiles and Biographical Directory.* Missoula: Bureau of Government Research, University of Montana, 1980.

______ and Paul B. Wilson. *Atlas of Montana Elections, 1889-1976.* Missoula: University of Montana Publications in History, 1978.

Walkowitz, Judith R. *Prostitution and Victorian Society: Women, Class and the State.* New York: Cambridge University Press, 1980.

West, Elliott. *The Saloon on the Rocky Mountain Mining Frontier.* Lincoln: University of Nebraska Press, 1979.

White, Edward G. *The American Judicial Tradition.* New York: Oxford University Press, 1976.

Wright, Carroll D. *A Report on Marriage and Divorce in the United States, 1867 to 1886.* Washington, D.C.: Government Printing Office, 1891.

Articles

Bishop, Joan. "A Season of Trial: Helena's Entrepreneurs Nurture a City." *Montana the Magazine of Western History* 28 (Summer 1978): 62-71.

Blackburn, George M. and Sherman L. Richards. "The Prostitutes and Gamblers of Virginia City, Nevada, 1870." *Pacific Historical Review* 48 (May 1979): 239-258.

Burnham, John C. and Robert E. Riegel. "Changing American Attitudes Toward Prostitution, 1800-1920." *Journal of the History of Ideas* 29 (July 1968): 437-452.

Campbell, D'Ann. "Was the West Different? Values and Attitudes of Young Women in 1943." *Pacific Historical Review* 67 (August 1978): 453-463.

Cott, Nancy. "Passionlessness: An Interpretation of Victorian Sexual Ideology, 1790-1850." *Signs* 4 (Winter 1978): 219-236.

______. "Eighteenth-Century Family and Social Life Revealed in Massachusetts Divorce Records." *Journal of Social History* 10 (Fall 1976): 20-43.

Faragher, Johnny and Christine Stansell. "Women and Their Families on the Overland Trail, 1842-1867." *Feminist Studies,* no. 2/3 (1975): 150-166.

Goldman, Marion. "Sexual Commerce on the Comstock Lode." *Nevada Historical Society Quarterly* 21 (Summer 1978): 99-129.

Hirata, Lucie Cheng. "Chinese Immigrant Women in Nineteenth-Century California." *In Women of America,* ed. Carol Ruth Berkin and Mary Beth Norton, pp. 225-253. Boston: Houghton Mifflin, 1979.

Jensen, Joan M. and Darlis A. Miller. "The Gentle Tamers Revisited: New Approaches to the History of Women in the American West." *Pacific Historical Review* 49 (May 1980): 173-213.

Kerr, William T., Jr. "The Progressives of Washington, 1910-1912." *Pacific Northwest Quarterly* (January 1964):16-27.

Lang, William L. "The Nearly Forgotten Blacks of Last Chance Gulch, 1900-1912." *Pacific Northwest Quarterly* 70 (April 1979): 50-57.

______. "Tempest on Clore Street: Race and Politics in Helena, Montana, 1906." *Scratchgravel Hills* 3 (Summer 1980): 9-14.

Larson, T. A. "Montana Women and the Battle for the Ballot." *Montana the Magazine of Western History* 21 (1973): 24-41.

Leonard, Carol and Isidor Walleman. "Prostitution and Changing Morality in the Frontier Cattle Towns of Kansas." *Kansas History* 2 (Spring 1979): 34-53.

Myers, Rex. "An Inning for Sin: Chicago Joe and Her Hurdy Gurdy Girls." *Montana the Magazine of Western History* 27 (Spring 1977): 24-33.

Roeder, Richard B. "Crossing the Gender Line: Ella L. Knowles, Montana's First Woman Lawyer." *Montana the Magazine of Western History* 32 (Summer 1982): 64-75.

Schaffer, Ronald. "The Montana Woman Suffrage Campaign, 1911-1914." *Pacific Northwest Quarterly* 60 (January 1964): 9-15.

Smith-Rosenberg, Carroll. "The Female World of Love and Ritual: Relations between Women in Nineteenth-Century America." *Signs,* no. 1 (Autumn 1975): 1-30.

Stoeltje, Beverly J. " 'A Helpmate for Man Indeed,' The Image of the Frontier Woman." *Journal of American Folklore,* no. 347 (January-March 1975): 25-41.

Welter, Barbara. "The Cult of True Womanhood, 1820-1860." *American Quarterly* 18 (1966): 151-174.

West, Elliott. "The Scarlet West, The Oldest Profession in the Trans-Mississippi West." *Montana the Magazine of Western History* 31 (Spring 1981): 16-27.

Unpublished Papers

Butler, Ann Katherine M. "The Tarnished Frontier: Prostitution in the Trans-Mississippi West, 1865-1890." Ph.D. diss., University of Maryland, College Park, 1979.

Dean, Patricia L. "The Jewish Community of Helena, Montana, 1866-1900." Honors Thesis, Carroll College, Helena, Montana, 1977.

Murphy, Mary. "Women on the Line: Prostitution in Butte, Montana, 1878-1917." M.A. Thesis, University of North Carolina, Chapel Hill, 1983.

Reiff, Jan. "Urbanization and Social Structure: Seattle, Washington, 1852-1910." Ph.D. diss., University of Washington, Seattle, 1981.

Schaffer, Ronald. "Jeannette Rankin, Progressive-Isolationist." Ph.D. diss., Princeton University, 1959.

Underwood, Kathleen. "Town Building on the Frontier: Grand Junction, Colorado, 1880-1910." Ph.D. diss., University of California at Los Angeles, 1982.

Ward, Doris Buck. "The Winning of Woman Suffrage in Montana." M.A. Thesis, Montana State University, Bozeman, 1974.

Index

About the Author

Paula Petrik is Associate Professor of History at Montana State University and a specialist in women's and business history. Petrik holds a BA degree from Cornell, an MFA in creative writing from the University of Montana, and a PhD from SUNY Binghamton. The recipient of Fulbright-Hays, NEH, Smithsonian, American Bar Association, and Littleton-Griswold fellowships, Petrik has written articles published in scholarly journals on several topics in women's and business history, including divorce, prostitution, female prisoners, family life on the frontier, and the American toy industry.